Acclaim for Maha

"*Mahabharata: The Eternal Quest* chronicles a vivid and timeless story that should be incorporated more often into our classrooms. . . Take the time to dive in and experience the epic from someone who honors the tradition upon which it came." *Kevin Cordi, PhD, Professor, Ohio Dominican U. www.kevincordi.com*

"Beautifully written and inspirational. Andy Fraenkel makes the Mahabharata come alive. . . a truly wonderful rendering of one of the great epics of ancient India."
E. Burke Rochford Jr., author of Hare Krishna Transformed (NYU Press) & Professor at Middlebury College

"Cinematic! What a great read! A compelling story and utterly engaging." *Rebecca Strowger, Independent Scholar*

"Well-written and concise. Excellent for college courses on philosophy, religion, or literature. It's clearer and gets to the point much better than many other Mahabharata tellings. . . The section at the end of the book on the Vedic Worldview will be very useful to the reader. I commend the author for including it."
Dr. Arnold Smith, Philosophy Dept, Kent State University

"To condense the profound wisdom and rich culture of Mahabharata into a book of this size constitutes a formidable challenge. In his offering, Andy Fraenkel has distilled the essence of the expansive scripture and has skillfully crafted a book which is accessible and comprehensible to a universal audience." *Varshana Swami, Author & Vaisnava Scholar*

"The importance of this book cannot be underestimated, and we are in debt to Andy Fraenkel for making it available in a readable and exciting format." *Thakor Topiwala, Lecturer on Hinduism & Bhakti Yoga, Hindu Center of Charlotte, NC*

"As a teacher of religious studies, I usually approach Hinduism as a set of concepts. Mr. Fraenkel, with his retelling of the Mahabharata, reminds us that this religious tradition is also rich with stories and all the elements that make stories appealing. He does so while not neglecting the religious poetry of the Bhagavad Gita."
Dr. David Torbett, Marietta College

"A stirring and authentic version. My prayer is that this Mahabharata will be enjoyed, studied and appreciated by people for years to come."
Dr. Laxmi Narayan Chaturvedi M.D, Author, "The Teachings Of Bhagavat Gita" www.teachingsofbhagavadgita.com

"Literature for those who want to step outside the box."
Mick Burk, West Virginia Public School Educator

"Andy Fraenkel provides us with a remarkable story in his adaptation of Mahabharata. . . He captures the essence of the epic and relates the unfolding action in a most interesting and exciting way." *Stephen Knapp, Author (Books on India's ancient Vedic culture) www.stephen-knapp.com*

"I loved reading Andy Fraenkel's wonderful version of the Mahabharata. . . I was thoroughly involved in the story's philosophy, family intrigue, and battle spectacle. The author captured my interest from the start, and knowing the plot did not diminish my excitement and fascination in its unfolding. Much of the Mahabharata brings to mind problems of more recent times; other wars and other warriors. This book, even though thousands of years old, offers us visceral and uncanny insights into our age." *Gail N. Herman, PhD, Storyteller, Professor and Educational Consultant www.gailherman.net*

Mahabharata
The Eternal Quest

Retold by
Andy Fraenkel

Foreword by

Subhash Kak, Ph.D.
Author and Regents Professor,
Oklahoma State University

*To Trivikram Swami
Thank you so very much
for your unflinching service
to our guru Srila Prabhupada
Sankirtana das
—Andy Fraenkel*

Flying Mountain Press

Copyright © 2013 by Andy Fraenkel
Cover-art Copyright © 2013 by Visnu Fraenkel and Jason Elliott

All Rights Reserved.
This book or any part of this book may not be reproduced in any manner without written permission from the author except for brief quotations in articles and reviews.

Printed in the United States of America
First Printing 2013
2500 copies

ISBN: 978-0-9896074-0-7
Library of Congress Catalogue-in-Publication Data
Information Pending
Fraenkel, Andy 1947

Published by Flying Mountain Press
For information on books and study guide
Visit   www.Mahabharata-Project..com
          www.flyingmountainpress.wordpress.com

For information on Andy Fraenkel's programs:
www.sacredvoices.com   email: story108@juno.com

COVER: Mystically guided by the sage Vyasa, the warrior-prince Arjuna enters a tropical valley high in the Himalayas. Ganga Devi, the Ganges River personified, sends her celestial waters to the Earth which flow down from the Himalayas. Ganga Devi is also the mother of Bhismadev, one of the Mahabharata's leading personalities and one of the twelve mahajanas (wisdom keepers).

To Josh and Visnu
who have taught me so much

To Ruth
whose love has sustained me

To the memory of my friend Lokamangala
Who was half of our two-men Mahabharata drama

And

To Srila Prabhupada
Whose compassion is without limit

Acknowledgements

I owe a great debt of thanks to the following individuals for their assistance and insights in helping to prepare this book: Rupa Devi Dasi, William Workman, and Madan Mohan Mohini Dasi, for their editorial work; Charlotte Jones, Emil Sofsky, Rich Knoblich, Mick Burk, Varada Bhat, Bill Gregor, Nityodita Das, Sukhavaha Dasi, Dr. Don Carrell and Dr. Robert Rosenthal (both of Hanover College) for their extremely helpful feedback; and my wife Ruth and son Josh for their invaluable input in the final edit.

I also want to thank my daughter Visnu Fraenkel and Jason Elliott for their work on the cover and map of ancient India.

I want to thank the following persons for their kind support and encouragement over the years and especially in helping to make this book a reality:

Mr & Mrs Yogesh & Pallavi Mody - Gopisa & Kalindi Fried
Joshua Nityananda Fried - Alina Chandravali Fried
Brian Feather - Mr & Mrs Vijaya Kumar - Pamela Ann Chabak
Mr & Mrs Laxmi Narayan Chaturvedi - Bhakta Josef Lauber
Anand M Chaturvedi - Preti B Chaturvedi - Jaya Rishi Dasa
Dvibhuja Dasa - Langaganesa Dasa (Louis S. Bernier, Jr.)
Mr & Mrs Rakesh & Poonam Beri - Sachimata Dasi & Prins Family
Vidyananda & Kirtida & Sarasvati (Halvorson) - Shyam Pandey
Dr & Mrs Madhu & Amy Dharawat - Dr A.R. Srikantiah
Dulal Chandra Dasa - Mr & Mrs Navin & Krishna Priya Jani
Mr & Mrs Suryaram Joshi - Mr & Mrs Thakor Topiwala
Mr & Mrs Vinodrai Shukla - Dr & Mrs Devender Batra
India Association of Huntington, West Virginia, Puja Group
My mother & sister: Waltraud Fraenkel & Nancy Furbish
Sacinandana Swami - Radhanatha Swami - Varshana Swami

CONTENTS

Map 2
Foreword 3
Introduction 5
Prologues 9
Chapter 1   The Vow 13
Chapter 2   The Curse 26
Chapter 3   Palace Intrigue 33
Chapter 4   The Summer House . . . 51
Chapter 5   The Contest 68
Chapter 6   The New Kingdom . . . 79
Chapter 7   The Dice Match 101
Chapter 8   Exile 111
Chapter 9   Incognito 139
Chapter 10   The Envoy 151
Chapter 11   The Cosmic Form . . . 167
Chapter 12   On The Battlefield . . . 178
Chapter 13   The Night Raid 227
Chapter 14   Grandsire's Story 237
Chapter 15   The Omens 250
Chapter 16   The Final Journey 261
Epilogue 269
Vedic Overview 271
Glossary 276
About Author 281

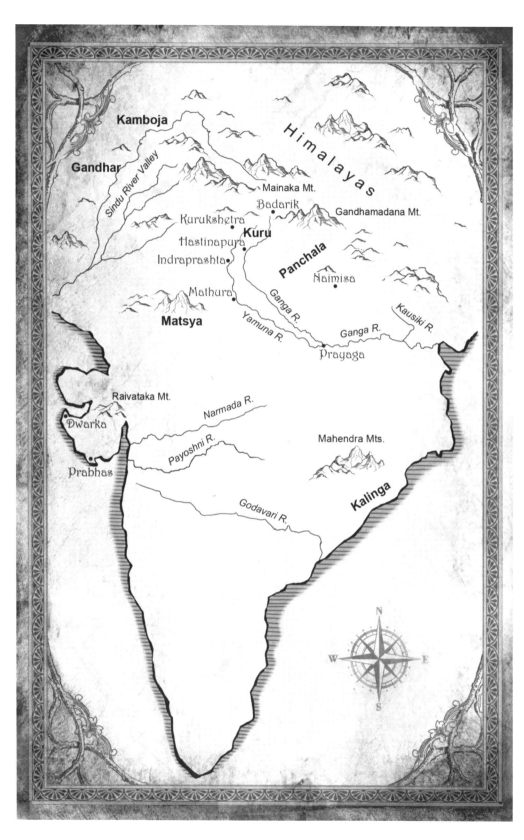

Mahabharata: The Eternal Quest

Foreword

A great book needs to be retold afresh for each generation. *The Mahabharata* is one of those books. Known as the fifth Veda, it is quite unlike the first four Vedas which are difficult to comprehend. It is an extensive book, seven times longer than the *Odyssey* and *Iliad* combined. An epic of ancient India, *Mahabharata* teaches the most abstract ideas indirectly, through stories. It highlights the most complex ethical dilemmas to take the reader to the deepest levels of spiritual wisdom.

The underlining contest in the book between the Pandavas and the Kauravas, who are cousins, is like that between the good and the evil. Its central event is the battle that takes place on the holy ground at Kurukshetra; but this battle also represents the living struggle within each individual's heart. As do the Greek philosophers, *Mahabharata* extolls examination of one's life, and it gives us the most uncommon wisdom to do so. The *Bhagavad Gita*, a jewel of world literature, is a part of it.

Growing up in Kashmir, *The Mahabharata* was a living text to us for its drama, action and wisdom. We chanted the *Bhagavad Gita* at home. Father exhorted his children to be brave and truthful like the Pandava brothers. In particular, he wanted us to learn to concentrate like Arjuna, whose challenge was to shoot the revolving fish above him while looking into its reflection in a pan of oil. Arjuna was so focused on the task that he saw nothing but the eye of the fish.

Mother felt a special relationship with the Deity Krishna, whose appearance day - Janmastami - was a big festival at home. The stories of Krishna's life were recounted. She decorated a swing for baby Krishna, and we fasted until midnight, the hour of His birth.

The Mahabharata is a living document in Indian and Southeast Asian culture, and beyond that, it has influenced world literature.

Mahabharata: The Eternal Quest

The story continues to be relevant to contemporary issues and concerns, especially in showing the havoc that blind ambition, greed and hubris can bring upon society. There are those who argue that selfless action and protection of Dharma, the moral law, taught by Krishna to Arjuna, should be somehow incorporated in the world of business to forestall repeats of our recent financial crises. The book's lessons on the nature and meaning of life bring enlightenment.

The Mahabharata inspires and provides strength as we go through the tribulations of life. It teaches fearlessness for it reminds us that our essence is immortal. Tulsi Gabbard, the congresswoman from Hawaii, writes that when she was on the combat tour of Iraq, the *Bhagavad Gita* brought her great comfort. She reminded herself that she didn't need to worry about death because her spirit-soul would continue to exist.

I still remember Andy Fraenkel telling the story of *Mahabharata* at an international conference in Atlanta over fifteen years ago. A hush fell over the hall as we listened with rapt attention, and at the end, when he came to the story of Yudhisthira and his dog, most had tears in their eyes.

Andy Fraenkel is a master storyteller who, in his performances at schools, colleges, and conferences, not only charms but awakens wisdom that has been largely forgotten in modern life. His writing is as direct as his spoken stories, and his *Mahabharata* has a fresh, fast-paced, cinematic quality to it. In this book he has captured the scope and breath of this great epic.

Subhash Kak, Ph.D.
Author and Regents Professor, Oklahoma State University

Mahabharata: The Eternal Quest

Introduction

Years ago, as a student in City College of New York, I discovered a book in the college library. The book jumped out at me - an old collectable that started me on a journey that I continue to this day. It was entitled *The Indian Story Book* by Richard Wilson (1914) and contained beautiful illustrations. Among the stories included were several from *The Mahabharata*. One story especially caught my attention; the story of King Yudhisthira and the dog. I worked it into a play for my theater class. The class decided to include the piece as one of four short plays we performed in elementary schools in the New York area.

At the time, my interest in Indian spirituality also grew. In 1971, after graduating college, my wife and I met A.C Bhaktivedanta Swami Prabhupada who, coming in a lineage of teachers stemming from the sage Vyasa (author of *Mahabharata*) introduced us to a deeper understanding of *Mahabharata* and *Bhagavad-Gita*. He explained, "In this age, *The Mahabharata* is more essential than the original Vedas." Eventually, I made several trips to India, which helped shape a two-man *Mahabharata* drama performed Off Broadway and my solo *Mahabharata* storytelling performances later on.

And what a tremendous story it is. Peter Brook, the British theater director, who years ago staged a nine-hour *Mahabharata*, reflected that the epic could not be compared with any one of Shakespeare's plays, but only to the Bard's entire body of work. *The Mahabharata* contains all genres: action-adventure, romance, humor, tragedy, horror, mystery, mystical and apocalyptical. It sheds light on all aspects of human nature. It is the living sacred story of an ancient land and an ancient tradition. *The Mahabharata* states that whatever is not found in its pages is found nowhere else.

Mahabharata: The Eternal Quest

Many Vedic scholars, and even the *Mahabharata* itself, establish the text as a history that tells of a civilization undergoing troubling changes at the height of its power. The story is driven by remarkable personalities and monumental events and conflicts. For millenniums the people of India have gone to *Mahabharata* for guidance on how to live a virtuous life, and is a source of inspiration for dance, music, drama, art, and storytelling. The great epic, however, should not be construed as being for India alone. *Mahabharata* has a rightful place in world literature since it addresses many contemporary issues and concerns. Throughout its 100,000 verses it espouses Dharma, which helps us to look at the meaning of our relationship and responsibility to the world around us.

Herein, I bring to bear my life's work in theater and storytelling. To shape these materials into this book was for me both exhilarating and a grave responsibility. I am honored and humbled to have had this opportunity. In my telling I have attempted to remain true to the story while envisioning it in the form of a movie on the big screen. For me, the storyteller's craft is essentially to tell the story in such a way as to ignite the imagination, and then let the listener, or reader, fill in the panoramic scenes and probe the depths of the story. I hope that this book may enrich readers' lives and inspire them in their own journeys.

In closing, I am indebted to Kisari Mohan Ganguli for his rendering of the first complete English translation of *Mahabharata* (1896), and to my spiritual teacher, A.C. Bhaktivedanta Swami Prabhupada, for his translation of the *Srimad Bhagavatam*, with its numerous chapters pertaining to *Mahabharata* and the nature of the Kali-yuga, published by the Bhaktivedanta Book Trust.

Andy Fraenkel
On Gita Jayanti, December, 2012
Commemorating Krishna's speaking the Bhagavad-Gita to Arjuna

Mahabharata
The Eternal Quest

"At the dawn of time,
the Lord sent forth beings,
bestowing upon them Dharma
and offerings for Vishnu,
saying, "Flourish, prosper,
and may all be well."

Bhagavad Gita

Prologues

One/ Endangered

Bhumi, the Earth goddess, soared heavenward, beyond the Moon and the Sun and through the starry Milky Way, up and up, all the way to Brahmaloka, the planet of Lord Brahma, the topmost Celestial. Her steps quickened as she ascended the grand, crystal stairway and entered his ethereal, multi-domed palace with its magnificent, stained-glass windows. As she knelt before the four-headed one, the grief she carried in her heart gave way and tears flowed from her eyes.

"O Brahma, born of a lotus from Vishnu's navel, you bear all things in this world. Please hear me. The Earth, like a small craft precariously adrift at sea, has become burdened by the military might of wicked men. It seems the Asuras, the demoniac forces, wish to seize control of my world. In the guise of royalty, and driven by insatiable greed, they ravage the Earth. No one can live in peace. The people, the animals, the birds and the land suffer terrible injustices. I implore you. Something must be done!"

Alarmed by her distress, yet sustained by inner calm, Brahma rose and reached out his hand. "Come with me, my child." Together they at once set out for Svetadvipa, Lord Vishnu's abode in this material universe. On their journey they were joined by Lord Shiva and the various gods of universal affairs: the thousand-eyed Indra, god of rain and king of Celestials; the wind-god Vayu ; Agni, the fire-god; Surya, the sun-god; the water-god Varuna, and many other Celestials. Arriving at Svetadvipa, they patiently waited on the shores of its milk ocean. Frothy waves lapped the shoreline laden with emeralds, diamonds, rubies and gems. The Celestials appealed to Vishnu, the God of gods. The crimson sky resounded with their prayers. But no response came from the Lord. Their prayers were met only by the sound of the waves crashing on that pristine beach. Their hearts were troubled by His silence. Why did not the all-compassionate Vishnu respond? At that moment, the Celestials experienced the anxiety and sufferings of those on Earth, and they understood Bhumi's plight and were humbled.

Vishnu channeled His message into the heart of Brahma who in turn revealed it to the gods. "The Lord of lords will descend to the Earth, into the realm of man, to alleviate the anguish created by the Asura kings and to counteract their military might. Many of His close friends and servants will also descend to assist Him, and He wishes you Celestials should assist them."

Two/ The Stolen Cow

She had to have it.

The kamadhenu cow held extraordinary powers. A cow of plenty, one that could fulfill all wishes. Whoever drank her milk would remain youthful for thousands of years. The cow, however, belonged to Vasistha, a sage who resided among the Celestials.

"Please get her for me," she begged her husband.

"You should not desire that which belongs to another," he chided her.

"It's not for me, my love. It's for a friend who is in need of the cow's powers. My dear husband, please." She touched his cheek. "It will not at all be difficult for you and your brothers. You are all great heroes. And Vasistha's hermitage is nearby. Please, Dyu. For me."

Dyu was one of the eight Vasus – the Shining Ones, protectors of Indra's celestial court. Dyu called the Vasus together and they quickly arrived at the hermitage of Vasistha, deep in the forest. They were cautious, and not wanting a confrontation with the powerful, mystic sage, made sure to take the cow in his absence.

Vasistha returned shortly after they left. He knew something was amiss and quickly searched the nearby meadows where the kamadhenu usually roamed. The cow was gone. To locate her, he entered samadhi, a deep meditation, and engaged the energies of the sun, clouds, trees, and the earth itself. Sitting in stillness, he projected his astral body in search of the cow and her abductors.

The skies darkened and fierce winds began to blow. The Vasus hurried along the path with their prize. They had gone some distance when a towering figure of the sage loomed before them, blocking their way.

"You dare take my kamadhenu! What insolence! I shall curse you all!"

Lightning streaked across the sky as the earth shook. The once brave Vasus fell to their knees. "Please, spare us!" they cried. Thunder boomed above the trees. Branches and leaves fell all around them.

"None of you are fit to reside in the heavens. As punishment for your reckless act, you shall take birth on the Earth for one lifetime."

"A lifetime on Earth!" The Vasus were aghast. "No, please don't do this to us. Be merciful. Anything else."

Vasistha paused to reconsider. "The curse has passed my lips and cannot be revoked. You must be born on Earth. But, if you can find a way to shorten your lives, you may return to the celestial realms quickly. But not Dyu. Dyu, you are the instigator of the group, and for your misdeed you will spend a long life on Earth. So be it."

Three/ Krishna Tells a Story

All was quiet. The night sky blanketed the valley. The stars sparkled, vying for attention.

Krishna pondered, "Can truth ever undermine Dharma? Or can a lie ever be preferable to the truth in upholding Dharma?"

Yudhisthira responded with a question. "But is not a lie under any circumstances still a lie?"

"My friend, morality might not be as easy to understand as you think. I'll tell you a story:

"In the forest there lived a sage by the name of Kausika who took great pride in always telling the truth. He was known far and wide for this unwavering quality. One morning, when he sat outside his hut, three men went rushing past and bound into the thick woods. Shortly, a murderous gang came in search of the three men. Knowing he would never tell a lie, they asked the sage, "Which way did they go?" Kausika told them exactly where the men went. The gang took off in pursuit. They caught the three men and robbed and killed them.

"Kausika thought by telling the truth he had protected Dharma, but it led to the deaths of three travelers. In truth, he was very foolish and unable to discern the subtleties of Dharma. Dharma may point the way for moral behavior, but that doesn't mean we should suspend our judgment when danger arises. At times, as in this story, truth may harm Dharma and falsehood may uphold Dharma. The wise men say Dharma protects us and sustains us. But we must also use our intelligence to understand the best course of action and protect Dharma."

Chapter 1

The Vow

"Your sons and their forces are ready," Sanjaya told the blind king. "As ready as they'll ever be."

King Dhritarastra listened with both expectancy and regret, hovering in a world of his own, molded of past and future. If only he had listened to Vidura, it would not have come to this. He feared for his sons, the Kauravas. What would happen to them now? If he could, he would make Duryodhan give back all the land he had taken from the Pandavas. But of all his sons, Duryodhan had always been beyond his control. Surely, Providence would now have its way.

Sanjaya, the king's aid and confidant, sat in the royal palace at Hastinapura by his side. Though Sanjaya's gaze was drawn within, he looked far beyond the city's streets and walls. With Vyasa's gift of mystic vision, he beheld the valley of Kurukshetra over a hundred miles away. There, as the two armies prepared for battle, Sanjaya could observe every aspect and scan every detail. He could hear any conversation and even know someone's thoughts.

"This is quite unusual," Sanjaya continued, and he paused in disbelief.

Dhritarastra impatiently stamped his jeweled cane for attention. "What is it?" He insisted on knowing.

"Yudhisthira has stepped off his chariot. He proceeds across the valley on foot and unarmed toward your sons."

"Unarmed? Does he mean to seek a truce or to surrender?" Dhritarastra inquired. His mind hoped against hope. Could there still be time for reconciliation, for peace?

The morning air was crisp. Yudhisthira, the eldest of the Pandavas, walked toward the expanse of Kaurava warriors and their allies. The army Yudhisthira beheld far outnumbered his own. In the distant ranks, amid his sworn enemies, he spied Bhismadev's splendid chariot, decorated with many weapons. He headed straight for it. Bhismadev was the respected Grandsire of the dynasty, the eldest and wisest. He was also Yudhisthira's ever well-wisher and like a father to him. Even now Bhismadev observed the solitary figure with pride. Yudhisthira took each step with such ease and grace. Bhismadev knew the last thing Yudhisthira wanted was this fight.

Bhismadev was surrounded by men impatient for battle, for blood and glory, for the sweet taste of victory. Duryodhan, Dushasana, Karna, Sakuni, and Ashwattama. They had waited years for this moment. The horses drawing their chariots whinnied in anticipation. The nobles snickered upon seeing Yudhisthira approach. Maybe this would be easier than they thought. Had Yudhisthira lost his nerve when he saw the sight of their intimidating forces? After all, he had retreated to the forest to spend thirteen years in exile without a word of complaint.

Bhismadev's mind drifted away from the moment at hand and settled into the past. How had he let it come to this, a civil war that would rip apart this exalted Kuru dynasty? It was the one thing he sought all his life to avoid. His mind wandered back to his youth, and to his father, King Santanu.

Mahabharata: The Eternal Quest

* * * * *

Santanu followed the maiden from the river to the far end of the village. She was of slender waist and golden skin, but above all, a remarkable fragrance emanated from her being. Santanu could not take his eyes off her. Actually, he could have closed his eyes and followed her just by her enchanting scent. He would do anything to have her as his wife. She looked back at the king riding upon his silver-encrusted chariot. She welcomed his unmoving gaze. This was the man and the world she would have. She smiled at Santanu and entered the house of her father, the chief of the fishermen.

* * * * *

King Santanu returned from his trip markedly sullen. No matter how much he tried, he could not hide his mood from his son. He was pensive for days afterwards. Time and again, Bhismadev tried to find out what weighed upon his father's mind. But Santanu only looked down and remained silent to all of his inquiries. Santanu loved his son. Bhismadev was the only surviving child born of Santanu and the goddess Ganga – the Ganges River personified. In his childhood, Bhismadev received his education and training from the Celestials, and especially from the sage Vasistha, in the heavenly regions from where Ganga had come. After his multifaceted education, Ganga brought the boy back to Earth to reside with his father. All the citizens knew this boy as Gangadatta – Son of Ganga – and they considered him the most blessed and fortunate person to walk the earth.

The king was unabashedly proud of Bhismadev and he continued to groom the youth with utmost care to become the future lord of the Kuru dynasty. In turn, Bhismadev loved his father, and as a faithful son, he would do anything and go to any length to ensure his father's happiness.

Bhismadev privately questioned the king's chariot driver about his recent excursions. When he informed the youth the king had lingered at the village of the fishermen, Bhismadev hastily proceeded there.

* * * * *

"Yes, your father came here seeking the hand of my daughter, Satyavati, in marriage," explained the fisherman curtly. He eyed the young man suspiciously. Had he come to make trouble for him and the village?

After a moment of strained silence, Bhismadev inquired further. "And what happened?"

"I told your father, the king, my terms for marriage." The fisherman paused again to gauge the youth's response and continued. "He can marry my daughter with the condition that her children must ascend to the throne and inherit the kingdom."

Bhismadev had not expected something like this, but now he understood the reason for his father's despondency. He considered the proposal and what it meant to the well-being of his father.

"If that's all you're worried about," he said rather nonchalantly, "I promise you here and now, and I will swear it before anyone you wish to bring forth as witnesses, that I relinquish all rights to the royal throne."

"This is indeed a generous offer," said the fisherman, "but it is not enough."

"Not enough!" Bhismadev's voice trembled with anger.

The fisherman continued cautiously. "Please. Let me explain. You're a handsome and courageous young man. In due course, you'll marry a woman worthy of you. In the future, you'll have children, and when they grow up, your children will become envious of my daughter's children. Your children will certainly feel they have been cheated out of a throne that is rightfully theirs.

Their enmity would rip apart the dynasty and lead to a war that would only threaten to destroy this great kingdom."

Understanding the human condition even in his youth, Bhismadev conceded, "It's a point well made. Therefore, for the sake of my father's happiness, and to preserve peace in the future, I make a vow to never marry and to never have children. I make a vow of lifelong celibacy."

When Bhismadev spoke these words, a thunderous applause was heard from the heavens and flower petals fell from the sky. The Celestials were amazed one of their own would make such a vow.

When Bhismadev returned home with his father's bride, Santanu was overwhelmed with happiness. The king was so grateful toward his son, he summoned all the power at his command to give Bhismadev a supreme benediction: he could choose the moment of his death.

* * * * *

Santanu and Satyavati had two wonderful boys, Citrangada and Vichitravirya. But fate would not let Santanu see them grow up. Even as he grew old, the king did not expect death to take him. There was yet so much to look forward to. Time passes all too quickly and the king was swept away from his loved ones by the wheel of samsara, the cycle of birth and death.

Tragedy struck the family again some years later when Citrangada, the eldest of Satyavati's two sons, died in battle. Again, she grieved and sought desperately to protect what was left of her family. She asked Bhismadev to arrange a marriage for his remaining stepbrother, Vichitravirya.

Bhismadev didn't know much about arranging marriages. He resorted to the easiest course for the kshatriyas, the warrior class. Bhismadev stole into the palace of King Kasi to take away one of his lovely and eligible daughters. He heard laughter emanating from one chamber. There he found all three sisters, the daughters of Kasi, together. When he entered the room they ceased their laughter. In turn, he was flustered and confused. He didn't know which sister to choose for his stepbrother, and so he took all three. After he returned with them to Hastinapura, he saw Amba, the eldest of the sisters, was distraught. She would not speak nor eat.

"I promise you," Bhismadev assured her, "you'll have a comfortable and prosperous life here in the court of the Kurus. I'll see to it."

"Comfort and prosperity are of no concern to me. I have already given my love to another," Amba retorted.

"If it means that much, then go to him. I shall arrange a carriage for you."

Amba quickly departed Hastinapura, eager to see her beloved Prince Salva.

* * * * *

"What are you doing here?" Salva inquired without a hint of affection.

Upon seeing Salva's stone-like countenance, Amba, at that moment, realized she had made a horrible mistake. She did not anticipate this reaction from her beloved, but how could she not have known? He was always proud to a fault.

"My beloved, my dearest, please don't reject me. You know I love you. There is no one else."

"Bhismadev took you from your father's house, did he not? You are now his responsibility. Let him take you in." Salva turned away and never spoke a word to her again.

Amba wanted to scream at the injustice of it all. *How is this happening to me? What have I done to displease the gods?* For months she and Salva had spoken of marriage. Her future was secure. Now, she felt herself adrift in a world of uncertainty. Her delicate body trembled. She struggled to regain her composure and to reassure herself. She was attractive and desirable. She thought of how Bhismadev had learned the finer arts of etiquette from the Celestials. *He is noble and just. Surely, he would be open to reason and accept me.* In an instant she was back in the carriage.

"Drive like the wind, back to Hastinapura," she instructed the driver.

She, like everyone, heard about the unshakable vow Bhismadev had made for his father. But she was confident she could entice him with her feminine charm. After all, this is what men want. Thus, she lied to herself to keep from falling apart.

* * * * *

Soon, Vichitravirya married the two willing sisters Ambika and Ambalika and afterwards Bhismadev enthroned him as king of the Kurus. But tragedy came upon the family a third time when the new king succumbed to a sudden illness. Satyavati, overwhelmed with grief, called for Bhismadev once again.

"Bhismadev, it seems the gods favor you. Everyone in the kingdom knows this. The Celestials have paved the way for you to ascend the throne."

"This I cannot do, for I have renounced the throne," Bhismadev said gravely.

"But you must! My sons were without heirs. Somehow the Kuru lineage must continue."

Bhismadev looked disapprovingly upon Satyavati, and she paused to offer up another approach, one Bhismadev might be inclined to pursue. "You may know of the ancient custom. If a man dies childless, or cannot beget a child, his brother is permitted to beget children with the man's wife to continue the family. The thing to do now is for you to approach the sisters and beget a child with each of them. In this way they'll both be satisfied."

"You know I can't do that."

"But this is only proper." She was frustrated. "Bhismadev, please be reasonable. The circumstances of the past have all changed."

"Everything in this world may change. The oceans may dry up and the stars may fall from the sky, but I have taken a lifelong vow of celibacy and I will never waiver from that vow. You must find some other way."

To his surprise, she countered, "There is." Satyavati told him a story of what happened before she met Santanu:

"One day the chief of the fishermen caught a large fish and when he cut it open, I was inside, just a tiny baby. He and his wife raised me as their own daughter. But from the time of my birth, my body smelled just like a fish. I had an awful time as a child. The other children made fun of me and wouldn't let me play with them. Even the adults wouldn't come too close. No one would be my friend. I was all alone. As I grew older, I thought I would have to spend the rest of my life like that. In my youth, I worked for my family ferrying people across the river. My passengers would sit at the other end of the boat. No one could stand my odor for too long. Then one day, the sage Parasara came on the boat. He wasn't like the others. He sat at arm's length from me. We were alone. He looked at me with longing as we crossed the river. I looked down and kept rowing.

'You're very beautiful,' he said. 'The only thing is you have a foul odor. But it can be remedied.'

He placed his hand upon my shoulder and the fishy odor left me forever. My body began to smell like a wonderful bouquet of heavenly flowers. But Parasara did not remove his hand.

'You're very beautiful,' he repeated and he drew me to him.

The waves gently tossed the boat. It seemed time was suspended.

'I've never been with a man.'

'Do not be afraid. You will not be dishonored. Today, you'll have a son who will do extraordinary things.'

At his beckoning, a thick fog descended out of nowhere, and under its blanket we made love. Afterwards, he steered the boat to an *island in the middle of the river and there I immediately gave birth to a son. The child miraculously grew into manhood before my very eyes.*

'It was time for my birth,' the man-child said to me. 'Thank you for becoming my mother. You will not regret it. Now I must take my leave and enter the great mountains of the North country. A strange time will soon be upon this world. I must prepare for the coming age, the Kali-yuga. But if you ever need me just sit down facing north and think of me.'

"The son I gave birth to is known as Dvaipayana Vyasa – the Island Born Vyasa. Afterwards, true to Parasara's word, I remained a virgin until I married your father. Vyasa is a member of our family. If you think it proper, he can be called upon to continue the dynasty."

Bhismadev gladly approved of her plan. It was time for Satyavati to sit down facing the north.

* * * * *

The Himalayan range stretched over fifteen hundred miles across the northern reaches of Bharata-varsa, ancient India. For millennia, sages and hermits had taken shelter and found solace in these formidable mountains. In some places, the wind had blown for a million years with no one there to listen. On a clear day the mountains were a world of pristine silence, as flocks of cranes and geese glided over their peaks. The mountains seemingly held out their secrets, enticing anyone who was brave enough, or crazy enough, to come and take them. The secrets they contained, however, were available only to those willing to sacrifice every ounce of their being. But to the Celestials, the gods in the heavens, these mountains were a mere playground.

Vyasa made his hermitage at the middle passage into the mountains, in the caves near the hamlet called Badarik. This place was only accessible to outsiders for several months out of the year.

During those months, the headwaters of the Ganges cascaded from nearby glaciers and cliffs. The air was crisp and the land where the gods could be seen was not far off. By the river, Vyasa sat in samadhi, sustained meditation, for months on end. Vyasa saw through the veil of time and understood the cycle of the four ages, and how the last age in the cycle, the Kali-yuga, would disturb and confound the inhabitants of the Earth. He understood in the coming Kali-yuga the Earth would withhold her abundance of fruits, vegetables and grains, and men would be forced to toil strenuously for their food and livelihood. Having to struggle in this way, men would become misguided, envious and quarrelsome. The brahmins, the women, the children, the elderly and the cows would be neglected and abused.

Vyasa gathered four of his most prominent disciples. "The Vedic knowledge is extensive and conclusive," he told them, "and it has come down through oral teaching since time immemorial. But the Kali-yuga will not allow the tradition to continue in this way. The four ages are like the four seasons. In the first three ages, men are endowed with keen memories, and by hearing something just once, they remember it for the rest of their lives. But the Kali-yuga is like the winter season. The path of Dharma, of virtue, will be icy and dangerous. Men's hearts will be hardened and their tongues and ears will be darkened. The span of their lives and memories will decrease. Their perceptions and conclusions will be feeble. Men will not know how to act or speak properly."

Vyasa's disciples shivered at his description.

For the benefit of all people born in the Kali-yuga, Vyasa divided the Veda into four parts: the Sama, Atharva, Rig and Yajur. The Vedas contained descriptions of the gods of universal affairs and ritual offerings to them, along with various teachings and instructions so men might understand the workings of this world and live harmoniously within it. Vyasa gradually trained each of his four disciples to become conversant in one of the four parts of the Vedas he chose for them. Each disciple was entrusted to teach his part to many new students who would in turn impart the teachings to others. Vyasa also ensured the clear transmission of the teachings by writing them down for the very first time. But he wondered if this would be sufficient for the populace of the Kali-yuga.

* * * * *

When Vyasa arrived at the palace he entered his mother's quarters and touched her feet with great respect and affection. Looking upon her son, Satyavati shed tears of love and embraced him. It didn't matter if he was unsightly. His hair and beard were long and matted. His body and clothes were caked with grime from the windswept mountains. Since the rivers and lakes froze over for most of the year, he could not bathe, and a stale, rancid odor had settled over him. Looking upon him, and smelling his odor, Satyavati remembered her own embarrassing youth, and suddenly realized the difficult task in store for Ambika and Ambalika.

Vyasa asked, "My dear mother, how can I serve you?"

His question brought her back to the moment at hand.

"The Kuru dynasty is threatened with extinction," she explained, "and you, my dear son, are the only one who can help." In this way, she went on to inform him of the role he was to play.

That night Vyasa went to the bedchamber of Ambika. She was so horrified by his appearance, she could not bear to look at him. During their time together, she kept her eyes tightly shut.

Before he left, Vyasa told her, "Your son will be exceedingly strong and proud, but because you have acted this way, he will be born blind. His name will be Dhritarastra."

The next night he went to Ambalika's chamber. She had heard what had happened from her sister and she made sure to keep her eyes open. But when she saw Vyasa she turned ghostly white. At the end of the evening, as he left, he told her, "Your son will be noble and kind, but because of your reaction toward me, he will also be unusually pale. His name will be Pandu."

Nine months later, Satyavati beheld her newborn grandsons, one blind and one pale. *They are so very fragile,* she thought. *We need one more child to insure the dynasty continues.* She asked Ambika to have union with Vyasa one more time. Once again the sage arrived in Ambika's chamber. To his surprise, Vyasa found a maidservant waiting.

"Please don't be angry," she said. "Ambika was too embarrassed to be with you again. She sent me in her place."

Although Vyasa was a frightful sight to most people, the maidservant saw his true, inner radiance. She happily welcomed him into her arms. They spent the night together and before he left, he told her, "Your son will be wise. His name will be Vidura."

* * * * *

Amba was outraged. Bhismadev wouldn't stray from his vow. She wanted him punished for ruining her life. She even appealed to the fearsome warrior-sage Parasurama, who called for Bhismadev and demanded he marry her. But nothing came of it. She felt abandoned. *Where is the justice?* she thought. *Where?* By and by, she went into the forest to perform austerities to petition the gods. She made a vow of her own. Amba deprived herself of food and society. She stood unmoving for twelve years and endured heat and cold, snakes and prowling animals. Every year she ate only one fallen leaf for her sustenance. Her skin became dry and withered, her cheeks hollow, her eyes sunken, her hair matted, and yet, a strange glow emanated from her being.

One day, Shiva appeared to the local rishis, the forest mendicants. He inquired about Amba. When they brought him to her, he asked, "My dear lady, I am curious as to why a woman of your beauty would come to the forest alone to engage in severe austerities and allow herself to become so emaciated?"

She told Shiva and the rishis her whole story: how she had been carried off by Bhismadev and was deprived of a normal, matrimonial life, and that even the exalted Parasurama intervened on her behalf, but he could not attain the justice she so much desired. She told them she had decided to take matters into her own hands. Her solution was to become a man in her next life to fight Bhismadev and kill him. That's why she had come to the forest to perform austerities. As she spoke, Shiva and the rishis listened to her plight with rapt attention, and tears welled up in their eyes.

She ended her story with an appeal to Shiva, "I want revenge. If you want, you can help me, but don't try to change my mind."

Shiva was charmed by her determination. "I assure you, you will achieve your purpose. In your next life you'll again have a king as your father. You will remember this previous life of yours. You will become a maharatha, a very powerful warrior. All I say will come to pass."

After Shiva vanished, Amba hurriedly gathered wood and proceeded to build a funeral pyre. In the presence of the rishis, she entered into the blazing fire, repeatedly uttering the words, "I want to see Bhismadev destroyed. I want to see Bhismadev destroyed."

Chapter 2

The Curse

Time passed. Soon the halls resounded with the laughter of the sons of Ambika, Ambalika, and the maidservant. The three boys grew up together. They were noble and courageous. They were the best of friends and loved one another as brothers.

Under Bhismadev's guidance the dynasty prospered and lived in peace with all its neighbors. Both kings and Celestials came to Hastinapura to offer homage to Bhismadev. But because of his vow he did not lay claim to the throne. Neither could Dhritarastra, the eldest of the youths. His blindness prevented him from ascending the throne. The king had to be in possession of all his senses to evaluate persons and situations in order to make effective decisions and rule properly. Thus, Bhismadev enthroned Pandu, the pale one, the son of Ambalika. Kings from far and wide came to pay tribute and homage to the new king. Seeing this, Satyavati was overwhelmed with joy. It seemed as if a new era had begun for the Kuru dynasty. King Pandu treated all the citizens kindly and justly, never speaking a harsh word. He was the most perfect king and the citizens all loved him. Meanwhile, feeling neglected, Dhritarastra grew bitter. Had Providence forgotten him?

But nothing ever remains the same for too long and one day Providence again intervened. While hunting in a dense forest, Pandu released his arrows and shot two deer in the midst of their mating. The deer were actually a sage and his wife.

"You fool!" said the dying sage, "Do you know what you have done? It is forbidden to hunt a creature while it frolics with its mate. My wife and I assumed the forms of deer only to enjoy in our lovemaking. This has cost us our lives. Thus I curse you: the next time you venture to enjoy the delights of love, you also will die."

Pandu was overwhelmed with grief for what he had done. "I will retire to the forest," he declared to his two wives, "to live a life of renunciation. I will live in peace and pray for the welfare of all beings. I will learn to neither rejoice in fortune nor lament in misfortune. I do not know when or if I will ever return to Hastinapura."

His two beautiful wives, Kunti and Madri, insisted upon going with him.

Kunti said, "We cannot enjoy our beds, comforts and meals in your absence."

Madri added, "As your devoted wives, we also vow to abandon all luxuries and go with you into the forest."

And so they did.

* * * * *

As a young woman, Kunti, before marrying Pandu, had received a boon from Durvasa Muni. While the mystic was visiting her adopted father's palace, she served him attentively. Durvasa wielded great and unimaginable powers. Being pleased with Kunti, Durvasa bestowed a gift upon her.

"I give you a mantra," he said. "With this mantra you can call upon any of the gods if you ever want to beget a child with them."

Kunti blushed at the thought. "I can't accept such a gift," she said.

"Do you dare shun my kindness? You must accept!" demanded the Muni. Kunti discovered what was obvious to everyone who knew Durvasa - he had a temper which could be aroused over the slightest provocation.

Thus, she reluctantly accepted the gift, and eventually Kunti's curiosity got the best of her. Using the mantra she called for the sun-god, Surya. Although she had no desire for a child at the time, Surya told her, "O beautiful one, you must know the power of the mantra. My coming to you cannot be in vain."

"But what shall I do?" she pleaded.

Understanding the intent of her question, the sun-god assured her, "Your chastity shall remain undisturbed, and after the child is born you will be as pure as before. And let it be known, your son will be born replete with golden earrings, armbands and armor. He will be a great and noble warrior, and as long as he has these ornaments he will be invincible in battle. He will be compassionate to all and will consider very few his enemies."

A child was thus born and Kunti smiled upon this strong and handsome new life. But how could she face her family and friends? And what man would have her as his wife now? She placed the baby in a basket and set it adrift in a nearby river. As she watched the currents take hold of it, she wanted to jump in the river and bring the child to her breast. She called upon his father the sun-god to watch over the child and to forgive her. With tears in her eyes, she forced herself to turn away.

The basket drifted downstream, past homes and villages, past children playing, past sages sitting in meditation, and past funeral parties burning the remains of dead relatives. Guided and protected by Surya, no one noticed the basket as it floated on and on until the river came to a bend where it flowed into the great valley of the River Ganges. There, at the end of the day, a charioteer watered his horses. He discovered the basket and took the baby home to his wife. They cried tears of joy, for they had been without child. Now the couple lit incense and gave thanks to the gods. They were struck by the baby's noble features and ornaments. They held him tightly and they raised the child as their own.

* * * * *

For the time being, in Pandu's absence, Dhritarastra assumed leadership of the dynasty. Deep in his heart he felt vindicated. Providence shone down upon him. His step was lively and his mannerisms jolly. As he took his place on the throne of Hastinapura he told himself and others it was only to keep it safely until the day his brother returned from the forest. "That day will be a joyous one," he told himself and others.

Dhritarastra had recently married a beautiful princess from Gandhar, the kingdom of the Northwest country, across the Sindu River and beyond the Kamboja Mountains. Her name was Gandhari, and she was a cultured and virtuous princess. Neither her father King Subala nor her brother Sakuni informed her the man she was to marry was blind from birth. When she first met Dhritarastra she made a silent vow to share in her husband's plight. Gandhari calmly wrapped a silk scarf around her eyes and tied the knot tightly in the back of her head. She never wanted to think of herself as better than her husband the king, and also she felt her austerity would insure she would be the mother of a distinguished lineage of kings.

* * * * *

One day, Pandu lamented he would be without an heir. Kunti told him of the mantra Durvasa had given her; she had the power to call upon the gods. She didn't know how her husband would react. She surprised herself at how readily this secret leapt from her mouth. Pandu was elated. He told her, "Because of the curse, I cannot give you a child. But the gods are like my brothers. Call upon them. They will help."

First Kunti called upon Dharmaraj, the lord of justice, and the pious Yudhisthira was born. A year later, she called upon Vayu, the wind-god, and Bhima of great strength was born. Then she called upon Indra, king of Celestials, and the mighty bowman Arjuna was born. At that time, Madri, Pandu's younger wife, asked to use the mantra. She called upon the two heavenly physicians, the Aswini Kumars who could cure the sick and restore youth to the aged. From them, the gentle twins Nakula and Sahadeva were born. These five brothers, fathered by the gods, came to be known as the Pandavas, named after King Pandu. Pandu was most pleased with his good fortune and celebrated the birth of his kingdom's new heirs.

* * * * *

Word arrived at the royal palace Kunti had given birth to Yudhisthira, the firstborn of their dynasty. Gandhari flew into a jealous rage. "Why?" she screamed. "It's been almost two years. Why is this happening?"

Gandhari had been with child for most of two years. Month after month she had anxiously awaited the birth of her own firstborn. But the child stubbornly remained in her womb. Now it seemed Kunti's child Yudhisthira would be heir to the throne. She felt the gods had cheated her. A silent fury festered within her. She entered a dark room and beat her protruding stomach with an iron rod. "Why don't you come out? Why don't you come out?" she screamed again and again at her stomach as angry tears streamed from her eyes. As she continued to beat her stomach, suddenly, her womb spewed forth a large ball of flesh. She was horrified and trembled uncontrollably. What on earth had she given birth to? She called for the sage Vyasa who shortly arrived in her chambers.

"Vyasa, you prophesied I would be the mother of a hundred sons. Your words are useless," Gandhari rebuked him as he barely entered the room. "I have given birth to nothing except this lump of flesh." She burst into tears.

"Do not worry my lady, you shall have your hundred sons," he comforted her. "I have never given a false prophecy."

Vyasa told her to prepare a hundred pots and break the lump of flesh into a hundred pieces and place each piece in a pot. In the meantime, he prepared a mixture of fresh herbs and ghee, clarified butter, and carefully poured the mixture into each of the pots. A hundred male children were formed. Duryodhan was the first to emerge from the pots, braying like an ass. His cries echoed throughout the royal palace and seemed to shake the walls to their very foundation. Violent winds blew down from the Northwest, bringing a monolithic wall of sand that engulfed Hastinapura. Day turned into night. Beasts wailed and jackals howled.

* * * * *

Vidura came before the blind king. As they grew up, Vidura had always been a close friend and a valuable advisor to his stepbrother. Being born of a maidservant, Vidura had no claim to the throne.

"Dhritarastra, I have come here to warn you, although my words will seem like daggers. In the past few days dreadful omens could be seen and heard throughout the land." Vidura had wanted to measure his words, but saw there was no easy way to voice what he had to say. "You must know what I'm talking about. It's your newborn son. In the future his unbridled desires will create havoc in the kingdom. You must renounce him and send him far, far away. It's for the good of the kingdom, my brother. You must forget he even exists."

Dhritarastra's head ached. He was well aware of the ill omens. This time he could not listen to Vidura's counsel. Dhritarastra shook with righteous anger. "How can you ask this of me? He is my own flesh and blood."

"This is very painful, I know. But it will avoid much greater pain in the future. You still can enjoy the pleasure of your many other sons. However, this first born son of yours will cause the destruction of your dynasty, just like the fire from one tree can ruin a forest."

Dhritarastra turned away. "Vidura, leave me and let me be. I forbid you to ever speak of it again."

* * * * *

In the forest, on a fresh spring day, a day that excites the heart and calls for love and adventure, Pandu approached Madri. He caught hold of her hand, and, despite her words of warning, he brought her to a soft patch of grass. They lay down together and he embraced her and kissed her again and again. The forest was hushed. Beams of sunlight streamed through the tall trees. At that moment, Pandu evoked the curse he had received years before and he died.

With tears streaming down their faces, Kunti and Madri built a funeral pyre by the bank of a nearby river. As Pandu's body was consumed by the dancing flames, Madri thought this was all her fault. What a wonderful life the three of them had together, along with their five noble boys. She wished she could pull back time. If only she had been firm with Pandu. Now, she dared not tell Kunti she had secretly longed for his touch. She braced herself and decided to perform the sati rite.

"My dearest Kunti, kiss the children for me," she said softly.

Kunti understood her intent. "Don't worry. I will raise your children as my own."

"You're a saint."

And after touching water to her forehead, Madri entered the fire to follow her husband into the next life.

Chapter 3

Palace Intrigue

Kunti and her five boys returned to the capital city of Hastinapura where they resided in the royal palace under the care of King Dhritarastra. The Pandava boys mingled freely and unpretentiously with nobles and commoners alike. Upon seeing them, all the citizens were reminded of the nobility and generosity of their father.

Dhritarastra, however, did not relish their presence. They were a constant ache in his heart. Dhritarastra only held the crown as a temporary steward for Pandu's eldest son Yudhisthira. The blind king had one hundred sons of his own who were known as the Kauravas, the eldest being Duryodhan. Dhritarastra longed for his own sons to be heirs to the kingdom. In one sense, he knew in his heart this desire was illicit. But was *he* not the first born? Why should he not be the king? What did it matter if he was born blind? Why was he forced to continue to live in his brother's shadow? Why did Providence continue to mock him?

The news of her grandson Pandu's death struck Satyavati in the core of her being. She felt she had every right to be happy and to see her family contented, but Providence was also cruel to her. Even as she looked upon her many great-grandchildren, the

Pandavas and Kauravas, she dared not allow herself to be happy. She could already see the signs. Too many times had she been full of hope. Too many times had her hopes been destroyed. *Is life only a bitter struggle?* she thought. *A string of hopes and defeats?* In the past, she had made every effort to guide the course of events. But she had grown old and tired, and she resigned herself to accept the will of Providence for her dynasty. She left the palace and retired to a hermitage deep in the forest for the remainder of her life.

The Pandavas and the Kauravas grew up together. From the very beginning, a rivalry emerged between them. Yudhisthira was heir apparent and Duryodhan could never forget this fact. Duryodhan was by nature envious and conniving. He became consumed with a desire for power beyond measure and he secretly vowed to let no one stand in his way.

* * * * *

Bhima's favorite trick was to jump in the river where the Kauravas were frolicking. He would grab six or seven of the boys and take them under the current with him. He was huge for his age. Bhima had no trouble staying under the water for a length of time. In his steel-like grip, his cousins struggled helplessly. At the last minute, he would let them go and they shot to the surface, gasping for air. Bhima was often frustrated with the gentle and respectful nature of his brothers, especially Yudhisthira, who patiently endured the taunts of their cousins. Numerically, there were a hundred cousins against the five of them. But Bhima was the equalizer.

Duryodhan always played to win and he was tired of being thwarted by Bhima. He resented Bhima with every ounce of his being. One night he approached his closest brothers, Dushasana and Chitra, with a wicked plan. "You know how much Bhima loves desserts," he started. Of course they knew. Often enough Bhima had muscled in on their share of the cakes, rasgullas, gulab jamuns, and other treats. "Well, this will be his undoing," Duryodhan assured them.

The next day the boys called after Bhima as he walked by the river. They came running toward him with a basket and smiles on their faces. *What type of game are they up to now?* Bhima wondered. But when they pulled out the cake, Bhima's eyes lit up.

"Bhima, we're getting older now and we're supposed to be more mature," said Dushasana in his most serious demeanor. "So we brought you this peace offering in the hope we could put aside our animosities and become friends."

Bhima's suspicions dropped by the wayside and he devoured the cake like a ravenous wolf. The cake accomplished what the hundred of them could not. Bhima fell to the ground like a log. The cake was laced with poison and he was out cold. The brothers bound him hand and foot and dragged him to a cliff overlooking the deepest part of the river.

"You like being under the water so much," said Chitra. "Well, you can join the fish."

"If you're lucky enough," added Dushasana, "maybe in your next life you'll be born a fish. Or a wolf. Or a bear."

The boys laughed with glee as they pushed his body off the cliff.

* * * * *

His brothers searched for Bhima until the last streaks of the sun disappeared below the horizon, and darkness covered the land. They returned home late that night, weary and cold. The next day Bhima was still missing. Kunti and her sons were perplexed at Bhima's absence. At each passing day, their hearts grew heavier.

"This is not like Bhima," Kunti repeated again and again. "He would never go off like this without a word to anyone."

The Pandavas approached Dhritarastra for the sake of their grieving mother, but the king seemed unconcerned. "Your brother is a strong boy. He can take care of himself. Sometimes, to seek adventure, boys will run away. Such things happen. So do not be alarmed. I'm sure he'll come back according to his own time."

As they left the royal court Arjuna was annoyed. "He doesn't really care about us. We're a thorn in his side."

"Arjuna, please don't speak like that," Yudhisthira pleaded. "The king loves us like his own sons."

"Yudhisthira, you're under illusion. He takes care of us simply because he is obliged to honor our father's memory, that's all."

"Let's look once more down the river," Yudhisthira suggested, wanting to move the conversation to a more positive note. "Perhaps Bhima had an accident and was swept away by the current."

"Haven't you seen enough?" challenged Arjuna. "It's Duryodhan and his brothers. They're always taunting us. And they hate Bhima because he won't let them get away with anything. They've plotted against him."

"But Arjuna, you have no evidence."

"Well, I'll get the evidence." Arjuna turned and ran down the lane towards the royal orchards and across open fields to a distant grove.

"Where are you going?" Yudhisthira asked as he and his brothers hurried after Arjuna.

"I'm going to confront Duryodhan and force it out of him."

"That would be unwise. To stir up this animosity will lead to no good," Yudhisthira advised. "Arjuna, please don't do anything rash."

But Arjuna did not heed his brother's advice. He raced ahead to where Duryodhan and his brothers played near the grove.

"Duryodhan, I want to have a word with you," Arjuna yelled as he approached the eldest of the Kauravas idling with his brothers.

Duryodhan could hear the agitation in Arjuna's voice and this filled him with a sense of both power and pleasure.

"What did you do with our brother?" demanded Arjuna.

"What are you talking about?"

"You know very well what I'm talking about. And I'm not leaving here until I get an answer."

Duryodhan turned to Yudhisthira. "Did you put him up to this?"

"Duryodhan, Arjuna is upset. He doesn't mean anything by it. Please excuse his behavior."

"And how many times would you have me excuse the behavior of your impetuous brothers?" Duryodhan sneered. "Yudhisthira, you're the eldest. You're supposed to know how to control your subordinates. I don't know what type of leader you'll make."

Hearing this, Arjuna lunged at Duryodhan. Yudhisthira caught hold of his younger brother and with great difficulty held him back.

"If he wants to fight me, Yudhisthira, let him try." Duryodhan jeered.

They were interrupted when some of Duryodhan's younger brothers called out. The boys had been playing and their ball had fallen into a dried out well.

"I have more important things to do," Duryodhan told Yudhisthira, excusing himself to tend to the lost ball.

The Pandavas followed cautiously behind. All the boys gathered around and peered down the well. They could barely make out the ball in the faint light that penetrated to the bottom.

"So who's going to climb down to fetch it?" asked Duryodhan.

One of the boys offered up his brother. "It's Soma's fault. He should go."

"I'm not the one who missed the ball." Soma retorted.

"I'll bet there are snakes down there," added a third boy.

"What's all this bickering about?" asked an older, unfamiliar voice. The boys turned to see who it was. A bearded stranger stood in the brush. "Doesn't this beat all," he mocked them. "A bunch of princes who can't get a ball out of a well. Don't they teach you anything, or do you just spend your time consumed in play?"

Grabbing up a handful of tall grasses nearby, the stranger moved toward the well. The boys opened up a path for him. He took off his ring and tossed it high in the air. He uttered a mantra turning the grasses into firm arrows. As the ring descended into the well, he swiftly drew his bow and fired an arrow that pierced the ring and penetrated the ball. Another arrow flew from the stranger's bow and entered into the shaft of the first arrow. And another. In this way, he quickly used up all the arrows, lodging each one into the end of the previous arrow. Finally, he leaned into the well and grasped the shaft of arrows and lifted up the ball and ring.

The boys were wide-eyed. Eagerly, Arjuna drew closer. "O dear sir, Bhismadev, the Grandsire of the Kuru dynasty, is looking for a master such as yourself to train us in the military arts. Would you kindly stay and be our teacher?"

"If he approves, it would be my honor," said the stranger. Giving Arjuna his crescent ring he added, "Bring him this. He will know who I am. In the meantime, I'll remain in the shade of these woods."

* * * * *

Bhismadev examined the ring and glanced toward Arjuna. "Is there any word of your brother?"

Arjuna sadly shook his head.

"Don't worry, and tell your mother everything will be fine," the Grandsire assured him. "I have spoken with Vyasa. He understands all things, and he tells me you and your brothers will all have full and prosperous lives." Bhismadev looked down at the ring again. For a long time he had been aware of Arjuna's innermost desire to master the bow and arrow. "It is said man proposes and God disposes. So my dear boy, be happy, for Providence has answered your prayers and has brought you a teacher like none other. This ring belongs to Drona, the illustrious brahmin warrior and student of the legendary Parasurama. Go tell your brothers and your cousins. We must give Drona a proper reception."

* * * * *

After Bhima was poisoned and tossed from the cliff, he sank down to the bottom of the riverbed, and even further, into a deep passageway to the land of the Nagas. In this dark, watery world, the snake-like Nagas wore luminous jewels on their foreheads to guide their way and spoke in a mysterious manner as they contorted their bodies.

Numerous serpents guarded the cave's entrance. They attacked Bhima, biting him repeatedly with their fangs, sending their venom into his blood. This brought Bhima to consciousness. Remarkably, the poison from the snakes and the poison from the cake counteracted one another. Bhima felt a surge of energy. With one mighty burst he ripped off the ropes that bound him and he flung the snakes against the cave walls. The snakes fled in terror to warn their lord. They streaked past underwater gardens, past statues of Naga heroes, and headed straight to the Great Chamber, where the serpent king presided on a coral throne.

"Vasuki, Vasuki. Beware! Misfortune is at our doorway, " they cried. "A mighty intruder comes. Please, protect us,"

"Do not fear. Whoever this fool is, I will dispatch him to the abode of Death." In one great bound, Vasuki grabbed his trident and raced forward, followed by the Nagas. When he came upon Bhima, the Naga king's ferociousness melted into curiosity. He recognized in this boy the manner and appearance of his old friend, Vayu, the wind-god.

"Tell me lad, who are you? What brings you here? And why do you trouble my people?" Vasuki inquired.

"I am the son of Pandu and Kunti," Bhima proclaimed. "But because of a curse on King Pandu, I was fathered by the wind-god. I have come here to your country only by chance. I was deceived by my cousins, the Kauravas, and upon awakening I found myself being attacked by your people and was forced to defend myself."

"So, you are of the gods and, more importantly, from my dear friend Vayu," said Vasuki, as he lowered his trident and embraced

Bhima. "Your arrival here is a special blessing upon us. Come, we must celebrate."

They sat down together in the Great Chamber and the Naga king called for a mug of *rasakund*, a celestial juice, to be placed before Bhima. He lifted it high and drank it down all at once. The mug was refilled again and again until Bhima had his fill. He looked around contentedly at his newfound friends with a smile as broad as his round face. The Nagas looked on in astonishment.

"I have never seen anyone drink more than three mugs and remain conscious," said Vasuki. "But you have consumed eight mugs in a row. How do you feel?"

"Fantastic!" Bhima bellowed.

"You should. Each mug of rasakund bestows the strength of over a thousand elephants. You will be invincible against your enemies. But now you must rest." All of the Nagas laughed heartily as Bhima rose slowly from his chair. His head swirled and their laughter echoed in his ears. With their help he gingerly made his way to his quarters.

Bhima slept for eight days straight. After rising from his slumber, he spent a jovial time with the Nagas, laughing and receiving gifts from them, and when the time came he sadly bid them farewell.

"My young friend," said Vasuki teary-eyed, "my people and I were happy to be of service to you. May victory attend you wherever you go."

Bhima left the Great Chamber and was escorted back to the surface of the river by a dozen Naga warriors. The Nagas blew their conch shells as a parting farewell. And as they churned the river with their tails, they disappeared beneath the foam.

Bhima made his way back to Hastinapura and was received by his mother and brothers through tears of joy.

* * * * *

The next morning Vidura heard the good news of Bhima's return. He made his way across the palace grounds to the Pandavas' quarters. After embraces, Bhima told of how he was poisoned and of his sojourn with the Nagas and the effects of the *rasakund*.

"Out of a bad experience something wonderful has come about," Vidura marveled. "Now you have far greater might than you ever thought possible. But Bhima, do not become enamored by it. Mere strength cannot always help you. Humility and stillness are greater than physical strength."

When his brothers heard Bhima's story, they did not like it one bit. The more they thought about the Kauravas' treachery the angrier they became.

Vidura cautioned them. "It would be unwise to confront Dhritarastra and his sons with their heinous act. Dhritarastra would not believe it and his sons would only deny it. There is no use mulling over it. Don't let your speech or actions be a cause of distress. There's already so much distress in this world. Better to use your words to benefit and comfort others. Now you must stay close together. Watch out for each other. Use this time to prepare yourselves."

* * * * *

At times, in Duryodhan's absence, the Kauravas and Pandavas would almost act civilly toward one another. One day, some of the princes sat together, eating lunch, talking about what it meant to be king. They were well aware that in the future Yudhisthira would most likely assume that mantle. Some of them imagined out loud how it would feel to assume the power, the majesty, and the honor, or to have anyone and everyone at their beck and call.

One of the boys turned to Yudhisthira who silently listened to the exchange. "Yudhisthira, what do you think it would be like?"

It seemed Yudhisthira reflected on the idea for the first time. "I really don't know," he said, and added, "but I would like to ask

Grandfather Bhismadev." The boys all agreed and they hurried off to inquire from him.

* * * * *

With the boys surrounding him, Bhismadev leaned back and considered their question. A satisfying smile radiated from his beard. When he saw the boys comfortable and ready to listen, Bhismadev told a story.

"Once a pigeon, pursued by a swift hawk, descended from the skies and flew into the throne room of King Sibi and landed on his lap. The pigeon appealed to the astonished king, 'You protect all the citizens of your land. I am also a citizen, therefore please give me your protection.'

'Of course my little friend, you have it,' the king assured the pigeon.

When the hawk heard the king's promise, he objected. But Sibi explained to the hawk, 'As king, it is my duty to give protection and care to anyone who seeks shelter of me.'

'What about my needs?' demanded the hawk, 'If you protect this pigeon, you are denying me my rightful food.'

'I will not abandon this pigeon, but I will open my storehouse of foods to you and you can take whatever you want.'

The hawk laughed out loud and said, 'O King, I am not interested in any of your human food. This pigeon is my lawful prey and I will only be satisfied when I sink my talons into his flesh.'

The king kept the hawk at bay and said he was prepared to offer anything for the life of the pigeon.

'I am getting very hungry,' replied the hawk, 'and if you're so keen on saving the life of this bird, I will accept, pound for pound, the flesh from your body as a substitute.'

Over the protests of his family and ministers, the king agreed to the proposal. After all, he thought, how much could this little pigeon *weigh? Sibi called for a scale and placed the pigeon on one side, and on the other side he placed a piece of flesh cut from his own leg."*

Upon hearing this part of the story, the boys squirmed and shrieked in a mixture of horror and delight. Bhismadev continued.

"But the scale tipped ever so slightly in the pigeon's favor. When he saw it wasn't enough, without hesitation, the king cut off another piece. But to his surprise, the scale still tipped in the pigeon's favor by a hair. Again and again, Sibi cut off pieces of flesh from his legs and arms, but the pigeon mysteriously grew heavier and heavier. Finally, the king sat on the scale, offering himself completely to the hawk. Even then, the scale still tipped in the pigeon's favor."

Here, Bhismadev, the master storyteller, paused briefly before he came to the story's lesson. "Boys, to make such a brave sacrifice and give such protection to anyone and everyone in need, *this* is what it means to be king."

The boys sat in stunned silence. One of them asked incredulously, "So the hawk ate the king?"

Bhismadev laughed heartily, "Oh no, not at all! You see, Sibi was always situated in the Dharma. He was known far and wide for his virtue, and the gods came to test it and see it for themselves. So Agni assumed the form of the pigeon and Indra came as the hawk. Afterwards, they restored Sibi's body and gave him numerous blessings, and at the end of his life a band of Celestials descended to carry him to the heavens."

* * * * *

After several months of instructing the princes in archery and other military arts, Drona took them out to a field for a test. He had placed a wooden bird in a nearby tree. Each boy lined up with his bow and one arrow. Drona told the group, "Quiet your mind, focus your attention, observe and act with your entire body."

First he called upon Yudhisthira to come forward and take aim at the 'bird.' Yudhisthira drew back his bow. Drona said, "Before I give you permission to shoot, tell me what you see."

"I see the tree. I see the bird. I see the clouds floating in the sky. I see the world before me."

"Put down your arrow and step back in line," Drona commanded. Next, he called for Chitra to come forward and told him to take aim. As Chitra drew back his bow Drona asked, "Before I give you permission to shoot, tell me what you see."

"I see the tall tree. I see the leaves and I see the bird itself."

"Put down your arrow and step back in line," Drona said. He called for Nakula. "Fix your arrow and draw your bow. What do you see?"

"I see the bird on a limb, the tree, and the sky behind the tree."

"Put down your arrow," Drona said. He called for Duryodhan to take aim. "What do you see?"

Duryodhan thought he had the clue. "I see you standing before me like a god. I see the branches and the leaves. I see the bird."

"Step back in the line," Drona said. He called for Arjuna to come forward and take aim. "Well, tell me," he said impatiently. "What do you see?"

Arjuna drew back his bow. "I see the eye of the bird," he replied.

"And what else?" Drona questioned.

"Nothing else. Just the eye of the bird."

Drona's no-nonsense demeanor hid the joy he felt in his heart. "Then you may release your arrow."

In an instant Arjuna's arrow penetrated the eye of the bird.

* * * * *

One day Drona gave a task to both Yudhisthira and Duryodhan. He wanted to see which of them would be more worthy to rule as king. Drona asked Duryodhan, "Bring back a man who is superior in nature to yourself." He turned to Yudhisthira. "I want you to bring me a man who is inferior in nature to yourself." The boys both left the palace compound and went on their separate ways to search the streets and lanes of Hastinapura.

As Duryodhan wandered about, he thought, *It seems Drona always gives me the more difficult task. To find someone lower would not be very hard at all. But no, he gives that to Yudhisthira. I imagine Drona expects more from me than from any of his other students. I'll see whom I can come up with.*

Duryodhan encountered a brahmin, and he reflected, *We of the princely class protect the brahmins. The superior gives protection to the inferior.* Next he encountered a working man and thought, *There is no question that I am superior to this man.* Then he came to the market and beheld the merchants selling their wares. *The nobles collect taxes from the merchants, therefore I am superior.* Soon, he encountered nobles who all offered their respects. He thought, *Even these nobles offer homage unto me. Wherever will I find a man who is superior to me?*

As Yudhisthira wandered about he also came upon a brahmin. He thought, *This man gives guidance and training to all who approach him, thus I am his servant.* He came upon a cowherd and thought, *Here is one who supplies us with milk. He tends to the cows whom are likened to our own mother. Thus, he is superior.* He came upon a farmer. *This man provides us with nourishment and thus I am indebted to him.* Yudhisthira came upon a man drawing water from a well. It happened to be a day of fasting, and an adult was not to take so much as a morsel of food or a drink of water. Yudhisthira thought, *Look at this man. He cannot control his senses. He would quench his thirst on this holy day. I have found one who is inferior!*

But the man did not drink. Instead, he brought the water to his thirsty horse. Yudhisthira thought, *This man had no intention of breaking the fast. In fact, it is I who am the lowest, for it was wrong of me to think badly of him.*

At the end of the day Yudhisthira returned to his teacher alone to submit himself as the lowest of men, since everyone he met performed such valuable service to the kingdom. And Duryodhan also returned empty-handed, since he could not find a soul superior to himself.

* * * * *

Year after year, Drona taught both the Pandavas and the Kauravas the art of combat and military strategy as well as many other subjects befitting royalty. Arjuna, fully absorbed in archery, practiced constantly. He practiced shooting while kneeling, standing, running and jumping. Arjuna was ambidextrous. His bow and arrows became an extension of his very being. He learned how to shoot from a moving chariot, from a galloping horse, and from atop an elephant. He also learned how to fight with sword, mace and spear.

Late one night Arjuna returned to the field quarters. As he sat on the patio taking his evening meal, a cool breeze came out of the north and extinguished the flames in the lamps hanging nearby. It turned pitch black. But Arjuna thought nothing of the inconvenience. He continued to eat, bringing the food from the plate to his mouth. Suddenly he realized, *If I can eat in the dark, I can also shoot my bow in the dark.* From that time on he practiced archery in the dead of night. He learned how to distinguish between various sounds in the dark and how far away they were. He learned to coordinate his breath with the use of his weapons. He learned the art of self-control and to call upon his inner strengths. He learned to unleash and guide devastating weapons by the use of mantra, sound vibration. Eventually, he learned how to fight alone against ten thousand warriors. He not only became renowned as the foremost archer in the world, but he also became known as Gudakesh, the one who conquers sleep.

Mahabharata: The Eternal Quest

* * * * *

The education of the princes was complete. The day for the tournament arrived. Drona had previously consulted brahmins who were expert astrologers to choose an auspicious day for the event. The arena, just outside the city, quickly filled up with all the citizens of Hastinapura. Everyone was dressed in their finery. Many sat in the stands, while wealthier citizens constructed their own platforms for their friends and family. A band of musicians played and when Drona came onto the field the crowd became hushed. Drona, with white beard trimmed, was dressed in white, and adorned with a white flower garland. He led a procession that included his son Ashwattama, the Pandavas, the Kauravas, and other princes from many lands. A thunderous applause greeted them. These young warriors carried skillfully crafted weapons, and wore silk turbans or crowns made of valuable gems. It appeared as if an army of Celestials had descended to the Earth. Ashwattama, however, wore no turban, for he wanted to display to all the world the brilliant jewel on his head, entangled in his hair, he had since birth. The jewel afforded him all protection.

The warriors fanned out across the field and engaged in mock one-on-one combat to display their prowess. They struck at each other with their swords and maces. They ran and jumped and turned as if performing a synchronized dance. They rode horses in a great circle, hurled their spears and brandished their bows and arrows, repeatedly striking their targets.

The best students in each discipline were paired up. Duryodhan and Bhima came forward to engage in fighting with maces. As each displayed his mastery of the weapon, their fighting took on a serious bent. Each struck forceful blows against the other. Drona signaled for trumpets to sound the end of the competition. With his glance he scolded both of them as they came off the field.

Mahabharata: The Eternal Quest

Finally, the field was cleared and Arjuna stood alone. From his bow he unleashed various weapons. The first arrow created streams of fire, and another torrents of rain, while a third created a cone of wind in the sky. From his moving chariot he shot a quiver full of arrows into a swinging gourd. With two arrows left, Arjuna used one to cut the rope from which the gourd hung. He used the last arrow to send the gourd sailing across the field to land at the feet of his teacher Drona. The spectators cheered wildly and Drona beamed with delight.

Only Duryodhan and Ashwattama did not share in the excitement. Duryodhan, his arms folded across his chest, looked on sternly. Then, to everyone's astonishment, a stranger, with bow in hand, ran onto the field. No one had ever seen him before. No one knew if he came as a friend or foe. Dozens of princes grabbed the hilt of their swords. Drona lifted his hand to calm them. He wanted to find out the intentions of this young man.

With one arrow, this stranger knocked the gourd into the air. As he circled the field, shooting in rapid succession, he shot the gourd higher and higher until he let it fall at Arjuna's feet. Upon seeing this, Duryodhan's heart pounded with excitement. He repeatedly shouted, "Wonderful! Wonderful" and led the applause for this stranger's feat.

"It's easy to charm an audience by the use of bow and arrow," said the stranger speaking to Arjuna. "Your admirers may be impressed with your displays of these cheap tricks, but I am certainly not."

"My friend, you should be careful with your words or they may get you into trouble," Arjuna warned.

"I am not your friend and I stand by my words until death."

"I don't know who you are, but if you are eager to die, I can surely oblige you."

"I'm tired of your words. If you want to speak, let us speak with arrows."

"So be it." Arjuna grabbed up a fresh quiver and knelt before Drona, seeking his permission to engage in combat.

Kunti, who had been looking proudly upon her son Arjuna, now looked intently upon the stranger. She looked to Arjuna and again to the stranger. She could scarcely breathe. Her world and her vision shrank into a narrow funnel. It contained only these two solitary figures challenging one another. As she heard the exchange of heated words, she felt faint. The past fell into the present and her future seemed to collapse. She did not know how or why this was happening. She gasped for air. She swooned. Her friends caught hold of her. Barely able to walk, she was escorted from the arena.

Yudhisthira saw his mother's condition and was concerned by this turn of events. Arjuna was impetuous and had spoken harshly. After all, the stranger was a guest to be respected. Yudhisthira did not doubt Arjuna was the most skilled of all warriors, but at the same time, he felt this mysterious stranger had some unknown quality that could undo them all. His body trembled at the thought.

Drona did not want to see this glorious day end in bloodshed, neither his student's nor this intruder's. He raised his hand to quell the crowd's murmuring and addressed the young man. "Arjuna is the son of Kunti and is in the lineage of the ancient and celebrated Kuru dynasty. Before I give Arjuna permission to fight with you, I must hear of your origins and know you are of equal birth to your opponent."

The stranger was struck by these words. He stood forlorn as his luster and vitality drained from his countenance. For years he had prepared for this very moment of combat. Now his life seemed uncertain in a world that would forever judge him based on his birth. He heard himself say, "My origins? I cannot say for certain."

Duryodhan, seeing a potential ally against the Pandavas, quickly stepped forward to give the stranger his support. With an upraised hand, he commanded the attention of all. "Hear me. The wise men tell us that heroes, like royal progeny, can also lay claim to nobility. Birth itself is a shallow argument for royalty. Have any of our births been so pure and spotless and holy? Not birth, but Destiny will decide who is higher and who is lower. One nudge by Providence can change the direction of our lives. So if some of you demand royalty as a qualification for this hero, by my power and authority I hereby bestow upon this warrior the province of Anga, which I own, along with the title 'King of Anga.' Thus, let the coronation begin."

Duryodhan immediately called for his own throne chair to be brought, and motioned for the stranger to take his place on it. He waved for the brahmins who hurriedly prepared for the ceremony. By reciting mantras alone, they ignited fire. They sounded conch shells and cut open coconuts. They sprinkled flower petals and scented water upon the stranger and offered him their blessings. At the end of the coronation the new king rose amid the cheers of the crowd.

Duryodhan stepped forth to embrace him, "O King, I would feel honored to count you among my friends. Tell me, what is your name?"

"Karna."

"From this day forth it is King Karna of Anga."

Karna bowed triumphantly. Although he had been raised by a charioteer, in the inner core of his being Karna had always sensed his own greatness. Now he felt at peace. He felt vindicated. For the first time in his life he was acknowledged for the noble spirit who dwelt within him. He told Duryodhan, "I give you my friendship. I give you my allegiance. I give you my very life."

Duryodhan radiated exuberance. On this day he had gained a formidable ally. Confidently, Duryodhan turned to Drona looking for his decision.

But Drona was not one to be intimidated. "The sun is about to set in the west. The day draws to a close. There will be no fight on this day. And since the stranger cannot or will not disclose his origins, there will be no fight on any day. I will not permit it."

Chapter 4

The Summer House

It was clear to everyone in the kingdom that in the not too distant future the rule of the dynasty should rightfully be transferred to Yudhisthira. The citizens waited eagerly for that time to come, and Duryodhan resented Yudhisthira all the more for it. Duryodhan knew something had to be done sooner rather than later.

He brought up the matter to his father whenever he could. "Father, you've given your life's energy to leading the kingdom. The people have prospered under your rule. Why should we turn over all you have achieved to Yudhisthira and his descendants? It's not right. The thought infuriates me. Listen to me father, I have an idea how we can avert this grave injustice."

"My son," Dhritarastra cautioned, "Yudhisthira, just like his father Pandu, has endeared himself to the people. It would be futile for us to usurp the kingdom."

"Father, you underestimate me. I've given it quite some thought. There is no need for a confrontation with the Pandavas. At this time of year, when the heat rises here in the capital, the atmosphere in the resort town of Varanavat is most pleasing and refreshing. The town is full of lakes and temples. I have instructed our ministers to describe the place in great detail to the Pandavas and instill in them a desire to visit there. In the meantime, Purochana and his men are completing a holiday villa for me. So when the Pandavas even casually express an interest in going, I will generously offer the villa for their use."

"And?" Dhritarastra was eager to understand further.

"Just leave the rest to me. While they are gone, we will have time to win over the hearts of the nobles and the people alike. And we'll be rid of the Pandavas soon enough," Duryodhan tactfully assured his father. However, he neglected to mention the villa he was having built, and especially the interior bedroom chambers, was being constructed with the most flammable materials and the whole place could be consumed in flames in an instant if a fire were to 'accidentally' occur.

* * * * *

Vidura had a sense something was amiss. It didn't sound right - Duryodhan inviting the Pandavas to use his newly constructed villa. Vidura knew Duryodhan. Duryodhan didn't do anything without some ulterior motive.

Before they left, Vidura took the Pandavas aside. "When you arrive at your destination, examine your new dwelling carefully," he warned, "and remember, a mole prepares for danger by digging an escape tunnel. One must respond to an enemy's cunning with greater cunning."

* * * * *

The Pandavas and their mother Kunti arrived in Varanavat and were greeted by crowds of well-wishers. They came to the villa and Purochana himself welcomed them and, along with the porters, he personally helped bring in their luggage. Purochana had overseen the construction of the residence to make sure of its lethal effect.

Now he remained on as the director of household affairs to execute Duryodhan's plan. Purochana bided his time. For weeks and months afterwards, he made every effort to assist the Pandavas, whether it was to help arrange their outings, or to receive guests, or to see their meals were prepared according to their liking. He also made sure the brothers and their mother had fresh clothes each morning and evening. Anyone who visited the Pandavas would see how meticulously Purochana attended to every detail of their daily needs. And everyone would comment that surely Purochana was the best of servants.

He would have to appear profoundly shaken when he announced to the kingdom the untimely demise of the Pandavas from a tragic fire in the villa as they slept. It must also seem that he himself had barely escaped with his life.

Thus began a game of cat and mouse. Purochana kept his eye on the Pandavas. In turn, the Pandavas were always observant of Purochana's movements. They also examined the house and discovered layers of boards soaked in scented oil or coated with flammable materials behind the walls and underneath the floors. The Pandavas learned well the art of diplomacy from Vidura. Careful not to alarm Purochana, they acted in such a way as to make him feel he was in complete control of the situation.

In the meantime, a man secretly arrived in Varanavat who was expert in digging tunnels. He had been sent by Vidura to help the Pandavas create an escape route beneath their villa. At a clandestine meeting they showed him where they wanted the tunnel to come out. Bhima thought hard about having to crawl through a narrow tunnel. The idea was repulsive to someone his size.

"I'm sick of all this intrigue," he blurted out. "Let's get it out in the open. I'm going to ring Purochana's neck." His brothers had to do all they could to stop him.

The digger reassured them he would make a tunnel for them to easily fit through. For a month, he worked throughout the night. After he finished, he left undetected.

* * * * *

The Pandavas spent their time walking throughout the area, conversing with the locals. In this way, they endeared themselves to the residents of Varanavat, and they also became very familiar with the surrounding terrain.

One day Yudhisthira entered the storehouse and saw the provisions were running low. It seemed Purochana had neglected to restock them. This was his mistake. Yudhisthira understood the time had come.

Yudhisthira ordered a sumptuous feast to be prepared along with fine desserts and wines. He invited the locals to come and dine to their heart's content. He also invited Purochana to dine with him and his brothers at their table. That great prince amongst nobles raised his glass. "Purochana, I salute you for your unsurpassed service to my mother, my brothers and myself. By your efforts alone you have certainly made this dwelling into such a wonderful and comfortable home for us that we cannot bring ourselves to leave." His brothers all applauded his words.

"It is my great honor to serve your illustrious family," Purochana replied as he rose from the table, "and it is my wish to be of continued service and to attend to you in any menial manner required of me. That is my pleasure."

The brothers all bade him to eat and drink to his heart's content, to relax, to enjoy himself, and, at least for this evening, to refrain from any service to them. They laughed heartily together. Bhima kept refilling Purochana's silver cup with wine. At the end of the evening, after everyone had left, Nakula and Sahadev helped the half-drunk Purochana to his quarters at one corner of the villa.

There he slept soundly, only to awaken to the scorching heat of the flames when it was too late.

The twins assisted Kunti as Yudhisthira and Arjuna led the way into the tunnel located in their bedroom. Bhima stayed behind. As he waited for the others to get a good head start, he helped himself to some of the leftover desserts. Then he lit a torch and, starting with Purochana's quarters, he set fire to various sections of the house. The house was immediately enveloped in flames, catching Bhima off guard. He passed through the dining room where he snatched up one last piece of cake. He realized it might be some time before he would eat such delicacies again. He wanted to reach for another piece, but the flames pressed in dangerously close and he made a hasty retreat. The building burned swiftly and majestically and the flames licked at Bhima's heels as he hurried into the tunnel.

Kunti and her sons had quietly made their way through the tunnel coming out into the forest. They emerged and waited anxiously for Bhima. *What's keeping him?* they all thought. No one said a word. They peered into the dark tunnel. In the distance, the crackling flames engulfed the villa. *What's keeping him?* Suddenly, Bhima spilled out of the tunnel and into their arms. They brushed the soot and dirt from his hair and clothes and proceeded down a wooded slope toward the river. Behind them, the building collapsed as the flames towered above the trees.

Neighbors from down the road came running. Quickly a crowd gathered. As the blaze continued, the people began to lament. "The Pandavas are dead!". . . "This must have been a trap set by Duryodhan". . . "Everyone knows he's envious of the Pandavas." . . . "And what about Purochana?". . . "He oversaw the building of this place, didn't he?" . . . "That fool didn't make it out alive either". . . "Serves him right!"

Purochana had done an excellent job in constructing his own death trap. And as the residents spoke, the villa and everything in it was reduced to ashes.

On the way to the river Nakula inquired of Bhima, "What took you so long?"

"Well," Bhima paused, "I wanted to make sure the fire was good and hot."

"You didn't go back for a second helping of cake, did you?" Sahadev teased.

"I was *busy* doing my job," Bhima insisted.

In the darkness he did not see the smiles on his brothers' faces.

The Pandavas and their mother climbed into two small boats hidden in the reeds. They pushed off and disappeared into the night.

* * * * *

The Pandavas paddled silently downstream. A mountain range was etched into the distant horizon by a low moon that shone behind it. They traveled all night and, as a faint morning glow emerged from the east and the last of the stars faded from the sky, they pulled their boats onto a lonely stretch of sand and sought refuge under the trees.

Bhima's limbs trembled, but not from the chilled morning air. He gazed upon his mother and brothers as they lay down exhausted and tried to sleep on the ground, using the gnarled roots of the trees as their pillows. *They are so kind, so noble and gentle,* he thought. *What have they done to deserve this? My mother and brothers sleeping on the hard ground like animals in the wild.* His mind couldn't make sense of it. His thoughts wandered to Duryodhan and his brothers sleeping comfortably in their plush beds. Bhima felt the outrage taking over his body and he vowed to tear the Kauravas limb from limb, and this brought him a little solace.

A crow shrieked, and a Rakshasa, resting in a large tree down river, instantly awoke. He scanned the view and saw them, the humans. His mouth watered as he contemplated their forms, for he had not had human flesh in a long time. He grinned and grunted, but did not allow himself to get too excited just yet.

"Sister, sister, wake up. Hidimbi, do you hear me?" He called to his twin sister sleeping on the branches below.

"What is it Hidimba? Why do you disturb my sleep?" She frowned and turned away.

"Hidimbi, don't be angry with me. I have good news. This morning Providence has blessed us by bringing food to our very door."

"We don't have a door you brainless brute of a brother. Because of your thoughtlessness, you let our cabin burn to the ground."

"Oh daughter of a deviled witch, cease your complaints. Now we have a real task to tend to."

"What are you talking about Hidimba?"

"Look, there, across the way. Delicious humans. After we capture them, we can eat that big one there," he said, pointing at Bhima, "and save the others for several days worth of dinners."

When Hidimba saw Bhima, he saw breakfast. But when Hidimbi set her eyes upon Bhima she saw a muscular, strong-armed lover. *I can't eat him,* she thought to herself, *that would be a waste of a gorgeous hunk.*

Rakshasa men are very hideous and horrid to behold. And Rakshasa women are even worse, but they have one saving feature: they can assume the form of a beautiful woman.

"Listen to me," Hidimba said, demanding his sister's attention. "Use your powers and change into a captivating woman. While the others sleep, entice that big one with your charms and lead him to me while I wait here in ambush. And make it quick. I can't wait to drink his hot blood."

Hidimbi liked the idea, at least the part about changing herself into a beautiful woman and enticing the 'big one.' As she walked toward Bhima, she thought about her brother's plan. *What's he ever done for me? Just gotten us into one mess after another. Even when I*

57

found a husband for myself, he decided to devour him six months later. I'd be stupid if I depended on him any longer.

Suddenly she heard a movement and she gasped. It was Bhima. He had seen her coming and surprised her as she walked, lost in thought.

"O young lady, who are you and why do you walk in the forest alone? I have never laid eyes upon anyone as lovely as you."

Hidimbi smiled at her perfect deception, but spoke truthfully, knowing there was not a moment to lose. "I have come here at the bidding of my brother. He is the lord of this forest and aims to make a meal out of your flesh and blood."

Bhima laughed heartily at the thought. "He can try to do whatever he wants."

Hidimbi was thrilled by this young man's confidence and drew closer to him. "But I have a better idea. Come with me now and together we can make a home for ourselves in these woods."

"I won't abandon my mother and brothers who are sleeping contentedly, knowing I stand guard."

"O great warrior, if you agree to come with me I will prove myself to you by killing my brother this very moment. I will care for you and satisfy you in every way possible."

All the while, the Rakshasa stealthily drew closer. Before Bhima could reply again, the Rakshasa bounded before them and looked menacingly from his sister to Bhima and back to his sister.

"My dear sister, have you lost your reason? You know I've been waiting patiently for you."

"You can wait all you want. I'm finished with you. From now on I belong to this warrior and he belongs to me."

"WHAT!!!" Hidimba was outraged at his sister's defiance.

"Can you please talk softly," Bhima asked of the Rakshasa, "My mother and brothers are sleeping nearby."

The Rakshasa couldn't believe his ears. He stared at Bhima uncomprehendingly. Hidimba stood head and shoulders over the human, and the human was telling *him* what to do.

Hidimbi took the opportunity to jump on her brother. She bit into his thick skinned neck. Hidimba threw her off without diverting his attention from Bhima. The Rakshasa let out a heinous snarl, opening his cavernous mouth that stretched from ear to ear, revealing several rows of jagged teeth.

"Keep it down," Bhima demanded, pushing the Rakshasa back. "If you wake up my mother I'm going to get really angry," he warned, waving a finger at Hidimba.

Hidimba flew at Bhima and they were at each other's throats. They fought like maddened elephants, pushing and tumbling. Locked together, they rolled over the ground, causing trees to crack and come crashing down around them. Hearing this, the Pandavas jumped to their feet to protect their mother and to find out the reason for the uproar. Arjuna dashed to the aid of Bhima.

Bhima waved him off. "Younger brother, stay back. I didn't call for your help."

As he spoke, Bhima took a blow to the chest, but he remained unfazed. Bhima couldn't tolerate that his mother and brothers had been disturbed from their sleep. He grabbed the Rakshasa and lifted him over his head. He whirled him around and smashed him to the ground. The earth shook and a cloud of dust engulfed them both. The combat continued amidst grunts and groans. Ribs crunched. A terrible, piercing cry made the Pandavas shiver. Then silence. And a moment later Bhima alone emerged from the settling dust.

* * * * *

Bhima and Hidimbi, the Rakshasa woman, went off together and made a temporary shelter for themselves in the forest. That night Hidimbi saw her Pandava was eager to return to his brothers.

"I don't want to keep you. I'll let you go back," she assured him. "But first you must give me a child who will provide for me and who can remind me of you."

A day later Hidimbi was pregnant with child. In the course of the day, her belly grew larger. Rakshasa women have the ability to give birth one day after conception, and by evening time she brought forth a baby boy. The child sucked fiercely at her breast and within an hour grew to manhood. His body displayed many of the ferocious features of his race, but unlike other Rakshasas, his head was totally bald. He looked adorable with his rounded chin, broad flat nose and several rows of sharp teeth. His parents laughed and named him Ghatotkaca - one with a head resembling a pot. Ghatotkaca also laughed heartily as he embraced his parents, not really understanding why they were laughing, but enjoying it all the same.

Ghatotkaca followed his father back to the Pandava camp. Bhima introduced his brothers to his new son. Together, they all journeyed south for several days, passing many other Rakshasas lurking behind the trees. Ghatotkaca would stare menacingly at them, and none of them dared to attack. As with other Rakshasas, Ghatotkaca was also attracted by the sweet smelling blood of these humans. With great effort, he summoned every ounce of his self-control to restrain himself from eating his own kinsmen. The Pandavas taught their nephew the finer arts of battle and of understanding the nature of an opponent.

After a time Ghatotkaca took his leave. Bhima told him, "Since your uncle, the lord of this forest, is dead, you must claim your rightful position as the lord of all the Rakshasas in these parts, as well as give protection to your mother."

"My dear father," he replied, "thank you for giving me life and making me who I am. If you ever need my help, wherever you are, face the direction of this forest and loudly call out my name. I, and the Rakshasas under my command, will come to your aid."

The next morning at sunrise Ghatotkaca returned to his mother, his people and his land.

* * * * *

Dhritarastra was stunned and saddened by the news of the Pandavas' sudden death in the fiery inferno. But that only lasted for a few minutes. He stepped out onto his balcony and felt the fresh morning air. The sun was rising over the distant mountains. It was the dawn of a new day for his dynasty.

Duryodhan was wildly elated. He struggled desperately to contain his happiness. He couldn't believe his good fortune. Purochana had also perished in the flames. Duryodhan and his scheme were safe.

The blind king and his family clad themselves in the simple cloth that was customary for mourners. At the state ceremony for the Pandavas and their mother, he and his son Duryodhan struggled to appear saddened by the events. All of Dhritarastra's sons also tried to look dejected. At the ceremony, Vidura and Vyasa also had to put on airs of lamentation, for they knew the Pandavas were alive and well.

*****

The Pandavas continued south through the forest. The next day they came to a river and found a ferryman to take them across. No sooner had they stepped onto his flatboat when a mighty current swept the craft mystifyingly upstream. The ferryman tried to control the boat, but his pole cracked in half. Bhima and Arjuna quickly grabbed two extra poles to redirect the boat. But their attempts proved futile against the current. Strangely, the waters of the river seemed calm, whereas their vessel was caught up in one narrow surge – a river within the river.

"This has never happened before," the ferryman assured them. "I don't know what's going on. Some wicked thing has taken control of the boat."

The strange current carried them some distance and ceased as abruptly as it had begun. The boat touched gently upon the shore.

An eerie stillness hung in the air. The ferryman sank down and cowered in the middle of the boat. With the poles in hand, ready to meet any challenge, Bhima and Arjuna jumped onto dry land.

"Well my boys, it's about time you got here," a voice called out. It came from a figure sitting serenely in the shade of a tree. "I've been waiting for you all morning. I have called you to me."

As the two brothers neared, smiles broadened their faces. "I can't believe my eyes," Bhima exclaimed. He turned and called for his brothers and mother to come quickly. The group approached the solitary figure in excited reverence and bowed before him. It was Vyasa. Vyasa waved for the ferryman to leave, tossing him a gold coin. Then he jumped up and hugged them all.

"I've been missing your antics," Vyasa confessed. "After I heard you perished in the fire, I thought I should come and pay you a visit. How are you faring?"

"It's been difficult for mother. I'm sorry she has to go through this," Yudhisthira explained, and added, "It's been difficult for all of us."

Vyasa listened and replied. "Know that every family has their share of happiness and distress. It's as inevitable as the coming and going of the summer and winter seasons. Best to remain undisturbed and simply let them pass. So do not lament your situation. Be content in all circumstances. This is the path to freedom. All things work for the good. You are all together. You have much to be thankful for."

The group tarried for a time, talking and laughing. Vyasa gave the brothers the saffron cloth of monks for them to change into. "You must remain in hiding a little while longer," he told them. He lead them to the town of Ekachakra and pointed out a home. "In that place lives a very pious family. They will welcome you. Maintain your disguise as wandering brahmins. After a time, a message concerning a grand event will reach your ears. You will know what to do next."

Vyasa watched the Pandavas go to the house. They waved their goodbyes. The man of the household came to the door and joyfully ushered them in. Before he closed it, he brought his hands together and bowed his head, offering pranams to Vyasa.

* * * * *

Every day, dressed in their robes, the five brothers wandered the streets and neighborhoods of the town. They lived a mendicant's lifestyle, going from house to house with their begging bowls. By midday they returned to their lodging, and along with their mother, they sat down together for their one and only meal of the day. On the third day Bhima stared at his empty bowl in frustration. As on the previous days, he had finished his meal ahead of the others. He missed his sweets and delicacies. He missed being able to eat as much as he wanted. He watched silently as his brothers lingered over their meals. He abruptly slapped his hand down.

"I can't stand it any longer. How long do we have to keep up this charade?"

"Bhima, please, control yourself," Yudhisthira said after carefully chewing the rice in his mouth. "We must wait here as Vyasa requested."

Bhima looked at him in disgust. "I'm going back to Hastinapura and take care of this once and for all."

"Boys, please. Let's not argue," Kunti pleaded. She knew what was really behind all this. "I've told you boys to divide whatever you receive equally amongst yourselves. But while we are here, Bhima will receive half of the food collection, and we can divide the remainder equally."

With this new rule, Bhima was appeased. But he became wildly elated with what came his way next.

Mahabharata: The Eternal Quest

* * * * *

One morning Kunti heard sobs coming from the next room. She heard the husband whispering loudly, trying to calm his family.

"You must be strong. Life is a perilous path, full of sorrow and misery. Happiness can never truly be attained in this world," he explained as tears ran down the faces of his wife and two children. "What can I say? I cannot delay another moment. You'll have to go on without me."

"My dear husband," implored the wife, "that would be impossible. If you die we will all perish. Better yet, I will go to the forest in your place."

The daughter spoke up. "Mother, you and father are the very foundation of our family. Both of you must live. I will go."

"Daughter, don't speak like that," countered the father. "You are young. You have your whole life ahead of you. There is nothing else for me to do but to sacrifice myself."

"Don't be afraid," said the son. Being the smallest and only seven years old, he stood up to make his point. The boy picked up a stick and held it proudly, imagining it to be a bow. "I'll take my bow and arrow and kill that demon."

The mother and father laughed through their tears and smothered their children with affection.

Suddenly Kunti entered the room. "I couldn't help but overhear you. Tell me what's wrong?"

Both the husband and his wife immediately jumped up. "No. No. You are our guest here. Don't bother yourself," the wife told Kunti. The husband added, "This has nothing to do with you. This is our problem."

Kunti inquired, "Please tell me. I might be able to help you."

"No one can help us," the husband said stoically. "We are subject to the will of Destiny. We can only take shelter in the Supreme Lord Narayana"

"That may be, but nothing is hopeless," Kunti assured him. "Please, tell me what happened?"

The husband cast his eyes to the ground, but his wife, eager for any help, spoke up. "For over a year, this town has lived under the threat of a fearsome Rakshasa. His name is Baka and he resides in the forest nearby. He's promised not to wreak havoc on our town, provided that on each full moon day we send him a cartload of food pulled by two buffaloes and driven by a human being - all destined to be his food. Each time a different household has to supply a sacrifice, and today it's our turn."

"And the king of this land?" inquired Kunti.

"The king doesn't care," the husband explained. "He just collects his taxes. The town is insignificant to him, so he doesn't bother to protect us."

Hearing of the king's neglect angered Kunti. "It shouldn't be a bother to the king. It is a matter of duty. The king is obliged to give protection to his citizens. He must be the first in the land to uphold Dharma. But fear not. I have a son. He will drive the cart in your place."

"I can't allow that. You are our honored guests."

"If a solution to your problem presents itself, you must take it," Kunti argued. "Besides, my son is very strong. There's no need to worry about him."

* * * * *

When Kunti told Bhima what needed to be done, a magnificent smile crossed his face. Bhima eagerly set out on the task. *Drive a cart full of food into the forest! What have I done to deserve this?* Bhima drove slowly, very slowly, reaching behind him all the while to partake of the cooked eatables. He was in heaven. And Bhima was also eager for a fight. He had enough of masquerading as a monk.

In the meantime, Baka had grown tired of waiting and walked along the road looking for his monthly tribute. He was wondering if he would have to go to Ekachakra to smash heads and destroy a few homes. Then he saw the cart come into view and a smile crossed his face. But upon a closer look, the Rakshasa couldn't believe his eyes. The food was practically all gone, and this broad shouldered human was the culprit. Baka saw Bhima taking yet another morsel, and decided to kill him immediately.

He thundered, "What do you think you're doing? That's my food you're eating!" Baka snorted like a raging bull, and lunged at Bhima, ready to pummel him.

Bhima, however, grabbed the Rakshasa's throat with one hand and held him at bay while he reached for yet another tasty item. Baka was incensed. With his face contorted and his red eyes bulging and his black, matted hair flying and showing his four rows of teeth, he raised a blood-curdling scream. Bhima threw him to the ground. Baka quickly rebounded and uprooted a nearby tree and hurled it at Bhima. Bhima dodged it, and in an instant, they both ripped trees out of the ground and charged at each other, smashing one another relentlessly. After those trees were shredded, they uprooted more trees, hurling them at one another. The forest around them became decimated and the Rakshasa turned to find another tree. But he did not get far. Bhima jumped and rammed his knee into Baka's back and broke his spine. Baka fell flat on his face. As he tried to get up, Bhima quickly twisted his neck. The Rakshasa's eyes bulged out. He vomited blood and fell dead.

Returning to Ekachakra that evening, Bhima left the mangled body outside the town's main gate. Next morning, word spread and the people streamed from their homes to behold the lifeless creature who had been the source of their dread for the last year. People soon hurried to the house of the family where the Pandavas stayed and asked the husband how the Rakshasa's death came about. He told them a brahmin with mystical powers had come to him wanting to alleviate the peoples' fears, and offered to kill the Rakshasa. The town's people cried for joy and they established an annual celebration to commemorate this event and honor the brahmins.

Chapter 5

The Contest

In the land of Panchala, King Drupada lived in fear of Drona. The powerful, brahmin warrior had invaded his kingdom for some seemingly slight offense Drupada had committed. The king told his priests he needed protection, and they conducted an extraordinary fire ceremony. From the blazing flame appeared two sparkling, clear-eyed children: a boy holding a sword and bow, and a girl of exquisite beauty and dark complexion holding a garland of wild flowers. The priests named them Dristadyumna and Draupadi, and Drupada accepted them as his own.

As Princess Draupadi grew into a maiden, she always meditated upon Arjuna day and night. From the very first time she heard Arjuna's name and the descriptions of his exploits, she knew he was the one and she would accept none other. In her heart she immediately took Arjuna as her husband and eternal companion. In the early mornings she prayed fervently at an altar to Shiva, "O giver of blessings, please grant me a husband who is noble, a husband who is strong, a husband who is chivalrous, a husband who is handsome and a husband who is wise."

But then came the news of the tragic fire at Varanavat. Draupadi was beside herself. No one could console her, until one day she was visited by Vyasa.

"My dear child, do not grieve. Arjuna and his brothers live. They are in hiding. To bring Arjuna to you, you must declare a svayamvara, a contest for your hand in marriage. In this way, contestants will come from far and wide. When Arjuna hears of it, nothing will keep him away."

A svayamvara! Yes, a contest of skill to win the bride! Draupadi liked the idea and agreed to it. This was the ideal way of a kshatriya marriage. Thus, messengers were sent across the land announcing the grand contest to be held in Panchala. Draupadi designed the contest in such a way that only a super-excellent bowman like Arjuna could win.

* * * * *

Receiving word of the upcoming svayamvara, the Pandavas and their mother moved to a village on the outskirts of Kampilya, Panchala's capital city. Still dressed in the guise of brahmins, they came into the capital and moved leisurely among the throngs of visitors. The magnificent boulevards were lined with seven-story apartment buildings. It was a festive atmosphere. Jugglers, jesters, acrobats, dancers, bards and musicians performed along the streets as crowds pressed in close to see them. Elephants and camels brought last minute supplies to various stations.

For sport, the princes from distant lands gathered to race their chariots. Many of them were excellent chariot fighters and drivers. Each vehicle was finely designed, encrusted with emeralds and crystals, and decorated with a variety of weapons and shields. In some contests the princes raced their own chariots. In others, the chariots were handled by their drivers, while the princes shot arrows or threw spears at moving targets. The festivities went on for a full week prior to the svayamvara.

* * * * *

The Pandavas had been noticed by two visitors from Dwaraka, Krishna and his brother Balaram. These two brothers looked stunning. Krishna's complexion glistened like dark lapis lazuli and he was dressed in yellow silk. Balarama, dressed in blue silk, shone like the moon.

"My dear brother, if I'm not mistaken, those are our cousins, the Pandavas, across the way." Krishna pointed them out with a nod of his head.

"I thought the Pandavas all died in a blazing fire at their vacation home in Varanavat."

"Yes, that's the story that's told. And there certainly have been enough tears shed to raise the rumor of their deaths into an irrefutable fact."

"What is real and what is unreal? What is truth and what is untruth? This has been the debate for ages," Balaram mused.

"Well, unless you see something with your own eyes how can you be sure?" asked Krishna, his lotus eyes sparkling.

"My dear brother, the sages tell us one can never understand everything by direct perception, and therefore we must rely on the authority of those with knowledge." And after a pause, with a hint of a smile upon his lips, Balaram added, "And the state authorities tell us the Pandavas died in the fire."

"Brother, I don't know about these authorities you speak of. I'll rely on my own eyes," Krishna said.

Balaram laughed out loud at the insistence of his younger brother.

* * * * *

At the center of the city, the arena was made ready. The stage was set, and the day of the svayamvara arrived. Prince

Dristadyumna, Draupadi's brother, addressed the audience. "O illustrious kings and princes, on behalf of my father and family, it is my great honor to welcome you. We pray you are comfortable in our fair city. Today, we offer the assembled nobles a vigorous contest my sister has designed for those seeking her hand in marriage."

At this moment, Draupadi walked to the stage. A hush fell over the crowd and all eyes followed her. She held in her hands a golden plate on which lay a garland of wild flowers. She would place the garland on the winner, her husband-to-be.

Dristadyumna continued. "Suspended from the arena's high ceiling is a fish on a rotating plate. Directly below the fish, a rotating wheel makes it difficult to get a clear shot. Those participating in the svayamvara must shoot an arrow through the spoked wheel into the eye of the fish. Another obstacle is the contestants cannot look directly at the ceiling, but must view their target by looking into a pan of clear water on the stage. But the very first challenge for the contestants is to bend and string the fabled bow of our ancestors, the Bow of the Panchalas. This challenge alone will humble many warriors who, even in their minds, will find it difficult to bend this unyielding bow. Good luck to you all, and may the best man win."

One after another, the nobles paraded onto the stage. They strained and trembled as they attempted to bend the Panchala Bow. Those few who managed to bend it were thrown off the stage when the bow sprang back in their faces. Each man left the stage a little less self-assured. When Karna successfully strung the bow on his first attempt, a great cheer arose from the crowd.

Draupadi raised her hand to speak. "Since Karna is the son of a chariot driver, I could never accept him as my husband. Thus, I respectfully ask him to desist from taking part in the contest."

Karna was stunned. Draupadi's words were like a blow to his chest. He felt cheated by Fate. Would he ever be fully accepted as a noble?

As he left the stage, a brahmin brushed past him. The brahmin knelt before the bow in veneration. He offered a prayer to the Supreme Lord Narayana who resides within the core of every atom and who is seated as witness within the hearts of all. The brahmin rose up and in the twinkling of an eye strung the weapon. With one knee firmly planted on the ground, he pulled back the arrow. He fixed his attention on the pan, and then on the reflection of the fish, and finally on the eye of the fish. When he saw nothing else, he released his arrow upwards. With a mighty sound, the arrow struck its mark. A tumultuous cheer arose from the audience. No one could believe what they had just witnessed. This unknown brahmin accomplished what the warriors of the world had failed to do. Duryodhan, Ashwattama, and Karna were steaming with anger. Other malcontents began to grumble.

Yudhisthira gestured for Nakula and Sahadev to come with him. He knew this was no time to bask in Arjuna's victory.

Draupadi was filled with joy. Her eyes were fixed on him. Her heart went out to him. She could instantly recognize her eternal love. She rushed forward with the garland of wild flowers and placed it around his neck.

"Will you come with me?" he asked.

"I am ready to follow you into untamed forests, through jungles, and across high mountains," Draupadi replied with unbounded affection.

"So be it."

As Arjuna and Draupadi left the arena, many of the princes began to talk among themselves.

"This upstart has made a mockery of the svayamvara ceremony."

"The svayamvara is meant only for kshatriyas."

"If Draupadi couldn't pick one of us, she should cast herself into a fire."

"Are we going to let this stranger take her away from us?"

"This is an insult and an outrage!"

The more they spoke the angrier they became. Drawing their weapons high, the princes hurled themselves toward the exit Arjuna and Draupadi had taken. Upon seeing the situation, Bhima uprooted a tree and swung it around, knocking the princes back. He tossed the tree on top of them and pinned them to the ground. He tore up a second tree to beat back a throng of warriors coming fast upon him.

A chariot driven by Nakula came for Arjuna and Draupadi. Horses obeyed Nakula like no one else, for he knew their language and could understand their every movement. Sahadev also came with a chariot for Bhima. But it seemed Bhima was having too much fun. Uprooted trees and disarrayed princes littered the landscape. Bhima climbed casually onto the chariot and they were off, following Nakula toward the city's western gate. Yudhisthira had already gone ahead in a third chariot to secure the gate. The chariots of Nakula, Sahadev and Yudhisthira sped through the gate and left the city. The enraged princes, spitting curses, wasted no time and headed for their steeds. Arjuna still carried with him the Bow of the Panchalas, and, as the princes raced forward, a mass of arrows descended upon the open gate, creating a tangled, impenetrable web that blocked their passage. In the distance, three chariots disappeared into the forest.

* * * * *

After reaching the village where they and their mother were staying, Arjuna hurried to the cottage to tell her the good news. "Mother, you won't believe it. I am so happy! I have obtained a most wonderful prize!"

"Arjuna, my son, whatever it is, you must share it with your brothers." Kunti proclaimed.

"But mother. . . I have won the hand of Draupadi!"

An awkward silence hovered in the room and Yudhisthira forced himself to speak. "Mother, you don't really mean what you said, do you?"

"My dear son, this must be so, for an untruth has never crossed my lips."

Arjuna didn't know what to make of it. He offered his own solution. "Yudhisthira is the eldest. Let him marry Draupadi since the eldest should marry first."

"Our mother's words must prove true," Yudhisthira countered, "and so we'll all marry her."

When Draupadi heard this pronouncement, she was startled. Marry all five brothers! But she recalled a recent dream, and suddenly she understood its import. "For months I had prayed at the altar of Shiva that I may have a husband who is noble, strong, chivalrous, handsome and wise," she told Kunti and her sons. "In my dream, Shiva came before me. It all seemed so real. He practically spoke the very same words I had uttered in my prayers to him. 'My child, you will get a husband who is noble, a husband who is strong, a husband who is chivalrous, a husband who is handsome and a husband who is wise.' Then Shiva smiled and vanished, leaving behind in my room the sweet fragrance of the forest. When I woke up, the fragrance was still there. All this time he thought I was asking for five husbands. And now his benediction has come to pass."

Just at that moment Krishna and Balaram came into the cottage. The Pandavas all jumped up with a start. But Krishna and Balaram were already bowed at Yudhisthira's feet, introducing themselves.

"We are the sons of your mother's brother," Balaram declared.

Kunti rose and threw her arms around each of them. "Krishna and Balaram! I cannot believe you have come to us!" She rejoiced, looking each one directly in the eyes. "I've been praying for your help," she whispered to them, and they knew she had.

The Pandavas expressed their relief and heartily embraced their cousins.

"We are living in disguise. How on earth did you find us?" Yudhisthira inquired.

"My dear cousin, fire, even when covered, can still be felt," Krishna replied. "From the minute we saw you in the crowds, we watched your every move. No one can exhibit such prowess and fight with such coordinated effort as you five brothers. It is the world's good fortune you have escaped the evil plan of Duryodhan. We were compelled to come here and offer our respects."

"Please sit down," said Kunti, "although I don't know what we can offer such exalted guests as yourselves."

"We'll have to save the pleasure of your company for a later date," Krishna said. "Soon the roads will be crawling with soldiers and spies. We don't want to call any attention to this place. With your permission we will take our leave now."

And the visitors were gone as mysteriously as they had come.

* * * * *

That night Kunti told her sons and daughter-in-law of Krishna's extraordinary birth.

"Balaram was the seventh son of my brother, and Krishna the eighth. My brother Vasudeva and his wife Devaki went through much tribulation. A celestial voice from the heavens had warned King Kamsa of Krishna's coming, that he would be the couple's eighth child. The voice said Krishna would kill him and that he would in time kill all the wicked kings. Fearful of the prophecy, Kamsa cast the couple into a dungeon beneath his palace. Cruel Kamsa even killed their first six children. He wasn't taking any chances. Balarama, the seventh child, miraculously survived the wrath of Kamsa.

When Devaki became pregnant for the eighth time, the king had his men guard the dungeon and surround the palace. They even surrounded the city of Mathura itself. Kamsa meant to kill Krishna the moment he was born. Krishna finally appeared at midnight. A brilliant light emanated from the dungeon. But no one saw it. Kamsa had fallen asleep. A mystic slumber enveloped the entire city and countryside, and all the guards and everyone fell fast asleep.

My brother received the child from his wife's arms and held him dearly. The door of the dungeon mysteriously swung open. To save Krishna, my brother took him away. He hurried through the courtyard of the palace and down the streets of Mathura, past the sleeping soldiers. He crossed the Yamuna River and entered the forest on the other side. It was a perilous journey. The cloud-covered sky rumbled as if to applaud the child's birth and lightening flashed to guide my brother's way in the dark. He walked for some distance and came to the village of the cowherd men. There he left the newborn child at Yasoda's side and returned to the dungeon, knowing Krishna was safe. Krishna grew up in the care of Yasoda and her husband Nanda, chief of the cowherds.

The next morning in Mathura, Kamsa was in a rage. The child was nowhere to be found. He called upon the Asuras and ordered them to kill all the children born within the last ten days. After a time, they heard about a wondrous child living in a forest village. They tried, but they could never kill him. They could never destroy the village nor kill anyone there. None of the Asuras who went there ever returned."

All night long the Pandavas and Draupadi listened to Kunti's story, spellbound by her every word. And as she came to the end, the sun's morning rays gloriously streamed from the horizon.

* * * * *

"He was incompetent! How could we ever have trusted him." Duryodhan had no kind words for Purochana. He was fuming.

Word was out that those suspicious brahmins who disrupted the svayamvara were actually the Pandavas. News spread through the land of Panchala like wildfire. The Pandavas had re-emerged, not only alive and safe, but together they wed the beautiful, wise and illustrious Draupadi. The citizens there were overjoyed that the Pandavas were now bound to their kingdom.

Duryodhan was inconsolable as he and his friends left Panchala, traveling in the comfort of a silver-encrusted carriage.

"Damn the Pandavas! Damn this place! Damn Drupada!" Duryodhan spat out the window.

Dushasana tried to reassure his older brother of their own prowess. "We should have gone after them and cut them down like dogs when we had the chance. But they tricked us by coming in the guise of humble brahmins."

"Whoever heard of a woman with five husbands. Isn't that a little obscene?" Ashwattama injected, truly perplexed.

"That's not the point." Duryodhan was annoyed. "The point is now the Pandavas' position is more secure and stronger than ever. They have Drupada as an ally. Did you see how many kings and nobles attended the svayamvara and how friendly they were with Drupada? With his power and influence, the Pandavas are no longer five brothers bereft of a father, but are a force to be reckoned with."

Dushasana mustered all his reasoning abilities to consider the matter. "We have to do something."

Ashwattama suggested. "We don't have to lift a finger. The Pandavas might very well become rivals for Draupadi's attention. Their jealousies will destroy them."

"Yes. That's it!" Duryodhan caught hold of the thought and made it his own. "It will be easy. We'll get my father to send some of his friends to Panchala and convince the Pandavas to take up permanent residence there. Father's friends could also remain and gradually sow seeds of jealousy and dissension among the brothers. The brothers will grow apart from one another as they vie for Draupadi's affections. We could have some loyal women nobles infiltrate Draupadi's retinue and incite her against her new husbands. Eventually, we'll send assassins to get Bhima out of the way. He's the rock they all rest upon. Without him, they'll be powerless."

"And what about Krishna?" Dushasana asked. "He seems to have taken an interest in the welfare of his cousins."

"What about Krishna?" Duryodhan was exasperated with the mention of Krishna. "He grew up in a village and has no military training. I tell you, my plan is infallible. Karna, what do you think?"

All this time Karna had been silently and carefully weighing each word. Karna spent his idle time as an astute observer. He could sift through the faintest of clues and derive the most profound observations. "Duryodhan, if you want my honest opinion, your plan sounds like a fantasy. We're not going to turn the Pandavas against each other, and Draupadi will never abandon them. And you've already schemed to kill them. How far did that get you? The Pandavas are blessed. As for Krishna, he is to be carefully watched. Who knows if the Pandavas and Krishna haven't already created an alliance. So I say forget all about your schemes. When we get back to Hastinapura, immediately put together the biggest army you can and march on Panchala and pound them into the ground. Then we'll be done with it. Finished in one quick stroke."

Chapter 6

The New Kingdom

The Pandavas were alive and Dhritarastra didn't like it one bit. From his spies he had known all along of his son's intentions for the Pandavas at Varanavat. Now he was irritated and afraid it would come back to haunt him. He called for Duryodhan and Karna the moment they returned from Panchala.

Dhritarastra spoke first. "Rumors about your involvement in the fire sprang up even as the ashes in Varanavat still smoldered. Now that the sons of my brother have returned from the dead, the citizens are wildly ecstatic. But I wonder what stories will come to light? What will the people think? Your ill-fated scheme could expose us all."

"Father, there's really nothing to worry about. Karna has a plan. This can all be resolved in one swift stroke."

Duryodhan sat back as Karna unfolded his plan to the king. Dhritarastra listened intently. He wanted to believe the plan could work. His excitement grew, and he chimed in. "An enmity has existed for quite some time between Drona and Drupada. In their youth they were the best of friends, but after Drupada became king he grew arrogant and cut off his ties with Drona, who was only a poor brahmin. I'm sure Drona would agree with us and be happy to see Drupada vanquished once and for all."

Duryodhan and Karna glanced at one another. Old age had made the king more vulnerable. Convincing him was easier than they thought.

Dhritarastra finished with, "I'll call for Drona and Bhismadev, as well as Vidura. We'll get their advice."

"Bhismadev and Vidura!" Duryodhan groaned. "You can't be serious."

"Be calm my son."

"I won't be calm. They've always favored the Pandavas. We'll get no place with them."

"We must listen to their wise counsel. They speak only for the benefit of all."

Duryodhan found it futile to say another word and gave a sidelong glance at Karna.

And so, the elders were called to the Great Hall. After hearing the plan, Bhismadev, spoke forcefully. "What is the value of prolonging needless hostility? War is not an amusement nor a means to satisfy one's goals. It's a waste of time and energy and ultimately of lives." Bhismadev directly addressed Dhritarastra. "But there's a very simple solution you have overlooked. A solution that can satisfy everyone. Divide the kingdom in half. Half for your sons. Half for the sons of Pandu."

Duryodhan's mind screamed, *That's ridiculous! Preposterous! It's not fair!*

Bhismadev continued, "We are fortunate Kunti and her sons did not perish in the blaze at Varanavat. The citizens love the Pandavas and their mother. The citizens loved your brother, Pandu, who brought great prosperity to the kingdom and treated everyone justly. Since the fire, people have accused you of the Pandavas' deaths, and they continue to speak ill of you. We don't want a fight with the Pandavas. Krishna would certainly come to their aid. Together, Krishna and Arjuna are invincible. They are the legendary

Nara and Narayana of old, the manifestation of man and God together."

Bhismadev paused briefly to let his words weigh upon the blind king. "To divide the kingdom in two is the only fair and honorable path. Yudhisthira can rule one half and your son Duryodhan can rule the other half. The citizens will be pleased by this arrangement and you'll be freed from the stigma attached to your good name. Life is short. In the end, all that remains is one's honor and reputation. This settlement will insure the peace and prosperity of our dynasty and will give you a place of distinction for generations to come."

After Bhismadev concluded, Dhritarastra turned to Drona for his advice.

"I am of the same mind as Bhismadev," Drona replied. "It makes no sense to attack the kingdom of Panchala. Call for your nephews and their new queen. Welcome them as you would your own sons. Shower Draupadi with gifts. Propose this division of the kingdom to them and to the citizens. Everyone will rejoice."

No. No. No. Duryodhan couldn't believe what he was hearing. Karna observed Duryodhan's reaction and felt he had to speak up.

"So *this* is the advice of our trusted friends." Karna crafted his words carefully. He continued by recalling an ancient history. "*There once lived a king. You may know his name - Ambuvica. The king was lazy by nature and not inclined to rule. He let his trusted minister make his decisions for him. Without the king's knowing it, the minister slowly began to usurp his wealth, his power, his property, and even his wives. But ultimately, without any effort of his own, the king kept his power and his kingdom. The king was indeed a lucky man. It was Fate that intervened on his behalf.* But sire, I wouldn't sit back and depend upon luck. I would firmly grab hold of my destiny and my sovereignty. These statesmen who advise you may seem like your trusted friends, but I say they are leading you astray."

Drona stood up in protest. "The advice Bhismadev and I have given will benefit everyone. Karna's hotheaded idea is simply to rush into a disastrous war." Drona looked at Karna with pity. "Better to conquer your pride than a kingdom."

Dhritarastra called to Vidura. "And you?"

Vidura rose to speak. "O King, none are better friends to you than Bhismadev and Drona. Take their words to heart. They are meant for your welfare. The schemes of your son and his friends are immature. The Pandavas can never be vanquished. They are protected by Krishna, and victory attends Krishna wherever he goes."

The words of Vidura, Drona and Bhismadev gave the king clarity of mind. The truth of their words shone like a brilliant sword cutting through the dark ignorance the king had allowed himself to be surrounded by. Their words calmed and reassured him. He now understood the proper course to take. He asked Vidura to extend Bhismadev's proposal to the Pandavas.

Duryodhan sat forlorn. He did not utter a word. He felt betrayed by his own father. What was the king thinking? This was all too much. Duryodhan mused that perhaps he too should let go of all his machinations and simply bow to the will of Providence. But the thought proved to be only a momentary distraction.

* * * * *

Duryodhan was not only relieved, but wildly exuberant. The old man came through for him. True, Dhritarastra had given the Pandavas half the kingdom. But the half he gave them was barren and rocky. His father proved to be a sly, old fox.

In times long ago, the king who ruled the region that the Panadvas obtained became consumed by greed. The rishis had cursed him as well as the land, and since then no one wanted to live there. Animals wouldn't go there. Birds wouldn't even fly over it.

For generations the land and the king's palace lay ruined and abandoned. A dry, hot wind constantly battered the landscape. Now this land belonged to the Pandavas.

Krishna arrived from his kingdom of Dwaraka by the western ocean and accompanied the Pandavas to their newly acquired land. He knew about the history of the region and could only smile at Dhritarastra's audacity. Yudhisthira also knew, but he did not complain. He was quite happy to accept Dhritarastra's proposal. He wanted only to live in peace, even if it had to be in the wilderness. Yudhisthira, like the righteous brahmins, remained always poised amidst happiness and distress, success and failure, good times and bad. He refused to hold a grudge, forever diligent to never commit the slightest offense to anyone. The *rishis* called him Ajatasatru, one who is without an enemy.

Krishna stopped his chariot on an expanse of land tangled with weeds and cactus as far as the eye could see. But Krishna looked pleased as his eyes danced here and there. He was not seeing the dusty landscape. He had something greater in mind for the Pandavas. With a glance, Krishna summoned the Celestials who descended from the heavens. With their help, a city was constructed consisting of wide streets, mansions, parks, gardens and numerous market places, all surrounded by a wall with magnificent gateways at regular intervals. The land was transformed into fertile fields with orchards, lakes, and roads. Flocks of birds covered the skies. In this once crippled land, nature's abundance again flourished.

Word of the new kingdom spread far and wide. People arrived from distant lands speaking a multitude of languages. Brahmins, farmers, merchants, craftsmen, and artists of all sorts, along with their families, flooded the roads, eager to dwell in the new city. Yudhisthira's city became known as Indraprasta since it was said to rival the celestial capital of Indra. Each day brought great happiness to Kunti, Draupadi and the five brothers.

* * * * *

One morning a man stopped Arjuna as he strolled leisurely through the marketplace. He told Arjuna his cows had been stolen the previous night. As the man spoke, a crowd gathered. Arjuna wanted to reassure the man, but the man wouldn't let him speak. He went on and on. "We are paying taxes to you. But it seems you and your brothers are inept. You have built a beautiful city, but in reality are you Pandavas capable of apprehending thieves and administering justice? It is well known that if the ruler cannot retrieve stolen property, he must replace it."

The crowd murmured in agreement.

Arjuna had to act. "My friend, you'll have both your cows and your justice. I promise you."

Arjuna was angry, mostly with himself, that he was not more vigilant. He headed straight for the palace to get his bow and several quivers of arrows. But then he remembered. That morning Yudhisthira and Draupadi relaxed together in the very room where he had left his weapons. Arjuna recalled the pact he had made with his brothers. When any one of them was spending time alone with Draupadi the others would not intrude.

I must heed this man's call, Arjuna thought. *If I do not, it will reflect poorly on our rule. But if I enter the chamber, I will break the pact and must accept some consequence. Yet, the man is waiting for me. Waiting for justice. I must go to his aid.*

Arjuna reached the chamber and did not hesitate. He barged through the doors. Yudhisthira and Draupadi were both startled by his intrusion.

"Please, don't mind me," he said without looking at either of them. "I'm just getting my weapons." And on his way out, with weapons in hand, and before Yudhisthira had uttered a word, Arjuna stopped abruptly. He turned to them and smiled affectionately. "I'm sorry, but this is important. Now that I've violated our little pact, you won't be seeing me for a while. I'll be going to the forest alone."

Yudhisthira felt saddened to hear his brother speak this way. "Arjuna, I know you must have a good reason for getting your weapons. Listen to me. You don't have to do this. Nobody wants to see you leave." Yudhisthira was almost pleading.

Draupadi agreed and tried to reach for Arjuna's hand.

But Arjuna would not hear of it. "A vow is a vow. If I am not my word, I am nothing."

And he was gone.

* * * * *

True to his word, Arjuna captured the thieves and retrieved the cows. Afterwards, he went on pilgrimage. He wandered through forests and across rivers until he came to a tirtha, the holy place of Prabhas, by the ocean and not far from Dwaraka. He followed streams of pilgrims to its many sacred sites. Arjuna sat in meditation and also performed menial service for the sages who resided there. He ate little and bathed in the ocean at sunrise and sunset. He relished this life. This simplicity.

But it would not last. Krishna arrived at Prabhas on a golden chariot and enticed Arjuna to return with him to nearby Dwaraka, his capital city, with its fifty magnificent gates. "When the citizens heard you were nearby they became anxious to see you," he told Arjuna. "You can't disappoint them." Krishna wouldn't take 'no' for an answer. But he also had something more in mind.

They arrived in Dwaraka where large crowds turned out to welcome the famed bowman. He was just in time for their annual 'Festival at the Mountain' celebration. The next day a caravan of hundreds of royal carriages left the city in great pomp. By evening they reached the campsite that had been prepared at the base of Raivataka Mountain. Brilliant flags, colorful festoons and bouquets of wild flowers decorated the large tents. Sumptuous foods and refreshments on plates of gold awaited them. The festivities began with a musical concert.

During the merriment Krishna introduced Arjuna to his sister Subhadra. Krishna had orchestrated everything. The moment was perfect. Krishna made sure it was a seemingly casual introduction. He even prodded Arjuna forward to meet others. But Arjuna couldn't help but to continually look back toward Subhadra. She, in turn, never let her gaze fall from the handsome Pandava prince with his long, flowing hair.

Krishna put his arm around Arjuna's shoulders and asked coyly, "My friend, tell me, how is it that the heart of one who revels in the simple life and has spent months visiting the holy places, is now so easily disturbed by the god of love?"

Arjuna was to the point. "Your sister is beautiful."

Krishna was to the point as well. "My brother Balaram wants her to marry Duryodhan."

"What!"

"It's true. And it's a pity that it's true."

"So you don't condone the arrangement?"

"Oh no. Not me. Nor our father. And Subhadra is certainly not inclined to seek Duryodhan's affection. It's only my brother who desires the arrangement."

"Well, we'll see about that."

Krishna smiled mischievously.

* * * * *

The next morning the camp was abuzz. Arjuna and Subhadra were nowhere to be found. Balaram was furious. He ran toward the open-air tent where Krishna leisurely conversed with a group of brahmins, as he was accustomed to do every morning. Throughout the camp, conches and trumpets sounded as Balaram burst into their midst. Krishna concluded his meeting with the brahmins and bestowed gifts upon them before turning his attention to his brother.

"Krishna, Arjuna has carried off our sister. I'm told he took her by force." As Balaram spoke, horse soldiers hastily came from all directions and gathered before the tent. "What are we going to do about this?" Balaram wanted to know.

Krishna paused to consider the question. Furious by Arjuna's conduct, the assembled warriors clamored for action. Krishna looked at them and again back at his brother.

"Why all this commotion?" Krishna asked.

Balaram immediately ran toward the horsemen with his arms upraised. "Quiet down. Quiet down. Give my brother a moment to consider a course of action for us." Then he turned to Krishna. "So how shall we punish this rogue? We wholeheartedly welcomed Arjuna to our city. No one in recent memory has received such a reception. And this is the way he repays us! For his offense, we should rid the Earth of the entire Kuru dynasty."

"Balaram, my brother, don't be so impetuous. Just think on it for a moment. The son of Pandu has treated our dynasty with great honor. Arjuna knows we are not mercenaries who trade off our sisters and daughters for wealth or to insure some social or political contract. He has made us no such offer. And that is not the way we treat our women. As kshatriyas often do, they steal away with their love in the middle of the night. We are noble warriors and honorable men, as is Arjuna. What noble men would not embrace Arjuna as a friend? I say bring them back here with fanfare and give them a proper wedding." When Balaram hesitated to respond, Krishna stepped toward him and sank to his knees. "Balaram, please. They love each other. I implore you, do this for me."

Balaram could not help but smile. Krishna acted perfectly in every respect. In this way, Arjuna and Subhadra were wed, and afterwards they departed for Indraprasta. A year later the couple gave birth to a son, Abhimanyu.

And over the next several years, each of the five Pandavas in turn begot a son with their wife Draupadi.

* * * * *

Krishna and his family soon visited with the Pandavas at Indraprasta. They all went on an outing to a lake resort near the Khandava Forest. After a splendid feast, as Krishna and Arjuna idled together away from the crowd, a haggard stranger emerged from the woods.

"Can you young men kindly provide me with food?" he begged.

Krishna invited the stranger to walk to their camp where plentiful food awaited him.

"I don't want your type of food," said the stranger, "I'm on a special diet. I know you are the illustrious Krishna and Arjuna, and I have come here to ask for your help."

Krishna and Arjuna looked at each other and nodded to assure the odd stranger. Krishna spoke, "Of course, we'll help you. Who are you and how can we serve you?"

"I'm Agni, the god of fire."

Krishna and Arjuna looked him up and down in disbelief. Agni was so pale and emaciated that he was beyond recognition.

"You look horrible. What happened to you?" Arjuna inquired.

"I've been quite ill. It's all because of a confounded king who was so intent on performing countless acts of sacrifice and charity that he exhausted a host of brahmins who were in his service. He had them perform an *agni-hotra* for twelve straight years, day and night. Throughout that time, they poured a constant stream of ghee onto the sacrificial fire. And I was obliged to drink it all. For twelve straight years! You can't imagine what the king put me through. It was cruel. I was forced to consume such vast amounts of ghee that I eventually lost my appetite, my complexion, and my very health. I'm just a mere shadow of a god. For all his pious acts, the king happily ascended to the heavens. But I was left to suffer. Where's the justice in this? It's not right, I tell you." Agni stopped himself from complaining too much. "I petitioned Brahma and he told me I could regain my vigor by consuming the Khandava Forest."

"That shouldn't be very difficult for you," said Arjuna.

Agni let out a feeble smile. "Normally it wouldn't be. But this forest is protected by Indra. Every time I try to devour the forest with my flames, he sends torrents of rain to drive me away. Please, I desperately need your help."

Observing the pained look on Agni's face Krishna reassured him, "Of course we will help you. But we've come here on vacation. You've caught Arjuna without his weapons. You may know Arjuna is renowned for his use of bow and arrows. Surely, you can provide him with weapons and a chariot suitable for the task."

Agni was delighted. In no time, he procured for Arjuna the celestial bow called Gandiva. He knew Arjuna to be ambidextrous and so provided him two magical quivers full of arrows that could never be depleted. Arjuna strapped a quiver over each shoulder. The fire-god also gave Arjuna a celestial chariot that bore the banner of Hanuman, the great monkey prince of ancient times. The chariot, adorned with a variety of weapons and shields, was drawn by four pure white horses that moved with the ease of the wind. Arjuna greeted each of the horses with great affection. He circled the magnificent chariot, examining every detail. As he stepped aboard, he trembled with excitement.

"The one who possesses this vehicle," Agni told Arjuna, "is envied by the Celestials. And the Gandiva is the bow of all bows. With its inexhaustible quivers, it is the multiplier of kingdoms, the chastiser of enemies, and the bringer of fame and fortune."

Agni didn't leave Krishna out of his gift-giving. Agni brought him a razor-sharp chakra, a discus known as Sudarshan that could cut thousands of enemies to pieces and return safely to its owner. Krishna also received an ornate club that roared fiercely every time it struck and killed an enemy. Krishna then mounted his own chariot nearby, and the two warriors were off.

Agni sprang upon the forest with renewed determination. He blazed with such intense heat it was as if the sun itself had fallen from the sky. But as before, Indra descended from the heavens on his elephant carrier Airavata, bringing with him an army of darkened clouds that stretched to the horizon. Indra orchestrated the attack. Lightning streaked across the sky and the thunder in the clouds triggered a deluge of rain.

Arjuna prevented the rain from extinguishing the fire by covering the sky with an unceasing blanket of arrows. In their chariots, Krishna and Arjuna circled the forest. Soon, the fire danced jubilantly as the trees fell upon one another and the lakes and ponds began to boil. Animals and birds dropped in exhaustion and cried pitiably as they were devoured by the fire. Their cries did not evoke the sympathy of Krishna and Arjuna for they recognized the animals and birds for who they really were. The forest had been seized by Asuras, and for some time, they had menaced the peaceful inhabitants of the land. Now, these animals and birds suddenly turned into ferocious, bizarre creatures. They rushed at Krishna and Arjuna from all sides, with weapons and claws raised, screaming, howling, cursing, their teeth bared and their eyes blazing with fury. Arjuna cut them down with a multitude of arrows, while Krishna used his mace and chakra. The roar of Krishna's mace resounded above the towering flames. Gradually, the attacks subsided. Suddenly, a disheveled and scorched figure fell in front of Arjuna's chariot, bringing the horses to an abrupt halt.

"Please, don't hurt me. I beg you, don't hurt me," he whimpered again and again.

Arjuna lowered his bow and arrow. The being before him looked like some strange phantom. The Asura covered his head with his arms and cowered in the dust as if he wanted to sink into the bowels of the earth.

"That's Maya Danava," Krishna warned. "He's the architect from the nether regions. He's the last one left here. Kill him!"

"No! He has sought my shelter, and thus, he need not be afraid. I will allow him to leave here safely." Arjuna looked with pity upon this being. "Go in peace."

"I will remember your kindness," he shouted as he retreated toward the nearby mountains.

Indra could not believe his attempts to save the forest had been foiled by these two upstarts. He called for a troop of Celestials who descended on Krishna and Arjuna with an array of dazzling weapons. Again, the two warriors sprang into action and released a barrage of arrows and easily drove off the attackers. Upon seeing this, Indra was both astonished and confused. He wondered, *Who are these two men that they could so quickly defeat my heavenly warriors?* Indra moved among the clouds for a closer look at the pair. He, with the thousand eyes, now clearly recognized Krishna, the One Without a Second, seated on one chariot, and on the other, he saw his very own son Arjuna, the greatest of bowmen. Shivers ran through his being at the sight. Still hiding within the clouds, Indra offered pranams to this fabled pair, Nara and Narayana, who were rarely seen in this world.

The fight was over. Indra returned to his heavenly abode. Agni was satisfied and regained his health. So it was that the Khandava forest, for the good of the world, had been destroyed. Its ashes smoldered for days afterwards.

* * * * *

After the battle, Maya Danava cautiously returned to see Arjuna. "You have kindly spared my life. Allow me to serve you."

"I cannot accept a gift or service for merely performing my duty."

"Please, ask anything of me and it is yours."

"It is forbidden for a kshatriya to enrich oneself from one who seeks protection." Arjuna looked from Maya Danava to Krishna. "If you want to show your gratitude perhaps you can serve my friend here in some way."

"Shri Krishna." Maya Danava turned and bowed before him. "It will be my great honor. What would you have me do?"

Krishna did not hesitate. "This will be your task. King Yudhisthira has a wonderful city but it needs a sabha, an assembly building with a palatial hall, as a finishing touch. I know you can build one, the likes of which have never been seen on Earth."

Maya Danava smiled, his mind already working on the sabha. "I will design a building which will captivate the mind, baffle the senses, and bedazzle all those who behold it. It will be one-of-a-kind, grand and refreshing, surrounded by columns of gold and adorned with exquisite gems gathered from throughout the world. Nothing like it has ever been built, nor will ever be built on Earth again. It will stand as a masterpiece of illusion."

When they arrived at Indraprasta, Yudhisthira warmly greeted them and gave Maya Danava the welcome he deserved as a renowned architect and craftsman. Maya Danava began by sectioning off a parcel of land ten thousand cubits square. He called upon a thousand broad-chested Rakshasa warriors and placed them in all directions to safeguard his secrets as he constructed this extraordinary building. It took him over a year to complete it.

* * * * *

Descending from the heavens Narada Muni beheld the sabha. He had heard talk of it and wanted to see it for himself, as well as to meet Yudhisthira. Narada was conversant in all branches of knowledge, both spiritual and material. He moved freely amongst the worlds of men and Celestials, traveling throughout the universe on the sound vibration of his stringed instrument, the vina. The vibration of the vina supported him and eased his descent. Below him, Yudhisthira with his brothers and ministers gathered by a crystal stairway that led down to a lake filled with lotuses. The group rushed forward to greet him. They bowed before Narada, who is worshipped by kings, brahmins, and Celestials. Even hunters, thieves and murderers were known to honor him and seek his advice, and were often transformed into saints by his grace. Nakula brought him a seat and Yudhisthira bestowed precious gems and jewels upon him. Narada appeared both serene and powerful. He made a gesture with his hand to bless the group, and waves of ecstasy stirred them.

Narada inquired, "My dear Yudhisthira, are you seeing to it that all the citizens are happy? This is the first duty of a king, or of any leader for that matter. Happiness must take the shape of justice and of economic prosperity. But take care that wealth is not used to bend justice to one's own liking. Nor should one manipulate justice to secure wealth. Justice and wealth are not playthings to increase our happiness, or to safeguard our prejudices. True happiness is reserved for those who are illumined from within, those who rejoice from within, those who see all things the same: be it a friend or foe, be it a stone, gold, or a clump of dirt.

"But you are a king, and to carry out your duty, you must make distinctions. Even though you maintain forts, soldiers, chariots, elephants and spies; and even though you have many men and resources at your command; and even though you are expert in collecting taxes and in the art of diplomacy, I hope you don't let your mind be consumed by the power you wield. I hope you don't let anyone whose passions are uncontrolled, or who would accept bribes and perform wicked deeds, near that power. I hope you protect the women, children, the elderly, the invalid, the brahmins and the cows. I hope you make sure the farmers, merchants, and craftsmen have order and opportunity to pursue a peaceful and prosperous life. My dear Yudhisthira, I hope you will always be devoted to the good of all."

"O Narada, your words are clear and concise and as sweet as nectar. I shall certainly imbibe them and do everything you have advised."

At Narada's request, Yudhisthira gave the sage a tour of the sabha and of the immaculate designs of Maya Danava. Afterwards, Yudhisthira inquired, "You must have visited the assembly houses of the gods of universal affairs in the celestial regions. Please, describe those places to us."

"In the heavens, the sabhas are many miles in length and breadth and height. Inside them, one is freed from all hunger and thirst, from all fatigue, fear and anxiety. No one speaks a word of untruth. No anger, nor envy, nor harsh words are found within their perimeters. The halls are filled with the light of wondrous colors and resound with the auspicious hymns recited by brahmins. In those halls it's never too hot or too cold. The Apsaras and Gandharvas, expert in dance, music and song, also perform in those chambers, composing wondrous melodies to the delight of the heavenly denizens. The bards tell inspiring stories nuanced with many meanings. All these dancers, singers, musicians, and story tellers are lavished with numerous gifts. But of all the palaces I have visited, the most stunning and extraordinary, without question, is the assembly hall of Krishna.

"Before I take my leave there's one last thing. The time has come for you to perform the legendary Rajasuya ceremony. Such an event has not been seen on this Earth for many generations. It is the desire of the Celestials, the sages, your forefathers, and of Krishna himself. They want to see you proclaimed as emperor of the world. Before you hold the ceremony you must send each of your four brothers and their armies in the four directions: to the east and west, to the north and south. They are to receive tribute and homage from the kings across the Earth or defeat them by force. The Rajasuya must be performed with utmost care, for it holds many obstacles. Engage expert brahmins who can navigate its myriad rules and regulations. In the shadows lurk brahmin Rakshasas who will surely exploit any weakness in the ceremony. Be vigilant to the minutest of details. If you are not, it could spell disaster."

Mahabharata: The Eternal Quest

* * * * *

The Rajasuya began with Yudhisthira and his brothers entering the arena in the wake of a thousand brahmins reciting Vedic hymns. The arena was built specially for the event during an auspicious month. A thousand trumpets welcomed kings and dignitaries from far and wide, including Duryodhan and other nobles of the Kuru dynasty. Poets and musicians sang the history of the dynasty. The Celestials were visible among the clouds, sitting comfortably in their sky chariots, and showering flowers onto the procession of brahmins and nobles.

All the paraphernalia in the arena was perfectly arranged. As in bygone ages, all the plates and utensils for the Rajasuya were made of pure gold, even the ones used to serve meals to all who attended. As they entered the arena, Krishna washed the feet and spoke kind words to each and every guest. It seemed he knew everyone intimately. The elderly were welcomed and seated first.

The brahmins had risen early that morning, hours before dawn, and bathed in the cold waters of the nearby river. With clay from its banks they placed the mark of Vishnu on their foreheads, arms and chests. They had also recited prayers during those auspicious pre-dawn hours.

At the Rajasuya, the brahmins ignited the sacrificial fires by the use of mantra. After several hours of ceremonies the coronation of Yudhisthira was completed. This was followed by much festivity, music, laughter and joyfulness. As the Rajasuya ended, everyone felt contented and at peace.

* * * * *

The Rajasuya culminated with the arghya, a ceremony wherein Yudhisthira showed his gratitude by bestowing gifts and honor upon the sages and kings who were present there. First, the assembly had to choose the most exalted personality who would be honored above all others and receive the First Honor. Yudhisthira called upon Bhismadev to give his assessment.

The Grandsire stood up and spoke in a resounding voice. "The First Honor should be given to none other than Shri Krishna, for he is the Ancient One, the origin of all things, and the author of Dharma. We are fortunate Krishna has blessed us with his presence on Earth, even as the Kali-yuga approaches. This is his boundless mercy. The very least we can do is to offer him the first arghya."

Yudhisthira felt great happiness upon hearing Bhismadev's choice. The way Bhismadev spoke of Krishna before the assembly sent waves of ecstasy surging through Yudhisthira's being. He asked of the assembly, "What do you all say?" A thunderous applause of approval rose up from the audience. He beckoned Krishna to step forward to be the first honored. As Sahadev presented him the arghya, everyone stood in respect.

Suddenly, a voice pierced the applause. Sisupala, the ruler of Chedi, rose up with his arms outstretched. "I cannot believe this folly! Have you all gone mad?" Sisupala made a sour face as he looked toward Krishna, and continued. "Many great personalities are in our midst: men who rule powerful kingdoms; sages and yogis who have performed great austerities; erudite brahmins whose knowledge is without limit. Who is this Krishna compared to them? Krishna is like a crow who feeds off the refuse of others. We don't even know his actual position in society. Krishna doesn't seem to belong to any caste. He grew up in a village and was raised by cowherds. He has no formal training as a kshatriya. All his life he's never cared about following Vedic injunctions. We don't need Krishna. To select him for First Honor is an insult to the nobles. I will not lend my name to this travesty."

The soft-spoken Sahadev tried to explain. "Giving to Krishna and honoring Krishna is like giving water to the root of a tree. When the root is watered, all of the branches, leaves and flowers of the tree are nourished as well."

Sisupala snickered. "You are young and impressionable. Your intelligence has been polluted."

"How can Krishna not be honored?" Bhismadev boomed. "He is Acyuta - the infallible one. He is Adhoksaja - the beginning and the end of all things, the Lord of past, present and future. He is Hrsikesa - master of the senses. Krishna is Bhagavan - complete in all six opulences: knowledge, wealth, strength, fame, beauty and renunciation. My dear Sahadev, pay no heed to this rogue and complete the ceremony of the First Honor."

Sisupala shook with anger and addressed his supporters. "The Pandavas have taken shelter in Krishna who is an imposter. He's not one of us. I am here to lead you, to guide you. If we hold together, their so-called strength will collapse like a house of cards."

"Your arrogant words only bring you closer to the abode of Death," Bhismadev warned.

Sisupala continued his ranting against Krishna and the Pandavas, and now even against the Grandsire himself. Sisupala's incessant flow of scathing words pounded at Bhima's brain. Bhima found it increasingly difficult to restrain himself. He was getting angrier by the minute. Sahadev tried to calm him, but to no avail since he was fuming mad himself. They both turned toward Sisupala, ready to strike him, but with a gesture of his hand, Bhismadev caught their attention and silently cautioned them to stand down.

The assembly had turned into a turbulent ocean. Some nobles grabbed the hilts of their swords, eager to put an end to the culprit, while others joined Sisupala's ranks, ready to defend him. Some nobles warned Sisupala to stop committing offenses against Krishna and the Grandsire. Nobles began to threaten one another, even as others called for calm. Many brahmins fled the Rajasuya not wanting to hear insults against Krishna, since these disturbances were ruining the ceremony.

In the midst of the commotion Krishna evoked his Sudarshan chakra. From his index finger, he sent it hurtling across the assembly, and that razor-sharp weapon severed Sisupala's head. Like a streaking meteor, Sisupala's spirit-soul emerged from his lifeless body and soared across the arena into Krishna's being. Everyone was stunned. Krishna, free from malice, had accepted Sisupala, his avowed enemy.

Bhismadev declared "Sisupala has been absorbed into that transcendent reality of Shri Krishna."

Everyone cheered, and Sisupala's stalwart supporters fled the assembly in fear of their lives. Finally, the brahmins completed this last part of the ceremony, honoring Krishna as the most exalted personality. Thus ended the Rajasuya.

* * * * *

The nobles could not understand why Krishna had waited so long to punish Sisupala, who was so wicked of heart. Bhismadev was knowledgeable about all things, and, after the ceremony, he told them a story to explain Krishna's seeming unwillingness to chastise this scourge of Chedi.

"Sisupala was born deformed. He had three eyes and four arms. He was prone to awful tantrums, and when he cried he screeched. His father, the King of Chedi, and his mother, the Queen, were often paralyzed with anxiety over their son's condition.

One day an eerie, disembodied voice informed them, 'Your child will shed his deformities when he sits on the lap of a particular visitor to the palace. Unfortunately, the visitor who is your son's cure will also one day kill him.'

The king and queen experienced both relief and dread in the same instance. From that time forth, they made sure to sit the child on the lap of whoever visited the palace. After hundreds of visitors, still nothing happened. Then Krishna came to visit the queen, his aunt, and when she brought the child to sit on Krishna's lap, the boy was immediately cured. The parents, overwhelmed with joy, danced round and round with their child. The queen abruptly stopped and rushed to Krishna, tears streaming from her eyes, and fell at his feet. 'O Krishna, I'm afraid for my son. Please, you have to promise me something.'

'Of course, my dear aunt. Whatever you want.'

'Don't kill him. Don't kill my son. If he makes any offense against you, or transgresses the Dharma, promise me that you'll spare him.'

'I'll spare him. I'll spare him not just once or twice, but I'll overlook a hundred transgressions.'

The king of Chedi eventually died and Sisupala assumed the reign of the kingdom. He became intoxicated by the power and privilege at his disposal, and as a result, he delighted in performing sins and misdeeds. He forced himself upon women, he wantonly killed innocent citizens, he kidnapped men and women and held them as slaves, he disrupted ceremonies, and he spoke ill of others, spreading false rumors. There was no sin this wretch had not committed. But Krishna tolerated everything because of the promise he had made to Sisupala's mother. Today Sisupala exceeded his one hundredth offense, and Krishna finally gave him the punishment he deserved."

* * * * *

After the Rajasuya, Duryodhan had a chance to examine the ingenious sabha, the crown jewel of Yudhisthira's already prosperous kingdom. Duryodhan's heart burned with envy. In that splendorous sabha, he saw Yudhisthira seated amid the throng, calm and assured, surrounded by Draupadi and his brothers. Duryodhan hated the Pandavas for their good fortune. This building should have been his. Draupadi should have been his. Their fame should have been his.

He wanted to flee from this sight. He tried to walk through a doorway, or what he thought was a doorway, and smashed his head against a crystal wall. Some of the ladies of Indraprasta saw Duryodhan's encounter with the wall and tried not to laugh too hard, covering their mouths with their hands. After that,

Duryodhan came upon what he thought was a deep pit and carefully walked around it. But after an usher walked across it, Duryodhan realized it was just a wonderful design of marble.

Next, he came upon another design on the floor. He went closer to examine it. *Very clever,* he thought to himself, *this amazing craftsmanship of marble on the floor appears to be exactly like a pond of water.* And when he tried to walk across it, he fell in. It was a pond, and Duryodhan was drenched and fuming. The ladies nearby laughed again at the sight, and Duryodhan made a hasty retreat. He stumbled out of the hall. Yudhisthira was pained to see this king of the Kauravas so humiliated.

Chapter 7

The Dice Match

Duryodhan and Sakuni sat together in the carriage on the way back to Hastinapura. Duryodhan, wrapped in thought, did not speak a word. Sakuni knew why, and he tried to strike up a conversation several times. But with no result, only an agonizing silence. Out of nowhere, Duryodhan's silence exploded.

"I can't stand it. Everything turns into gold for the Pandavas. Wherever they go the Celestials, nobles and commoners honor them. They are constantly lavished with gifts and affection. Why them? And now, along with their city and lands, they have their magnificent sabha. It is said one should act before an enemy gets too powerful. I've tried everything to destroy them. But nothing has worked. So, my dear uncle, you are a clever man. I've always admired your resourcefulness. You're the only one who can help me. Help me destroy the Pandavas. Help me claim their sabha, their kingdom and their queen as my own."

Sakuni smiled with satisfaction at Duryodhan's confidence in him. "My dear nephew, I'll help you get everything your heart desires. You won't even need weapons. No. The Pandavas are blessed and cannot be defeated in battle even by the Celestials."

"So what are you saying?"

"I'm saying don't sulk. You'll have your glory yet, just trust your uncle. Isn't Yudhisthira fond of dice? I think he even fancies himself an expert."

"Everyone knows this weakness of his."

"I am a wizard at gambling. I have in my possession a pair of dice that obey my every command. My nephew, all you have to do is invite the Pandavas back to the capital city for a few days of friendly sports and games. You make all the arrangements. One evening, we'll have them come to the Great Hall for a game of dice. With my dice I'll take away everything they have. But first you must speak with your father. He must be of the same mind or else he could ruin everything. In fact, let the invitation come from him."

* * * * *

Back in Hastinapura they went to Dhritarastra. Duryodhan made Sakuni speak first.

"My dear King," Sakuni began, "I come to you because I'm concerned about Duryodhan. He looks sickly of late. He has no appetite and seems depressed."

The blind king was concerned. "Duryodhan my son, tell me, is this true?"

Duryodhan did not answer.

Dhritarastra appealed to his son. "I'll do anything in my power to help you."

"My dear father, at Yudhisthira's Rajasuya I saw thousands of nobles and ambassadors from all over the world waiting in line to gladly give him tributes. He received thousands of elephants, thousands of horses, thousands of chariots, thousands of ornate clothes and textiles, and countless pots filled with gold, and magnificent gems from the sea. The riches I beheld in his court surpassed those of even the king of heaven. The thought of Yudhisthira's wealth and opulence sickens me. I only want to die."

The blind king was saddened. "Duryodhan, I am surprised to hear such words. You are not in want. You wear clothes woven from the finest silks. You carry the best weapons. In your stables are the fastest horses. You live in a mansion made of the finest marble. I've made you heir to the throne. You carry the fame and honor of the Kuru dynasty. Hastinapura is the crossroads of the world. There's nothing you can't have. Why should you be discontented?"

Duryodhan would not let up. "Even if one man has a richer purse or a faster horse or a finer palace, I am discontented. Yes. I want to be discontented. I relish being discontented. From discontentment comes ambition. With ambition comes the drive to fulfill one's desires, and by fulfilling one's desires one can be happy. My father, if you want to see me happy again then help me. Sakuni has an idea. He is a master at dice. Sakuni will challenge Yudhisthira to a game and take away everything he has. All you need to do is to invite him back to Hastinapura."

The blind king was flustered. "Let me consult with Vidura about this."

"Always Vidura. Why don't you just let me kill myself, and then you and your Vidura can live happily together."

"My son, don't be angry. Please. Of course I will help you."

Duryodhan and Sakuni looked at one another. Their plan had worked.

* * * * *

The Pandavas returned to Hastinapura upon Dhritarastra's invitation. They were welcomed with pomp and honor. Their quarters were beautifully decorated. Yudhisthira, his brothers and their queen received many fine gifts. Then came the suggestion for an evening game of dice.

Sakuni said, "We princes of the royal court are warriors and are apt to engage in sports as well as games of chance. Yudhisthira,

103

I know how much you enjoy a game of dice. Surely you can indulge us for one evening."

Yudhisthira understood why they had been invited back. He had been warned by Vidura who came to know of the plan. Yudhisthira hesitated to play. But when his hosts pressed him, he thought, *They have been so kind and have made every possible arrangement for our comfort. How can I refuse?*

That evening, the Great Hall was filled with elders and respected leaders of the Kuru dynasty. Yudhisthira played for the Pandavas. Sakuni played on behalf of Duryodhan. Karna and Ashwattama came and sat by Duryodhan as the gambling began. Bhismadev, from his prominent seat in the assembly, looked on in dismay. *Why would Yudhisthira agree to this game?* he wondered. *What is the sense of it? Yudhisthira must know Sakuni cannot be defeated in dice.*

Stakes were wagered. Jewels and diamonds of the finest quality. Sakuni took the dice in his hands and threw them on the board. "I have won!" he shouted. Yudhisthira wagered a thousand gold coins and next ten thousand. The dice were cast. "I have won!" Sakuni proclaimed again and yet again.

Yudhisthira wagered his silver-encrusted carriage, drawn by eight horses as white as moon beams. He wagered a thousand royal elephants with the mark of a lotus on their foreheads. He wagered a hundred thousand cows who all provided an abundance of milk. Sakuni's dice held a strange spell over Yudhisthira. Sakuni's voice continually resounded in the Great Hall, "I have won again!"

The tension was palpable. The assembly hovered in stunned disbelief. Grandsire Bhismadev looked pained, but could do nothing. He could only wait for fate to take its course and know, that in the end, justice would be done. Yudhisthira quickly lost everything he had: his army, his wealth, his lands, his sabha, even the weapons, jewels and royal garments he and his brothers wore. His world was being devoured by Sakuni.

"I have won again!"

Sakuni's words rang in Yudhisthira's ears. It seemed to him he had fallen into a dream. He watched himself. He saw his feet in the glistening snow. Mountains towered all around, holding great secrets. Their silence was deafening. He felt himself dangerously suspended over a precipice, losing his balance. Overhead, a clear, limitless sky. He fell into oblivion. Falling. Falling. Not knowing if he was falling down or up. A bird shrieked. Then Sakuni called his name and Yudhisthira snapped back to the moment.

Sakuni taunted, "My dear Yudhisthira, tonight Providence shines upon me. You have lost all of your wonderful possessions. But my friend, I am a reasonable man. I'll give you a chance to win it all back. Just find something, anything at all, that you can wager."

In desperation Yudhisthira gambled away his brothers, and himself. Finally, he wagered their lovely wife Draupadi. Sakuni rolled the dice and raised his arms in triumph. "I have won again!" The Pandavas had lost everything, even their freedom and their wife.

* * * * *

Dushasana gleefully ran to Draupadi's quarters like an impish child. He knocked impatiently on the door and when she appeared he insisted she come with him at once. When she hesitated, his countenance darkened. He grabbed her roughly by the hair and, in spite of her protests, he dragged her before the assembly of nobles and warriors. Draupadi looked in disbelief upon her husbands who, stripped of their weapons and wealth, sat with heads bowed in shame. Across the way sat Duryodhan, Karna, Ashwattama, and Chitra, all filled with pride and smiling in great satisfaction. It appeared to Bhismadev that Draupadi was a lamb in the midst of hungry jackals.

Duryodhan told her of her fate. "My dear Draupadi, rejoice. Now you belong to me. Yudhisthira foolishly lost you and everything he owns in the dice match. Your husbands are paupers. In fact, they are my slaves."

Draupadi couldn't believe her ears. Pained and humiliated, she tried to remain composed as hot tears streamed from her eyes.

Duryodhan felt triumphant. "Come here Draupadi and sit on my lap." He slapped his thigh in an effort to entice her, but she defiantly stood her ground. Duryodhan was relentless. "Draupadi, do you understand? You are my slave. I can do whatever I want with you, and if I want to see you naked, no one can stop me."

With a gesture from Duryodhan, Dushasana began to pull off her sari. Draupadi looked across the Great Hall towards her husbands, and then towards the nobles. All of them appeared forlorn and helpless. Dushasana continued to unravel her sari.

At first Draupadi held tightly to her garment. She soon realized her resistance was futile. She raised her hands in supplication. If no warrior or elder or gentleman came forward to protect her honor, she would take shelter of that transcendent personality, Shri Krishna. "O Soul of the Universe," she called out, "please hear me. You are the friend of the innocent and the destroyer of all obstacles. O Krishna, save me from this injustice. You are my life and soul. Please, protect me!"

The Kauravas snickered at Draupadi's misplaced petition. They all knew Krishna was hundreds of miles away in his own city of Dwaraka. But unknown to them, Krishna heard her cries. Dushasana continued to unravel her brilliant colored sari. As he pulled off the cloth, more cloth appeared in its place. Heaps of cloth covered the floor, but Draupadi remained clothed. The scene turned into a spectacle. Bhismadev and Drona, who had felt powerless to act, now laughed out loud. Dushasana looked around uncomprehendingly. All of his muscles ached. He staggered away, exhausted.

Unseen, that supreme mystic Krishna had supplied Draupadi with endless cloth. Krishna laughed and laughed. Bhismadev felt

Krishna's presence. He knew Krishna ever-delighted in playing tricks. Bhismadev remembered a story:

As a child in the village of Vrindavan, Krishna frolicked in the fields with his playmates. One day his childhood friends came running to his mother, Yasoda, to tell her that Krishna had been eating dirt.

She immediately called for Krishna. 'What have you been up to?' she demanded to know.

'Nothing mother,' he innocently replied.

'Have you been eating dirt?'

'No mother.'

But Yasoda knew how mischievous Krishna could be. 'Open your mouth and let me see.'

Krishna complied. And when Yasoda looked in Krishna's mouth she was amazed. The universe came spilling forth and she quickly became engulfed by countless galaxies hurtling through unlimited space. She beheld innumerable stars and planets along with the myriad forms of life that inhabited them. On the Earth she saw mountain ranges, forests, deserts, jungles, and vast oceans. She saw great herds of elephants, buffalo, and gazelle roaming freely across the plains. She saw people of all colors and creeds, speaking a variety of tongues. She saw the sweep of humanity and all the shades of their emotions. She saw the thread that runs through all life, which is lodged in every atom and molecule, and connects all things. She even saw herself in her own home attending to her household duties as little Krishna came running in to embrace her.

She tried to fathom what all this meant. She became perplexed. It was too much. Krishna was her little child to protect and care for, to hold and to love. That's all she needed to know.

'Krishna, go wash your hands and get ready for dinner,' she told him.

'See mother, I told you, no dirt,' he said as he walked away smiling.

* * * * *

No longer able to restrain himself, Bhima rose like a mountain in the midst of the Pandavas. "Dushasana!" he yelled, "Do you think you can simply walk away from your evil deeds and be done with it? Sometime, somewhere, we will meet again under different circumstances. I promise you, I will rip out your heart and drink your blood. And you Duryodhan, I would have jumped up and killed you and all you brothers before this assembly. But out of respect for my elder brother Yudhisthira, I did not. Some day I'll find you and smash the thigh you showed to Draupadi. Hear me, O assembled warriors. If I do not keep these vows, I am not worthy to enter into the celestial abode of my ancestors."

Suddenly, the earth rumbled and fierce winds blew and crows shrieked from the nearby trees. Dhritarastra trembled, for although he was blind, he recognized these ill omens, and remembered the omens years ago that accompanied the birth of Duryodhan. He remembered the prophetic words of Vidura. He could understand the gravity of his warning, and how Duryodhan's greed and envy were leading his dynasty toward an abyss. Fearing for his sons, Dhritarastra called out to Draupadi.

"My child, come forward. You and your husbands have been greatly wronged. Somehow or other, a dark cloud has fallen upon the nobles assembled here and we have allowed such an injustice to take place against you. Draupadi, I beg you to please find it in your heart to forgive us and to forgive my sons. I will give you a boon. Ask from me whatever your heart desires. I will give it to you gladly."

"I want the freedom of my husbands," she said without hesitation.

"Surely my child," said Dhritarastra, with a relieved smile. "That's easy enough to give. But please, ask for something more."

"My husbands should have their weapons returned to them."

"Of course. Of course. I'll give you that, and name whatever else you desire."

"Sir, I don't have to ask you for anything else. " Draupadi spoke with conviction. "Now that my husbands have their freedom and their weapons, they can easily regain whatever rightfully belongs to us."

The Pandavas rose and gathered their garments and weapons. Along with Draupadi, they made ready to leave the Great Hall as the assembly looked on.

Dhritarastra's voice was shaking when he called out again. "Wait! Before you leave, I return to you everything you have wagered and lost. Take it all back. I beg you to forget the abomination that has taken place here this evening."

The Pandavas bowed to the king, and Yudhisthira touched his feet in respect. The blind king let out a sigh. He felt a catastrophe had been averted, and a monstrous burden lifted from his back. Now his sons would be spared and his good name had been redeemed.

Duryodhan whispered to Sakuni. "We can't let them leave in this way. They'll grow more powerful than ever. Whatever the Pandavas may say or do now, they will not forget this night. You must do something."

Sakuni was not one to be without a scheme. He rose to address Yudhisthira. "Listen to me. You live a blessed life. You have been favored by the gods. Everyone desires to see you and your family well attended to and honored properly. This is a fact. But ultimately we alone must accept responsibility for the decisions we make in life. Yudhisthira, you have gambled and lost. That the king has seen fit to give it all back to you is fine with Duryodhan and myself. But you cannot deny Duryodhan could have easily lost the wealth he wagered. So only to be fair to all parties concerned, we should play one final game of dice. Whoever loses this game forfeits their wealth and the comforts of their home for twelve years. Whoever loses must enter the forest to live in exile. Before they return, they must spend a thirteenth year living incognito. If, however, their identities are discovered during that thirteenth year, they will have to repeat their exile for another twelve years. Yudhisthira, this one last throw of the dice is the only honorable thing to do."

A silence hung over the assembly. Everyone waited, transfixed.

"So be it," Yudhisthira said, motioning for Sakuni to proceed.

Sakuni shook the dice and cast them on the board. When the dice stopped he turned toward the assembly. He dared not be overjoyed. "I have won again," he said plainly.

Chapter 8

Exile

The day the Pandavas left Hastinapura a blistery wind engulfed the city. Many citizens saw it as an ill omen, that they themselves were condemned and the Earth was doomed. They cursed Duryodhan for his cruel and envious nature. When the citizens learned Draupadi had decided to join her husbands in exile, they were taken aback. From birth she had only known the comforts of palace life with its rich foods, perfumes and fineries. The people heard she had sent her five sons to Panchala to live with her brother Dristadyumna for the duration of the exile. They wondered from where did she gather up the strength to renounce her luxuries, to be away from her children, and not to care for them, nor to see them grow up. Men and women cried out and clutched their hearts at the mere thought of such hardship. A multitude followed the Pandavas into the forest and surrounded them and pleaded with them to turn back. But if the Pandavas were intent on going into exile, the citizens vowed to join them in the forest as well. Yudhisthira beseeched the people to return to their homes, to comfort one another, and to let him and his brothers meet their destiny, since all things ultimately work for the good. And so, with heavy hearts, the people unwillingly retraced their steps.

The Pandavas and their entourage of brahmins continued to a place by the Ganges River known as Pramanakoti, where an ancient and sacred banyan tree stood. They camped underneath the great banyan where they meditated and fasted all night long as the brahmins chanted Vedic hymns. Their prayers seemed to ascend into the clear night sky, bedecked with millions of stars, to bless heaven itself.

The next morning, before sunrise, Yudhisthira also requested the brahmins to return to their homes. "You are gentle men, dedicated to your studies, prayers and meditations. The forest is full of difficulties and discomfort. It is said a proper host must always lavish kindness upon a guest. A guest must be given a comfortable seat, sufficient food and drink, and pleasing words. Treating a guest in this way is certainly a religious duty, and a man can attain even greater merit by greeting a complete stranger who comes to his door in this fashion. But, while living in the forest, I will have nothing to offer you and I will not be able to maintain you properly. Please return to your dwellings."

The brahmins mused over the recent events. "This is a world of contradictions. The pious suffer and the wicked, seduced by their own senses, seem to have their own way. Strange indeed. And more of this is in store in the Kali-yuga. Yudhisthira, do not abandon righteousness, nor your desire to maintain the brahmins. If you want to provide them meals, this is our advice to you. The sun is the source of all food. Therefore, pray to the sun-god Surya for a solution to your conundrum. With concentrated mind and heart, worship the rays of the morning sun which bring health and prosperity. Stand in the river, facing toward the lord of light who is the sustainer of the Earth with her thirteen great islands, and absorb yourself in the hymn to the sun-god which was composed by Brahma at the dawn of creation."

"My dear sirs, thank you for your guidance. A king can never realize the wealth of this life nor of the next without seeking the wise counsel of brahmins who are well-versed in Dharma and who seek the benefit of all."

At dawn, wading into the river, Yudhisthira, in all humility, offered prayers to Surya again and again. After a long time, being pleased, the sun-god appeared before him with a gift. "O King, I know your only concern is for the well-being of the brahmins who travel with you or who may visit you in your exile. Thus I bestow upon you a gift - this copper bowl. Once every day place whatever food you have prepared into this magic bowl. The food therein will expand unlimitedly. All who are present can eat to their full satisfaction. Draupadi will be the last to partake of the meal. Afterwards, wash the bowl and put it away safely to be used the next day."

With their new gift, the Pandavas, followed by the brahmins, proceeded happily into the forest.

* * * * *

One day Vyasa approached the Pandavas' camp. He could hear the raised voices of Draupadi and Bhima chiding Yudhisthira.

"I still don't understand it," Draupadi threw up her hands. "Whatever possessed you to gamble away our freedom and wealth to that evil-hearted wretch? When I see you all idling here in the forest rather than raising your weapons to punish the wicked, it infuriates me."

Yudhisthira tried to console Draupadi. "My love, do not set your heart on grief. The forest abounds with plenty. We can surely live here in peace. Please, be patient and forgiving. Forgiveness is holy."

"But forgiveness is not always the right course. The wise say a first offense should be forgiven. An offense caused by ignorance can also be forgiven. But in this case, the Kauravas have made offenses over and over again."

Bhima interjected, "Yudhisthira, unlike you, I can find no peace living in the forest." His proud voice almost trembled. "You may have adapted to the life of a mendicant, my brother, but I would rather die in battle."

"Bhima, anger clouds one's judgment. A man who acts in anger cannot distinguish between friend and foe, between when to speak and when to remain silent, between what is a proper and improper course of action. If one who receives anger only gives anger and if one who is insulted only gives insult, how can there ever be peace in this world? That's why we must live a life of virtue, as difficult as it may be."

Bhima persisted. "What is this virtue you always speak of? Virtue, virtue! I say only the wealthy and the strong can be virtuous. As warriors, we will not find our wealth by remaining in the forest."

"The sages tell us real wealth is found within."

"My brother, the spiteful words of Duryodhan and Sakuni do not bother me. But you certainly know how to torture a man with words. When we do not strike back at the injustice in this world, it is not a virtue but a vice."

Vyasa revealed his presence with a smile. "Children, children. This is no time for arguments. Above all, don't remain in anxiety. Prolonged anxiety fosters ill health. Just like a hot iron rod heats up a bowl of water, anxiety in the mind affects the rest of the body. Use this time now to your advantage."

The Pandavas and Draupadi all turned their attention to Vyasa and welcomed him with a flurry of salutations and smiles. They ushered him to a seat and bathed his feet with scented water and placed before him a bowl of fruit for his pleasure. After settling down around him, he began in a grave voice.

"In your absence Duryodhan, Karna, Ashwattama and Sakuni are busy making alliances and increasing their strength. In the future, if there is to be a battle, both Bhismadev and Drona are duty bound to fight on behalf of the Kauravas. Together, these two remarkable warriors possess the most powerful of earthly and celestial weapons. You must act accordingly and prepare yourselves. I have come to you with a plan. One of you must take a dangerous journey. Who will it be?"

Without hesitation Arjuna jumped up. "I'll go."

"Arjuna, yes, of course. You shall be the one. You must begin your journey immediately. Follow my voice."

Arjuna put on his protective breastplate and a short-bladed sword, and snatched up his Gandiva bow, along with a quiver of inexhaustible arrows. After offering prayers, herbs, and ghee into the fire, Arjuna set forth from the Pandava camp, following Vyasa's disembodied voice.

"Arjuna, I will give you a mantra. Always keep it on your tongue. This mantra will guide you and protect you on your journey. On the far side of the Himalayas, there is a mysterious valley. The path that leads across the mountains is inaccessible, covered by ice and snow. The trip is impossible for a mere mortal. But the mantra will clear the way for you. Arjuna, go to those mountain heights and just try to please Shiva, the Three-Eyed One, by performing meditations and austerities in the forest near the river. In this way, you can gain entrance into the world of the Celestials. Surely, they will grant you the use of their extraordinary weapons."

Vyasa chanted a secret mantra, and gradually Vyasa's voice faded. Now the mantra guided Arjuna as it danced on his tongue. The path opened up before him and he effortlessly traversed raging rivers, dark forests, and dangerous mountain passages. Arjuna walked day and night without food or rest. The mantra sustained him. Remarkably, within only a few days he had gone the distance and arrived in the valley at the top of the world. There, in a lush forest, he set his bow and quiver at arm's length and planted his feet firmly on the ground. The branches of the trees were laden with fruits of indescribable tastes. Innumerable birds lived there and, in the morning, the forest resounded with their sweet songs.

Flocks of geese gathered in the waters nearby. Instantly, they were airborne, honking joyously in their flight.

* * * * *

Day after day, Arjuna stood absorbed in meditation, his only food being the fruit that fell from the trees close at hand. In the first month, he ate once every three days. During the second month he ate once every six days. In the third month he ate twice. In the fourth month he did not eat at all, but existed on breath.

One day, Arjuna's meditation was disturbed by shrill sounds and rustling in the underbrush. When he looked up, his eyes met the eyes of a boar. The creature's hairs stood on end. It snorted menacingly and attacked. In one motion, Arjuna rolled out of the way and retrieved his bow and quivers and released an arrow. From another direction, a second arrow whizzed through the trees. Simultaneously, both arrows struck the boar and it fell dead to the ground. In death, the creature turned into his actual self, a hideous Rakshasa. Arjuna cautiously approached the creature.

"Don't touch him. He's mine," a voice warned through the trees.

Arjuna looked but saw no one. "Who are you? Show yourself," he demanded.

A tall, bearded man dressed in buckskin stepped forward. "I've been tracking this Rakshasa. He has terrorized the residents in these parts for some time. I've saved you from a horrible death and there's my arrow to prove it," he said, pointing to the arrow in the Rakshasa's neck.

"You didn't save me. My arrow struck him first," Arjuna challenged.

"I don't think so," laughed the hunter lightly as he spoke.

Arjuna was annoyed. "Do you think I need your help?"

The hunter's mood turned grave. "You're a proud fellow, aren't you?"

"Behind my pride is my prowess."

"You need to be taken down a notch or two. Stand and fight, or face your doom."

The hunter and Arjuna began firing arrows at one another. The hunter laughed all the while as he leapt behind one tree and then another, dodging Arjuna's arrows. The forest resounded with his laughter. He then appeared in full view, as Arjuna continued the barrage of arrows from his mighty Gandiva bow. The hunter merely swatted the arrows away as if they were insignificant flies.

Arjuna reached in his quiver for another arrow. Nothing. His hand searched desperately. The quiver was empty. This was impossible! Arjuna began to perspire. *Who is this mysterious opponent? How could this be happening?* He had journeyed all this way to seek blessings from the gods and not to arouse anyone's anger.

But at this moment Arjuna would not be deterred from the combat. Using the Gandiva bow as a club, he rushed at the hunter. With a swift gesture, the hunter knocked the bow out of Arjuna's hands. Arjuna drew his sword and struck the hunter, but the sword disintegrated into dust. With one blow, the hunter brought Arjuna to his knees. Arjuna rebounded, but found himself locked in the hunter's arms. Arjuna felt faint in the hunter's ever tightening grip.

As if in a dream, he heard the words of Vyasa, "Just try to please Lord Shiva." Arjuna began to utter the mantra. In his mind's eye, in profound reverence, he placed a garland of lotus flowers upon Shiva. Arjuna bowed again and again as the Three-Eyed One danced around him accompanied by his consort, the goddess Parvati. Apsaras and other heavenly nymphs joined in, dancing, singing, and laughing well into the night. The combined momentum and sound made Arjuna's head spin. It was almost too much to bear, even for the strong-willed Arjuna. He felt himself carried away in the delight of a thousand dancers and singers. And in the middle, Shiva joyfully danced like a child, whirling madly around and around.

Arjuna summoned every ounce of his being, and he found himself back in the grip of his opponent. There, he saw the garland of lotuses around his neck. *That's strange,* Arjuna thought as the hunter's laughter echoed throughout the forest. Before Arjuna's eyes the hunter turned into the Three-Eyed One. The hunter's overpowering grip turned into a warm and friendly embrace.

"Shiva! Shiva!" Arjuna called out and wanted only to fall to the ground in full prostration. But the hunter would not let him go. *How could I not have recognized that all along the hunter was Shiva?* It seemed the broadening smile on Shiva's face was simply a reflection of his own.

"Arjuna, this combat with you has been most enjoyable. You have pleased me very much. How can I repay you?"

Arjuna was dumbfounded.

"You've come here to seek a favor of me, haven't you?" Shiva inquired.

"Yes," Arjuna admitted. "My brothers and I are in need of your divine weapons."

"My most powerful is the Pasupata. You can use it if you like." Shiva offered it unhesitatingly. "This weapon can be unleashed from your bow. If that is not available, you may unleash it through the vibration of your voice or by the gaze of your eyes. If nothing else, it can be guided by thought alone. This weapon must only be released against a deadly enemy. If you use it against an unworthy foe or at an improper place, the Pasupata will destroy you, along with your entire race."

As he waved to Arjuna, Shiva ascended into the sky. Shiva's waving had an extraordinary effect. It opened Arjuna's eyes to another dimension. Shiva's departure had opened a portal in the sky. One by one, upon beams of light, Celestial lords descended: first came Varuna, lord of waters and leader of all aquatics, accompanied by a host of Nagas; and Kuvera, of golden hue, the lord of wealth, and with him a battalion of Yaksa warriors; and Yama, the lord of death, with the power to vanquish all creatures and planets; and Indra, bringer of rains and wielder of the thunderbolt. As if one, they spoke.

"O Arjuna, your eyes have been freed that you may perceive us directly. We bring to you our most cherished weapons and the ability to release them and recall them at will. With them, you will consume the ranks of your foes. You and your brothers have descended as mortals to assist the Lord of lords in His mission, and thus, we assist you by offering you our weapons. In this way, we humbly serve the Supreme Lord by serving His servants."

* * * * *

After the Celestial lords departed, Arjuna heard the sound of rolling thunder. It grew louder. The clouds broke open and light flooded the sky as a wondrous chariot appeared, drawn by a thousand shining horses and moving like the wind. Indra had sent the chariot to bring Arjuna to the celestial kingdom. The chariot came before Arjuna and hovered slightly above the ground, allowing him to step aboard, and then rose majestically into the sky. There he beheld the vast expanse of the Himalayas stretching as far as the eye could see in all directions. He shivered at the sight. Arjuna brought the palms of his hands together and offered his respects to those imposing mountains. While traversing them, he felt like a child playing on the lap of his father. As the chariot ascended, Arjuna heard the clear voices of sages chanting Vedic hymns, echoing from the canyons below.

Countless Celestials, eager to behold Arjuna, lined the route as the chariot coursed through the Milky Way. As the chariot approached Indra's capital, the residents applauded the Pandava prince. Colorful banners streamed down from an armada of sky ships floating above the city. Music resounded in all directions. Fragrant gardens, lakes, terraces, and emerald columns dotted the panorama below. The chariot descended into the plaza of Indra's majestic palace where he was seated on a magnificent emerald throne. Arjuna descended from the chariot and bowed before him. Indra gestured for his son to come sit with him, to share the same throne. Out of affection Indra smelled his son's head. They enjoyed each other's company as attractive, slim-waist Apsaras danced for their pleasure.

Urvasi danced at the head of a thousand maidens. Arjuna watched her every movement and gesture and, in turn, she watched him. She was thrilled by his attention. She observed his confident and relaxed manner amid this splendid assembly of Celestials. She would make sure to keep the other women away from him. She wanted him all to herself. That evening she went to his chambers, dressed to delight the senses, with her hair in braids and bedecked with wild flowers.

When she came before Arjuna, he turned his eyes down and spoke mildly. "O mother, how can I serve you?"

"I am here to serve you," she replied. Her eyes sparkled. "To serve any little whim you have, for I have been pierced by Love's arrows."

"It is sung on Earth that ages ago one of the earliest Kuru kings fell in love with you."

She was thrilled Arjuna had heard of her. "Yes, and I had fallen in love with him."

"Thus, I must say, you are like a mother of my dynasty."

"Don't be silly," she laughed, wanting to give him a kiss.

He held her back. "Why do you find my words so amusing?"

Urvasi's smile fell away. "No one has ever refused my advances. How could you be so cruel?"

"I only meant to honor you."

"You should honor me by paying attention to me, not by keeping me on a pedestal. Thus, I curse you to lose your manliness and live as a eunuch for a whole year. You won't even be able to touch your famous Gandiva bow."

With her ego bruised, she hurriedly left his chambers.

* * * * *

At that time, the sage Lomasa also visited Indra's court, and the lord with a thousand eyes took him aside and bade him to visit the Pandavas in the forest. Indra told him, "Console them, and reassure them of Arjuna's well-being and eventual return. While Arjuna spends time with me in the heavens, take the Pandavas on tour to the holy places. This journey will free them from any sins they have accrued and will wash away all their misgivings and anxieties."

* * * * *

One day the sage Lomasa came into the Pandavas' camp. After hearty greetings he told them he had seen their brother in the court of King Indra. Lomasa, as Indra had suggested, came to take the Pandavas on a tour of the tirthas, the holy places.

Lomasa told the Pandavas: "At the tirthas, one can easily draw close to the everlasting, transcendent reality. As we visit the tirthas, you must shed all pride. Be content with what may come. Eat and sleep in moderation. Look upon all beings equally, and treat all as you would want to be treated. Only then will the mysteries of the tirthas be open to you. Visiting the tirthas can be done by anyone, rich or poor, and it exceeds even the benefits of opulent rituals and ceremonies that are performed at great expense. At the holy places one also has the opportunity to meet the pure souls who reside there. While at a tirtha one may fast, perform service to the brahmins, offer gifts, and chant the sacred hymns in praise of the Supreme Lord. By journeying to the tirthas, you pray with your feet. At the sacred place, by bringing your hands together and bowing down, you pray with your body. Pray also with your words and thoughts and wealth. Pray with your very soul."

Guided by Lomasa, they first went to Naimisa Forest, which is such a wondrous place that even if one only thinks of going there, half of one's sins are mitigated. At Naimisa the Pandavas gave cows and wealth as gifts to the local residents and bathed in the sacred waters. The small group traveled south to Prayaga and on to Hemakuta where the hills resounded with the Vedic hymns sung by invisible Celestials, which delighted the hearts of all. There, everyone observed silence since any other sound would disturb the rocks and boulders, causing them to shake and roll.

    The Pandavas turned east, journeying to the Kausiki River and made their way down the river to where it met the Ganges and, after a time, they came to where the Ganges spilled into the ocean. There they plunged from cliffs into the mighty waters of the ocean. Afterwards, they journeyed south, down along the coastline to the kingdom of Kalinga, and to the Mahendra Mountains to receive the blessings of the many rishis who dwelled there. They came to the sacred Godavari River, whose waters could wash away all misgivings. The Pandavas traveled down the coast, eventually reaching the western coast where they traveled north up to Prabhas where they fasted for twelve days drinking only water. Krishna and Balarama came from Dwaraka to greet them. The Pandavas told them stories of their travels and the people they had met. After a time, they continued their pilgrimage to the Payosini River whose rushing waters sounded like music. They continued on to the Narmada River where they bathed. It was said that those who bathed in its soothing waters would bring prosperity to a hundred generations in their family.

    The party turned north in earnest towards the Himalayas. In this way, they circled the very heart of Bharata-varsa. On their pilgrimage, the Pandavas offered both menial service and charity to thousands of brahmins. Many of the holy places had been pilgrimage sites since antiquity. Wherever they stopped on their grand tour, Lomasa, skilled in the art of narrating histories, would tell many stories of the events that made those places sacred. Four years had passed as the Pandavas finally crossed into the Himalayas. As they came into view of one mountain, Lomasa fell to the ground to offer his respects. He told the group a story about that mountain.

"In ancient times, mountains had wings and could fly about. But they were clumsy and when they landed, they often crushed people and their homes. The people lived in fear of the mountains, and so the rishis appealed to Indra. Indra immediately took action. He lined up the mountains wherever he found them and cut off their wings with his thunderbolt weapon. But Mainaka, the son of Himalaya, wanted to keep his wings. As Indra menacingly raised his weapon, Vayu, the wind-god, came to the aid of his mountain friend and swept him up. Mainaka spread out his wings and, carried by Vayu, he glided south over the ocean. There, he came to rest on the ocean floor. He remained in hiding from the wrath of Indra for millennia.

"Then one day, Hanuman the monkey prince flew overhead, crossing the ocean on his way to Lanka in service to Lord Rama. Mainaka heard Hanuman was the son of Vayu. There's a saying that if you can't please the father then please his child, and the father will undoubtedly be pleased. And so, wanting to please his old friend Vayu, Mainaka jumped up from the ocean bottom and offered Hanuman a place to rest during his long flight. It was a big risk for Mainaka as Indra could have seen him and, in fact, did. The mountain trembled as the god of a thousand eyes approached. But Indra looked kindly upon Mainaka and assured him, 'You need no longer be afraid of me. Your selfless act to aid Hanuman has won me over. By serving Hanuman you have served Rama. My dear Mainaka, you can go where you please.' And after a long absence, Mainaka returned here to his place among the Himalayas."

The Pandavas all marveled at Lomasa's account. They bowed to the mountain and continued to Badarik. There, Lomasa pointed to another mountain.

"At that place, since time immemorial, the sages Nara and Narayana have engaged in penance for the benefit of all beings. Indra came there once, foolishly thinking they were striving to become powerful enough to usurp his position in the heavens. He wanted to *appease them with gifts, but they ignored him and he flared up with anger. He sent leopards, lions and elephants to threaten them. He sent storms, earth tremors and wild fires. But Nara and Narayan remained undisturbed in their meditations. When nothing else worked, Indra turned the region briefly into a paradise and sent a hundred Celestial women to allure them and captivate their minds. Narayana, in turn, created a hundred women even more beautiful who maddened Indra with lust. The most beautiful was Urvasi who emerged from Narayana's thigh. Nara and Narayana cannot be defeated in any way. They are none other than your Krishna and Arjuna."*

The group continued into the Gandamadana Mountains which led to the regions where the Celestials would often descend to sport on Earth. Arjuna had followed this very path in pursuit of the celestial weapons.

The way was steep and treacherous. All around them the skies darkened. Fierce winds were suddenly upon them and enveloped them in a dust storm. They lost sight of one another. The winds howled so fiercely that the Pandavas were nearly swept off the mountainside. The group held on tightly to boulders and scraggly trees as the winds ripped at their faces and took their breath away. Angry winds lashed at them from one direction and then another. But soon the winds ceased as suddenly as they had come.

The Pandavas felt relief only momentarily. Pounding rains came fast upon them as thunder flashed against distant clouds. The group scurried higher, frustrated and in tears and not knowing where to turn. Out of nowhere, or perhaps as if the Celestials had placed it right in their path, they came upon a cave. There they took shelter from the storm, which continued to rage throughout the night.

Seeing how Draupadi trembled from the cold, Yudhisthira cursed himself. She experienced nothing but hardship since she had become their wife. His brothers faithfully attended to her. Yudhisthira thought of Arjuna who always seemed to draw good fortune to himself. How was he faring in Indra's court surrounded by luxury? Yudhisthira longed to see him again. Although safe, the Pandavas found no comfort among the jagged rocks in the cave. That night they huddled together as best they could.

Morning arrived with clear skies and a glorious sun rising in the east. The group was thankful, but exhausted. They languished on the mountainside not knowing what to do next. Bhima saw that Draupadi had been pushed to the breaking point. They all had. Their bodies ached and they could hardly go on. Bhima sat down, facing the forest home of his son Ghatotkaca, and summoned him in silence. Ghatotkaca, with a band of Rakshasas, leaping great distances, arrived within moments to assist them.

Ghatotkaca carried Draupadi, and Rakshasas carried the Pandavas upon their shoulders, while others removed boulders to create a path. Lomasa preferred to go on unassisted, and moved gracefully forward by dint of his mystic powers. That day, the party easily crossed the mountain range and came to a hidden valley, the playground of the Celestials, with its refreshing lakes and waterfalls. Magnificent flowers bloomed year round and ever-ripe fruit-bearing trees adorned the landscape. A thousand varieties of healing plants and herbs proliferated throughout the valley, and the air was filled with evocative aromas. Here, the Pandavas remained. It was certainly a reprieve from the long and arduous journey they had undertaken. They relaxed and sported in this heavenly resort. But their thoughts and their talks always turned to Arjuna. They longed to see him again and anxiously awaited his return from the heavens.

The Himalayas stood serene and immovable. The world below them basked in glory. "It won't be like this much longer," Lomasa warned them. "It's coming soon, the Kali-yuga. The Celestials will disappear from our vision. In the Kali-yuga, the splendor of the earth will shrivel up. Virtue will be abandoned. Sickness will ravage the land. Deformities will be commonplace. The earth will shake from calamities. No family will be spared.

"The so-called kshatriyas will not protect the citizens, but rather exploit them for their own gain. Others will assume similar habits. Hypocrisy will rule the day. Uncultured men will put on fancy attire and procure wealth by nefarious means. Indeed, decisions will be based solely on how much wealth can be made, and wealth alone will determine a favorable outcome in a court of law. People will be overwhelmed by anxieties and will be forced to work hard like asses simply to maintain themselves. Any sane person will want to flee to the mountains. The people of the Kali-yuga will forget that one earns happiness by making others happy. It is especially our duty to please and protect the cows, the children, the women, the elderly and the brahmins."

One morning, after many days, the Pandavas beheld Indra's chariot descending gracefully from the sky, radiating the splendor of a dozen suns at sunrise and emanating a melodious symphony. Drawn by multicolored steeds and accompanied by a hundred celestial chariots, Indra's chariot carried, to their unbounded joy, their beloved Arjuna. He had stayed with Indra for almost five earthly years, which was only a matter of days in Indra's realm. During that time, Indra gave Arjuna his personal weapons, and trained him how to deploy and control them. Indra also had Arjuna learn the celestial arts of music and dance from the Gandharvas. Indra knew of Urvasi's curse and he assured Arjuna that he would not only require his weapons, but these arts as well.

* * * * *

The Pandavas left the mountains and made their camp once again in the forests of the lowlands. Word of where the Pandavas were staying soon reached Duryodhan's ears. He decided to taunt them by having a grand picnic nearby. He called for colorful tents to be brought along, and the finest of foods to be cooked, and the best musicians to perform, and he invited hundreds of his friends to frolic to their hearts' content. Duryodhan planned that the aroma of the foods would scatter in the breeze, and the music would fill the air, and the laughter of his friends would resound throughout the forest. The Pandavas, living in austerity, with no comfortable place to sleep and eating only the simplest of meals made from roots, herbs and berries, would surely be agitated to the core of their beings. Duryodhan would relish the moment. He would delight upon seeing the faces of the Pandavas, and of the beautiful Draupadi, pained and dismayed. *Bhima will be enraged,* Duryodhan thought, *and there won't be a thing he can do about it. Let him try.* Duryodhan laughed out loud as he imagined Bhima's reaction.

Duryodhan, however, learned that Gandharvas were already vacationing in the pristine forest where he had planned to set up camp. Refreshing lakes dotted the countryside and the aroma of wild flowers filled the air along with the sweet cooing from flocks of multi-colored birds. Majestic waterfalls tumbled out of the distant mountains. This would certainly be a desirable destination even for the Celestials. As he approached, Duryodhan sent a messenger with an escort of warriors to the Gandharva encampment. They were cordially greeted by their chieftain as a host of his warriors looked on.

"Please hear me. I have a message from the powerful King Duryodhan, the ruler of this land. He is on his way here with his entourage which includes many nobles and thousands of warriors, and wants this area vacated as quickly as possible."

"We were only planning to spend a few days here," said the chieftain.

"The king wants you to leave immediately. He's on his way here now."

The Gandharvas looked at one another in amusement. "Has your king taken leave of his senses?" the chieftain asked.

The messenger ignored the question. "He has made elaborate plans for this excursion."

"This is no way for him to treat visitors to his country. We are not his servants, but rather, we are denizens of heaven. We have come here to sport with our consorts in these lakes."

"Nevertheless, he wants you out of here," the messenger insisted.

"Having brought his message, you are as much of a fool as your king," the chieftain declared. "Now you better move along, unless you want us to send you to the abode of Death."

* * * * *

When Duryodhan learned of the Gandharvas' defiance, he immediately commanded his soldiers to attack. But they were no match for the Celestials on their flying horses. These sky warriors roamed with ease on the earth and in the sky. They closed ranks and unleashed a deluge of arrows and spears. It seemed the Kauravas held an advantage since they fought with their backs toward the sun. But the sky warriors drew their swords high, and the brilliance of the sun's reflection blinded the Kauravas who panicked and fled.

But Karna was not one to run from a fight. His chariot stealthily wove its way forward as his arrows felled dozens of the enemy. The Gandharvas seemed momentarily stunned by his prowess. Duryodhan and his brothers, Dushasana and Chitra, regrouped their forces and made a second charge with Karna at the fore. Duryodhan hoped their surge could turn the tide. But these sky warriors were in no mood for a prolonged fight. They hurled hundreds of clubs and cleavers at Karna's chariot. Seeing this devastating array of weapons pouring down upon him, Karna, with sword in hand, quickly leaped from the chariot before it was smashed into a thousand pieces. Wounded and being no fool, he made a hasty retreat. The Kauravas fled the battle. All except for Duryodhan. He persevered alone, and soon he found himself surrounded by enemy warriors. Rather than die fighting, he surrendered to them. Many nobles and their women had also been captured.

Nearby, the Pandavas heard the commotion and rushed into the fray to help their cousins. The Pandavas first appealed to the Gandharvas. It was improper for the Celestials to engage in battle with human beings. They should release their captives.

The chieftain and his sky warriors, still incensed by the battle, would not listen to reason. When they threatened the Pandavas, Arjuna sent forth a wave of arrows that mercilessly fell upon their ranks. Arrows from Bhima, Nakula and Sahadev quickly followed. There were attacks and counter-attacks, but ultimately the Gandharvas were no match for the Pandavas. Finally, they brought Duryodhan, bound in strong ropes, before the Pandavas. Duryodhan looked pitiful.

The Gandharva chieftain was perplexed. "Why do you Pandavas want to save this wretch? He came here to humiliate you. To mock you. To flaunt his wealth and power. Are you sure you want us to turn him loose?"

Yudhisthira spoke. "It was foolhardy of Duryodhan and his warriors to pick a fight with you. But please release him and all of the captives as a favor to me. Thus, my family's honor will be saved and I will be greatly indebted to you. Ask anything of me. I am always at your beck and call."

"Yudhisthira, you are truly noble. May your deeds be forever sung on the earth and in the heavens." The Gandharvas and their chieftain affectionately embraced Yudhisthira and his brothers and departed for their celestial abode.

The freed captives profusely thanked the Pandavas for saving their lives. They praised the Pandavas and saluted them, and told them they were ready to die for them. Upon returning to Hastinapura, they continued to sing the Pandavas' glories.

All except for Duryodhan. Everything had gone horribly wrong. He felt a tremendous ache in his brain.

* * * * *

Duryodhan was morose for weeks after. Life was bitter and had lost its meaning for him. His existence was as hollow as a reed. He had been so humiliated that he obsessed over it for weeks. *The Pandavas fought the Gandharvas to save me. Yudhisthira bargained with them for my release. Everyone loves the Pandavas. Am I supposed to feel indebted to them?* He felt plagued. His feeling of emptiness wouldn't go away. He saw no reason to go on. He wanted to kill himself. No one could talk him out of it. Karna, Sakuni, Dushasana. They all tried. They had good arguments, but Duryodhan would not be swayed. He went to a spot in the forest, away from everything and everyone, and there he sat to fast until death.

It was the Daityas and Danavas who finally changed his mind. They had too much at stake. Ages ago these two demoniac races had conspired to rule the Earth. At that time the Celestials had intervened, and these Asuras were repelled back to the nether regions, the lower planetary systems, from whence they came. Now they were ready to try again, and Duryodhan was indispensible to their plan. Duryodhan: arrogant, sullen, impetuous, greedy, addicted to sensual pleasures, and always determined to have his own way. All the qualities they looked for in a leader.

From their realm, the Asuras cast a spell and summoned him. Duryodhan heard the sound of fire crackling. He looked up to find himself in a lifeless landscape. Only smoldering skeletons of trees and jagged rocks. The sun could not penetrate the haze. Birds shrieked. He found himself with a group of Asuras encircled by a wide ring of fire. Duryodhan did not recognize this place. The group hailed him as an emperor and hero. Three of them stepped forward, getting right to the point.

"Greetings, O King."

"Rejoice, for you have many great heroes at your command."

"Do not kill yourself. It will not serve you."

"Such an act will only gladden your enemies."

"Your purpose was never to bring them happiness."

"And no dead man ever defeated his foes."

"So stop your grieving and take what is rightfully yours."

"There's no fault in that."

"We have been preparing for your victory."

"Know that many Asuras have taken birth in royal families."

"You have Sakuni who was born to destroy righteousness."

"You have your brother Dushasana, like a dagger in the dark."

"And your friend Ashwattama with a gem on his head that makes him immune to death."

"We have provided you with many stalwart warriors."

"Including the Samsaptakas, who were created simply to destroy their enemies."

"A holy man will come to help you."

"You will rule the Earth."

"What more can you ask for?"

"Take up this task."

"Even if it brings ruination, you will be glorious."

"The coming Kali-yuga will be our time to rule."

"The Earth will drown in chaos."

"Confusion and ignorance will reign supreme."

"Men will be blinded by lust and anger."

"They will shed all compassion."

"And strike dead anyone who stands in their way."

"Be it fathers, mothers, brothers, friends, or elders."

Suddenly, an Asura child jumped on Duryodhan's back. "Even children will not be spared," the boy shrieked in joy. Duryodhan spun around, trying to shake the boy off. The boy held tightly onto his neck, almost choking him. Duryodhan grabbed the boy and threw him to the ground. The boy rebounded and ran off giggling.

The three continued.

"O Duryodhan, the time is ripe."

"O hero, fix your mind."
"Achieve your victory."
"So be it."

The words reverberated throughout Duryodhan's body. *'Achieve your victory. So be it.'* And when he opened his eyes, the Asuras were gone, and he was sitting in the forest, in the very spot he had chosen to fast until death. His neck was sore. He wondered what had happened. *Was it a dream?* It seemed so real. The sounds. The smells. The child on his back. He couldn't quite remember everything, but he remembered their words, *'You will rule the Earth.'* Duryodhan's body shivered with anticipation. He raised his clenched fists in defiance of the heavens. "Yes! I will rule the Earth!" he proclaimed. "It is my destiny!"

* * * * *

One day, there was a great tumult in Hastinapura. Durvasa Muni, leading a procession of his ten thousand disciples, made a grand entrance into the city. People spilled out onto the streets to greet the acclaimed holy man. The people knew if they pleased Durvasa, he would undoubtedly bless them. They also knew if they displeased him in any way, he could condemn the city to ruination with his mystic powers.

Duryodhan, however, viewed the scene indifferently from the balcony of his palace. But as he continued to observe the excitement below, an idea sprung to mind. *Holy man. Of course.* Duryodhan was always ready to exploit any situation for his own ends. *Durvasa Muni at my disposal! Could it happen?* His mind reeled. For the first time in a long time Duryodhan came alive.

He rallied his brothers and threw out commands to the palace servants. He told them that Durvasa must be pleased in all respects. Duryodhan and his priests welcomed the ascetic along with his ten thousand disciples and worshiped them in great pomp. Duryodhan personally attended to Durvasa's every need and saw to it that his every request was immediately and faithfully fulfilled.

Durvasa's habits were quite peculiar. Sometimes the Muni would announce, "I'm hungry. Bring me a meal." But when the meal was placed before him, he would seem uninterested and only pick at his food. Sometimes he would say, "I'm going for my bath. Have my meal ready when I return." But when he got back he'd say that the hour was late and retired without eating a morsel of food. Yet at other times, he would wake up in the middle of the night and demand that food be brought to him.

Durvasa was impressed that Duryodhan attended to him without ever getting angry or annoyed. *Duryodhan,* he thought, *has played his hand quite well.* After a week, Durvasa offered the king a benediction. "You have pleased me very much. Ask from me whatever you want. I'll be happy to grant your wish."

In his heart of hearts Duryodhan was overjoyed. The scheme had worked beautifully. Now he spoke the exact words he and Karna had formulated together. "My cousins, the Pandavas, are residing in the forest. I'm sure they would consider it a great honor to host you and your ten thousand disciples. But one thing. Please arrive at their hermitage late in the afternoon while they are resting after having finished their meal."

Durvasa well understood Duryodhan's intent. The next morning, Duryodhan and his family members bid the Muni and his disciples farewell. Afterwards Karna threw his arms around Duryodhan and gave him an elated hug, lifting him off the ground. "You've done it! You've pulled it off!" Karna was wildly exuberant. "You've skillfully avoided Durvasa's wrath, and you have sent that wrath hurling in the direction of the Pandavas."

* * * * *

Durvasa Muni showed up precisely as planned. At first, the noble-hearted Yudhisthira was overjoyed to welcome the Muni and his followers. He wasn't aware that Draupadi had washed the magical bowl after everyone finished eating. When he found out, his heart sank. Not because he was in jeopardy of being cursed by a hungry and slighted Durvasa, but because he felt badly that he could not properly accommodate his guests. The Pandavas quickly gathered in their hermitage to consider their options.

"We have to make something," Yudhisthira insisted.

"What! A meal for ten thousand?" Bhima was incredulous.

"Does Durvasa actually expect us to feed them all?" Sahadev asked.

"Imagine what he'll do if he doesn't get his meal," Nakula wondered out loud.

"I'll bet anything Duryodhan is behind this," Arjuna speculated.

With that revelation, they all excitedly started talking at the same time.

"Listen to me," Draupadi commanded with a loud whisper, not wanting to alarm their guests. "Just stall them. I'll think of something,"

With that as the plan, Yudhisthira and his brothers calmed themselves and approached Durvasa with folded hands and bowed heads. "O exalted sage, famous throughout the world for having subdued your passions," Yudhisthira began, "welcome to our humble abode. You must certainly be tired from your long journey. Please go down to the river. Refresh yourselves and perform your evening prayers. Upon your return we will provide some repast for you and your disciples."

In the meantime, Draupadi knew there was simply nothing to be done. The situation was overwhelming. And in her helplessness she meditated on Krishna. "O Lord of the Universe, bestow your kindness upon us. You are the unshakable refuge of the helpless. You are the soother of miseries. The protector to those who seek your protection and the guide for those who seek your guidance."

In the distant city of Dwaraka, Krishna turned from his friends. He heard Draupadi's prayer and gave it his immediate attention.

Instantly, Krishna appeared before her and the Pandavas. "So, how can I help you?"

Draupadi explained the dilemma, but Krishna only asked to see the sun-god's copper bowl, saying, "As a matter of fact, I'm a little hungry myself."

"But Krishna, the bowl won't provide any more food."

"Bring it here and we'll see."

Draupadi brought the bowl and Krishna examined it inside and out. He found a tiny morsel of rice stubbornly clinging to the outer rim. With the tip of his finger Krishna scooped up the grain of rice, brought it to his lips, and licked it up. He savored the taste for a long time. "That was soooo good," Krishna proclaimed. Then he called for Bhima. "Go tell your guests their meal is ready."

At that very moment, Durvasa Muni and his disciples bathing in the river felt strangely satisfied, as if they had just finished a feast. From where this satisfaction came, they could not fathom. They were so satiated they couldn't bring themselves to take a bite of food. When Bhima called them to dine, the ascetics turned to their mentor for their cue.

"We had better move on," Durvasa announced. "I have my suspicions about men who are so devoted to Krishna."

He gave a curious glance toward the Pandavas' hermitage. With that, he and his disciples, their stomachs full, waddled out of the river like ducks. They gathered their things and disappeared into the fading day.

And with Draupadi's permission, Krishna returned to Dwaraka.

*****

It was the last month of their exile. One day, a deer wandered innocently into the Pandavas' encampment. He lifted up in his antlers two special sticks used by one of the brahmins in their retinue to ignite a sacrificial flame each day. Instantly, the deer bounded off. With a disturbed mind, the brahmin ran to the Pandavas. He frantically told them what happened and the brothers grabbed their weapons and took off after the deer. For hours they pursued it, but the creature proved to be elusive, always appearing in the distance, challenging them to capture it. Unsuspectingly, the Pandavas wandered ever deeper into the jungle.

Soon the midday sun beat relentlessly down upon the brothers. After hours of traveling, their limbs grew heavy. Their throats were parched and dry. Exhausted, they sat down in the shade of a large banyan tree. Yudhisthira asked Nakula to climb to the top to see what he could see. Nakula adroitly scaled the tree and called down, "I see in the distance tall trees that usually grow near water."

"Take your quiver to fetch us water and hurry back."

Nakula went some distance when he came upon a lake of crystal waters. He was overwhelmed with thirst. He had to drink. He brought his cupped hands, brimming with water, to his lips. Nakula, however, did not know that in the lake there lived a Yaksa, an unearthly, warrior-like spirit with feathers laced in his long hair and a variety of weapons hanging from his belt. The Yaksa had, in fact, been waiting for the Pandavas. Just as Nakula was about to drink, the spirit in the lake called out, "Stop! This is my lake. Before you drink you must answer my questions."

The Pandava did not heed the voice. He considered it a trite nuisance. The spirit, however, cast a spell upon the water and when Nakula drank, he fell dead.

Soon, Yudhisthira sent Sahadev. This Pandava came to the lake and saw the lifeless body of his brother. He saw the crystal waters of the lake. He was overwhelmed with thirst. He was about to drink, when the spirit called out. "Stop! This is my lake. Before you drink you must answer my questions."

Again, the Pandava did not heed the voice. Again, the spirit cast a spell, and again the Pandava drank and died.

One after another, Arjuna and Bhima approached the lake. They responded in the same way and met with the same fate. Finally Yudhisthira himself approached. He found the four lifeless bodies of his brothers. He saw the crystal waters of the lake. He was overwhelmed with thirst. He was about to drink when he heard the Yaksa's command. "Stop! This is my lake. Before you drink you must answer my questions."

The others had been overcome by the powerful urge to drink. But Yudhisthira stood quietly. He did not drink. "Ask your questions and I will answer."

"Tell me, what is quicker than the wind?"

"The mind."

"And tell me, what is more numerous than the blades of grass in the fields?"

"The thoughts that spring from the mind."

"What is it that, when lost, causes no regret?"

"Anger."

"Who appears to be alive but is among the walking dead?"

"A miser."

"And what is heavier than the mountains?"

"The love of one's mother. The words of one's father."

"What is the best gift bestowed upon man by the Celestials."

"A wife who is both a friend and companion."

"What is another friend?"

"A peaceful mind."

"And another companion?"

"Wisdom."

"And how is it to be acquired?"

"Serving the wise brings us wisdom."

"What must we renounce to make us wealthy?"

"Our desire for riches, fame and adoration."

"Tell me, what is wealth?"

"To look equally upon happiness or distress, upon a pebble or a piece of gold."

"Tell me, what is the greatest possession?"

"Knowledge of things to come."

"What is our foremost duty in life?"

"To seek the welfare of all beings."

"What is the best kind of happiness?"

"The happiness from within."

"And finally, tell me this - what is the most astonishing thing in this world?"

Yudhisthira considered the question. He became lost in its many answers. Finally he replied, "Death is lurking all around us. Our fathers and grandfathers grow old and die before our very eyes. Indeed, all life is rushing into the mouth of Death, and yet we behave as though we will live forever. What can be more astonishing than this?"

A calm silence surrounded the lake and the spirit rose from beneath the waters to reveal himself. Gradually, before Yudhisthira's eyes, the Yaksha changed into Dharmaraj, the lord of justice, his Celestial father. Yudhisthira and Dharmaraj embraced one another through tears of love.

"My son, I lured you here to meet you. To examine your wisdom. To test your forbearance. You have pleased me very much." Dharmaraj waved his hand over the bodies of the lifeless Pandavas. "Now, I bring your brothers back to life. Yudhisthira, my son, all blessings upon you, and upon those who hear this story of our meeting. They will never seek evil, nor will they seek the wealth of others. Their minds will be serene and clear - even at the moment of death."

The four Pandavas gradually stirred and stretched themselves as if awakening from a deep slumber. By then Dharmaraj had vanished into mist.

Chapter 9

Incognito

At the end of the twelfth year, leaving their retinue behind, the Pandavas slipped into the kingdom of Matsya where they hid their weapons in the hollow of a large, old tree. Embracing one another they said their good-byes and, one by one, they entered undetected into the capital city to begin their year of life incognito.

Yudhisthira posed as a brahmin by the name of Kanka. He made his way to the court and came before Matsya's ruler, the aged and virtuous King Virata. Yudhisthira took from his pouch a pair of dice made of gold and set with lapis lazuli. He cast them down on a table three times, and each time he rolled the same auspicious number. The king was amused.

"With my dice I entertain and delight both young and old," Yudhisthira said. "But playing at dice can often bring about disastrous results, just as it did with King Yudhisthira. But unlike him, I am an expert at the game. When I play, I always win. Know that I have never cheated anyone. Nor have I ever spoken an unkind word. I only speak what is palatable and uplifting."

Virata was captivated by this brahmin, tall and noble in stature and self-assured. "From where do you hail?"

"Years ago I resided in Indraprasta and was the friend and confidant of the famed Yudhisthira. O King, Providence has brought me to your city. Today I stand before you in search of a livelihood. Accept me in your service and I will bring you good counsel and good fortune."

Virata sensed this stranger's companionship would do him good. "So be it. The gods have seen fit to guide you to my kingdom. Now you will be my friend and confidant."

And through Yudhisthira's influence, the other Pandavas quietly gained positions in Virata's palace. Bhima, the lover of food, became the chief cook. Arjuna, the mighty bowman, evoked Urvasi's curse and became an effeminate, eunuch dance instructor. He taught the maidens of the palace, including Virata's own daughter, to dance and sing. The handsome Nakula, an excellent swordsman, had a special affinity with horses. He understood their every move and whinny. The horses at the royal stables became overjoyed to have him as their caretaker. Sahadev, soft-spoken and always giving in charity to the elderly, knew the nature of cows. Through his care, the royal herd became content and provided an abundance of milk. The stunning Draupadi bound her long, black hair behind her and dressed in simple cloth. She became the personal servant of Virata's wife, Queen Sudesna.

The queen inquired of Draupadi, "You have such fine skin and a fragrant body with full breasts and rounded hips and a glow that rivals the full moon itself. It seems you are more like a goddess than a maidservant."

"My lady, I am blessed to be the wife of Gandharva princes, but I am an independent woman by nature, and so I travel freely and maintain myself by my work. My husbands are very jealous and are like lions in battle. They don't want any man coming too close to me. So please take heed and warn any man who desires me, for if such a man makes one wrong move, he will be struck down on the spot."

* * * * *

One day Indra came before Karna in the guise of a brahmin. Indra knew well of Karna's vow of gift-giving, and this so-called brahmin made a strange request. "Kindly give me the earrings, armbands and armor from your body."

"My dear brahmin, I've had this armor since birth. It would be very difficult to remove it. However, I am prepared to give you land, cows or damsels. Whatever you like."

"I have no need for these. I want only your armor."

"But the armor serves to protect me. It renders me invincible. O brahmin, allow me to give you anything else. I offer you great riches. I will even win the Earth for you."

"You are famed for giving in charity for whatever is asked of you, but yet you hesitate. This is unbecoming of you."

Karna now revealed what he had suspected all along. "I know who you are - O Indra, King of the Celestials. And I say it is unbecoming of you to approach me like this, seeking gifts in the guise of a brahmin. What need do you have of anything I can bestow? You, with your unimaginable riches and powers, should bestow gifts upon me."

"Karna, you are wise," Indra said, enjoying Karna's praise.

"My vow of giving gifts to anyone who makes a request is well known. But if I give you what you want, I become vulnerable to defeat."

"I say you can maintain your glorious vow and still have protection."

"What do you mean?"

"Other than the thunderbolt weapon which is solely at my disposal, I'll give you any weapon you want."

Karna considered the proposal, confident that ultimately his own prowess would be sufficient to protect him. "Arjuna and I are equally matched. The problem is that the infallible Krishna is always shielding him like a doting mother. Surely, you must have a weapon which can tip the scales."

"Yes. The Vasavi. It cannot be foiled and is certain to destroy the one you target. But you can only release the weapon once, and only if you are in mortal danger. Otherwise it will fail you. The Vasavi is yours. Simply cut the armor from your body and give it to me, for I proclaim you will not be scarred."

The exchange was made. Each of them smiled, thinking he had made the better bargain.

* * * * *

For ten months everything went well for the Pandavas until Keechaka set his eyes upon Draupadi. Keechaka was the general of Virata's army and Sudesna's older brother. One day he made a rare visit to his sister's inner chambers, and there he beheld Draupadi. Afterwards, he could not stop thinking about her. He returned several times to get glimpses of her. Her form was a feast for his eyes. He had to have her. He casually questioned his sister about her maidservant. Sudesna knew exactly what was on his mind.

"Forget her. She's already married to some Gandharvas."

"So."

"I guess that's never stopped you before. But Gandharvas might be a little more troublesome than the ordinary husbands of the women you lavish your affections on."

"My dear sister, you underestimate me."

"My dear brother, I think this girl is out of your league."

"This servant girl... out of my league." Keechaka was infuriated by his sister's remark. He stormed off. But he couldn't keep away. Keechaka returned the next day at a time he knew Sudesna was out.

He found Draupadi alone and came up behind her and whispered in her ear. "Your beauty drives me mad. I desire to be with you."

Draupadi turned around and saw his large frame looming over her. She moved away quickly. She kept her eyes down as she humbly offered him advice. "I can't help you my dear sir. Your desire is like a thorn that torments your mind. It would be best if you learned how to control your senses."

Keechaka laughed out loud. "There's no need for me to control myself. I am practically like the king of this land. Old Virata depends upon me. Everyone in this kingdom depends upon my protection. It would serve you well to get to know me better."

"I know you have several wives who are quite shapely themselves. I suggest you find your satisfaction with them rather than give way to illicit activities."

Keechaka was delighted she was aware of him. "If you know about me, you should know I am very determined to get what I want. And I want you as my wife. I'll even forsake my other wives for you. I can give you a life of luxury. You'll have fineries and dozens of servants to attend you. On my word you will rule over the entire kingdom, and I myself will serve your every whim."

"The only thing I require from you is that you leave my presence."

He was taken aback, but he obeyed. He withdrew from her almost against his will. She had rebuked him with such authority, with the certainty and the grace of a noble. This made him want her all the more. He waited until his sister returned.

"My sister, you have to help me. I am burning up with desire." Sudesna was about to scold her older brother when he raised a finger to her lips. "I beg you. Please say you'll help me."

Sudesna felt obliged to her flesh and blood. Since they were children, he had always sought her help. She relished his dependency upon her. "Tomorrow I'll send her to your place on some errand. When she arrives, don't be your usual, brutish self. Don't try to force yourself upon her as you've done with other women. Speak sweet words to her. Serve her. Charm her."

* * * * *

The next day, Sudesna told Draupadi, "My brother has just received a new batch of wine. Go to his place and bring back a jug for me"

"Madam, I won't go there. Your brother will only try to have his way with me."

"He knows you're my servant and on an errand from me. He won't try anything."

"You have so many servants. Please send another."

"Don't be silly. My brother is harmless. Go quickly and fetch me the wine. I am eager to taste it."

Soon, Draupadi found herself hesitating at the door as a servant showed her into Keechaka's chambers.

From inside she heard Keechaka call, "Come in. Come in. Don't be shy. How may I serve you?"

She came before him. "My mistress has asked me to fetch wine for her," she said without looking up.

"Of course. Of course. " Keechaka was in high spirits. He called for a servant to bring a jug of wine from the storage rooms and turned his full attention to her. "It's a pleasure to see you again."

Draupadi did not offer a response, and he tried to make light of it. "Please don't look so uncomfortable. I'm not going to bite you." For a long moment he gazed upon her, upon the curves of her face and her breasts and her hips. "You know what would bring me the greatest pleasure?" he asked.

She remained silent looking down at the ground, hoping against hope he would not continue in this line of thought and would let her be off once the wine arrived.

"I'll tell you," he continued, "I'd like to see you in the finest silk dresses with precious jewels and gems hanging from your neck and ears, and I'd like to see your wrists adorned with gold and silver bracelets. I'd like to see you happy in all respects. Won't you let me do that for you?"

"My mistress is expecting her wine."

"Don't fret, I'll send a jug over with one of my servants. Make yourself comfortable. Try one of these pastries." He motioned to plates on a low table that were filled with delights. "I had my cooks prepare them especially for the occasion."

"I'd better go."

Keechaka was getting impatient. The smile on his face receded. He felt his anger rise. After all, he had made every effort to be cordial to her. "Who do you think you are? You are a menial servant. Do you think you can shun my kindness?"

When Draupadi did not answer and turned to leave, he bounded toward her and grabbed her wrist.

"Where do you think you're going?" He yanked her to him. "I didn't dismiss you."

"You're hurting me," she told him. "If you continue in this way, you'll spell out your own doom."

He laughed out loud, "You poor, misguided woman!"

She pushed him back and tried to run from the room.

Keechaka caught her. "Wench! You dare threaten me. You, a nothing! If you want, I can really hurt you."

He hit her in the face and knocked her down to the floor. As Draupadi tried to get up, he kicked her in the back. She groaned and shivered in pain. He was about to turn away when he decided to kick her again. If she would not willingly let him caress her, he would still have his way.

But Draupadi remained defiant. "You're like a child who wishes to catch hold of the moon," she told him.

Keechaka kneeled down beside her and whispered into her ear, his cheek against hers. "Listen to me good. We'll try this one more time. Tomorrow night. You decide the place. Prepare yourself to greet me properly. You'll talk to me sweetly. You'll glance at me tenderly. You'll show me your affections. Do you understand me?"

Draupadi nodded. After he left, she picked herself up. Her face throbbed. Her back ached. Every step was painful. With great effort she went to speak to King Virata about this injustice. Virata clearly favored his general and was indifferent to her plight. Yudhisthira, always by the king's side, clenched his fist. He struggled to suppress his anger. What could he say, lest their true identities be found out?

* * * * *

That night Draupadi stole into Bhima's room off the side of the kitchen.

"Bhima wake up. I need your help."

Bhima happily awoke to find himself in Draupadi's arms. He realized she was trembling and saw her face. His delight turned to rage. "Who has done this to you? What fool is eager to leave this world for the abode of Death?"

Then her tears came. "I hate living like this. This charade. I might as well be dead. I hate seeing my husbands, who are the lions of the Earth, living like menial servants. This is worse than living in the forest. There, at least, we had our dignity. Why has my fate now been placed in the hands of arrogant fools. I must have done something in my youth or in my previous life to warrant this. So much suffering has come my way. I just want to know a little happiness again. I want to know that life is fair and just."

"My love, I will make everything right. Tell me, who did this to you?"

Draupadi told Bhima everything that had transpired: of how Keechaka had tried to force himself upon her; how he struck her as she fled; and how afterwards, she had even appealed to Virata.

"Don't worry. I'll smash this wretch like an earthen pot," Bhima told her. "Send a message to Keechaka. Tell him he's been right all along and that you look forward to meeting him tomorrow night."

* * * * *

Keechaka received the message the next day and he was elated. He spent hours bathing and received a massage with precious oils and perfumes. He went through his wardrobe again and again to select his finest and most becoming garments. He constantly thought of this woman whose beauty put all other women to shame. She had finally come to her senses and offered herself to him. She wouldn't regret it. He danced and he drank. For one last time before he left his mansion, he looked in the mirror and reveled in what he saw.

At the appointed hour, in the dead of night, he arrived at the designated place – the hall where Arjuna gave lessons in dance and music. At night the hall was dark and vacant. There, at a couch in a corner alcove, Keechaka dimly made out the silhouette of a figure wrapped in a shawl, waiting. His heart pounded wildly. He came up from behind.

"Have you been waiting long?" he asked.

"All my life for this moment."

Keechaka ran his hand down the back of his love's spine. At the same time he felt a hand caress his thigh. "Your touch is electrifying," he practically moaned the words.

"Come closer," he heard his love say.

"Yes. Yes. I want to melt in your arms."

"You will." With that, Bhima threw off the shawl to reveal a wide grin on his face.

Keechaka was dumbfounded. "Aren't you the cook?"

"Yes, and I'm going to make mincemeat out of you."

Bhima fell on Keechaka with his fists, his chest, his head and teeth. Keechaka, being very powerful himself, grabbed Bhima and they tumbled onto the floor. Bhima battered Keechaka with the fury of a hurricane. Keechaka tried desperately to defend himself. He lunged for Bhima's neck and began to choke him. Bhima grabbed his hair and threw him down and struck him with his powerful fists, all the while laughing loudly. Bhima would not let Keechaka die easily. With his bare hands, he crushed each of his bodily limbs. Keechaka cried out in pain and begged for mercy. But Bhima gave none. Holding Keechaka's head with his mighty hands, Bhima crushed his skull. Bhima's fiery eyes were the last thing Keechaka saw. Bhima's laughter, the last thing he heard. Bhima rammed Keechaka's appendages into his torso. In the end, Bhima reduced him to a large, round, bloody lump of flesh.

Bhima called for Draupadi who was hiding nearby and, lighting a torch, showed her Keechaka's remains. Draupadi did not withdraw her gaze. She felt at peace. "This is good," she said. "Justice has been served."

* * * * *

That morning, palace guards came upon what was left of Keechaka. The gruesome sight churned their stomachs and nausea overwhelmed their senses. In an instant their breakfasts were all over the floor. Word of his death spread throughout the city. "No human could have done that," the citizens conjectured. "It must have been the handiwork of the servant woman's Gandharva husbands." Keechaka had some faithful followers, as all powerful men invariably do, but for the most part people were relieved by his demise.

* * * * *

Crows flew overhead. Bhuminjaya stood in the empty courtyard of the palace, dejected. His father, King Virata had taken the army to thwart an invasion from the north by their constant rivals the Trigartas. All able-bodied men were gone. Virata even invited Yudhisthira, Bhima, Nakula and Sahadev to join him. Although he didn't know their true identities, Virata suspected they were capable warriors. The Pandavas gladly mounted the chariots he provided, for they had surmised their year of living incognito had come to an end.

But the attack from the north was a diversion. The real threat came from the Kaurava army entering the kingdom of Matsya from another side. Duryodhan himself masterminded this plan after he heard that the formidable Keechaka was dead. Now, the Kauravas were stealing away Matsya's herd of sixty thousand cows, without a man to stand in their way. Bhuminjaya received news of this calamity from the cowherds who had escaped the Kauravas' net. He wanted desperately to challenge them, but he had no capable chariot driver.

Arjuna heard of his plight and came to Bhuminjaya. "I'll drive your chariot."

"You?" Bhuminjaya snickered. "The dancing instructor of girls?"

"If you want a song and a dance, I'll be happy to provide one for you later. Time is of the essence."

Bhuminjaya was hesitant. His father hadn't even taken this one with him. "Can you drive a chariot?"

"I do have other talents besides dancing." Arjuna threw on a coat of mail with ease. He called for Bhuminjaya's chariot and took the reins. "We don't have all day."

Bhuminjaya's face brightened. He wondered how this effeminate dancing instructor could be so bold. *Why not?* he thought. *There are stranger things in this world.* And he climbed onto the chariot and lifted his bow. "This will be my Gandiva, and just as the great Arjuna smites his enemies, I will smite those who dare usurp our property. "

The maidens came running out of the palace to see their dancing instructor in his new role. Uttara, Bhuminjaya's sister, teased her teacher. "Gentle sir, in your coat of mail you look just like the famed Arjuna." The other girls giggled excitedly, and even Arjuna had to smile.

* * * * *

Arjuna brought the chariot to a bluff overlooking the valley. Below, the cows, stretching as far as the eye could see, were being herded away. When Bhuminjaya saw the might of the Kaurava forces his face turned ashen. He saw Bhisma, Drona and Kripa, as imposing as deadly sharks in a vast and dangerous ocean. What was he thinking? How could he stand against them? His body trembled at the mere thought of a fight. He knew he wouldn't last a moment. Bhuminjaya moaned and cursed himself as hot tears streamed down his face.

Bhuminjaya sighed. "Let's go back."

Arjuna gave him a quizzical look. "Go back? I won't turn my back even on an army of Celestials and Rakshasas combined."

Arjuna turned the chariot down a wooded road until they came to a great tree. There he retrieved his Gandiva bow and two golden quivers of inexhaustible arrows and other magnificent weapons. Stunned by this arsenal, Bhuminjaya's mouth hung open. "Who are you?"

"I am Arjuna, the son of Pandu. So don't be afraid, for this chariot will become our citadel, and today I will vanquish your enemies." He tossed Bhuminjaya the reigns. "Here, you drive and I'll do the fighting."

As they headed toward the enemy, that master bowman who could fight single-handedly with thousands of warriors, plucked his Gandiva bowstring, and the sound of it reverberated throughout the sky, announcing him to all the world. And Bhuminjaya knew the day was all but won.

Chapter 10

The Envoy

The Pandavas revealed their identities. Virata was overjoyed. He placed himself and his kingdom at their beck and call. To augment their allegiance, a marriage was proposed between Arjuna's son, Abhimanyu and Virata's daughter, Uttara. In the Pandavas absence, Subhadra and her son Abhimanyu had resided in Dwaraka with her brother Krishna. Now, at age sixteen, the boy had grown into a noble and powerful youth. He, his mother, and many family members streamed into Matsya to unite with Draupadi and the Pandavas. Abhimanyu rushed into the palace and fell at his father's feet. Arjuna proudly raised him up and smelled his head. He was almost as tall as his father and just as handsome with his flowing hair and infectious smile. Arjuna's joy knew no bounds. When Abhimanyu and Uttara met, they instantly fell in love. A grand wedding celebration was held with much gift-giving, not only to the wedding couple but to the brahmins, nobles and commoners alike. After the wedding, the mood turned serious as the Pandavas, along with their allies and Krishna himself, met to devise a strategy to regain their kingdom.

"We'll send an envoy to the Kaurava court to find out their intentions," Yudhisthira suggested.

His words were met by groans and protests. Everyone knew Duryodhan's character and no one believed he would cooperate and actually return the Pandavas' share of the kingdom.

Drupada offered his assessment. "You can try to placate Duryodhan till the end of time, but it won't work. He'll never relent. He wants everything his own way. When you try to be cordial with him, he thinks you're weak and you've given in to him. Or he'll suspect it's some sort of ploy. In the end, he'll only try to take advantage of you. O King, at your Rajasuya, I vowed my unwavering allegiance to you. I am prepared to fight at your side that you may reclaim your land."

Virata rose from his seat. "The Pandavas have suffered enough. We must force Duryodhan to meet our demands."

Satyaki rose to make his point. "I agree and I say send warriors rather than envoys. The only way this is going to be resolved is with Duryodhan's death."

"Please," Yudhisthira persisted, "let us first beseech them before we jump to conclusions."

"Beseech them with arrows and spears," Satyaki retorted. "That's the only thing they respect."

"My friends, over the last thirteen years Duryodhan has strengthened his alliances, and their forces are far greater than yours," Krishna noted.

Satyaki was adamant. "So we'll summon our allies and increase our ranks."

Krishna offered a two-pronged approach. "I suggest you do both. Rally your forces and also try to reason with Duryodhan. Yudhisthira, send an envoy to Hastinapura to seek the return of your kingdom. There's no harm in asking." And Krishna added with a sigh, "I'd be surprised if he gave anything back."

"Yes," Yudhisthira agreed, "let us move forward on both courses. We are equally capable of war and peace. But we must give Duryodhan a chance to do the right thing. That would be best."

Drupada conferred. "Allow me to send one of my brahmin counselors to the Kuru capital. He is mild-mannered, well-versed in Dharma and can bring together opposing points of view. Hopefully he can appeal to Duryodhan."

Krishna added, "If he cannot gain Duryodhan's favor, I will personally go to Hastinapura myself."

* * * * *

Duryodhan employed a network of spies to keep close track of the Pandavas now that they were out of hiding. *How devious of them,* he thought when he found out the Pandavas were preparing for the worst by amassing warriors and making strategies. Even though Duryodhan's forces greatly outnumbered Yudhisthira's, he still felt uneasy. His spies told him that after the council at Matsya, Krishna returned to Dwaraka. Yudhisthira grew increasingly apprehensive and had urged Arjuna to leave for Dwaraka to seek Krishna's help in the emerging conflict. Duryodhan's head was in a spin. *This would be disastrous!* Krishna's army was made up of the finest fighters anywhere in the world. They were bold and skilled and could fight under the most grueling conditions. Whoever had those warriors would certainly be victorious.

"Get me my fastest horses" he shouted to his servants "I must leave for Dwaraka at once."

Duryodhan made good time. He arrived at Krishna's palace moments before Arjuna and he rushed into Krishna's chambers to find Krishna asleep on the couch. Duryodhan sat down in a chair by Krishna's head. Arjuna arrived, surprised to find Duryodhan waiting. Arjuna took a seat by Krishna's feet. They waited, and when Krishna awoke his glance fell first upon Arjuna. Krishna jumped up, "Arjuna, pray tell, what brings you here?"

Duryodhan cleared his throat to get Krishna's attention. "My dear Krishna," he spoke up "I happened to be waiting here long before Arjuna."

"And how can I help you?" Krishna asked Duryodhan.

"It seems that forces are gathering for the coming conflict, and I am here to ask for your help."

"I see. And you Arjuna. Why have you come?" Krishna inquired.

"I have also come to seek your help."

"This presents somewhat of a problem," Krishna pondered.

"There is no problem," Duryodhan retorted. "Obviously, since I was here first, I should get first preference."

"But I saw Arjuna first," Krishna explained.

"Krishna, you are known to be impartial," said Duryodhan. "Arjuna may be your good friend, and you may have seen him first, but I was here first and I insist you give me first consideration."

"Yes, yes," Krishna said, "somehow I must please you both. Therefore, one of you can have my most powerful military force and the other can have Me, alone and unarmed, for I will not actively take part in the fighting. Now, you must decide."

Duryodhan was elated. "Well Krishna, your terms are. . ."

"Duryodhan, please," Krishna interrupted. "Arjuna is just like your younger brother. You can understand that the youngest must be satisfied first."

Duryodhan's jaw dropped. All seemed lost. Beads of sweat appeared on his brow as he watched Krishna turn to Arjuna.

"So Arjuna, what is your choice?"

"I only want you and nothing else," Arjuna said without hesitation.

"Well Duryodhan," Krishna concluded, "that means you must take my army, headed by my renowned general Kritavarma."

Duryodhan's face lit up with joy. *Kritavarma and Krishna's army!* His victory was practically assured. He was beside himself. But he didn't want to appear too overjoyed. He feigned modesty. "I am unworthy. I don't deserve such a gift. But if you insist, then what can I do? I can only fall at your feet and thank you. I thank you a thousand times. May your glories be greater than ever. I thank you Krishna. I thank you from the bottom of my heart."

And as Duryodhan departed, Krishna could not help but smile.

* * * * *

Hastinapura was ablaze with word of Krishna's imminent arrival. Throngs of citizens lined the streets to welcome him, while more gathered on rooftops to get a better view. Everyone talked about how Krishna would make an appeal to Duryodhan on behalf of the Pandavas since negotiations with Drupada's brahmin had stalled. The brahmin had left without being able to touch Duryodhan's heart, and Hastinapura's citizens were amazed that Krishna would play the role of an envoy. Lavish tents had been set up along the road to the capital where Krishna and his entourage could stop to rest, but Krishna did not use those facilities. Elephants continually sprayed the way with scented water to freshen the air and prevent dust from rising on the well-traveled road.

That morning Dhritarastra and Gandhari entered Duryodhan's mansion with great fanfare.

"What brings you here?" Duryodhan asked, already knowing the answer.

"My son, come and embrace your father and mother," the blind king extended his arms. Duryodhan gave them each a quick embrace, and Dhritarastra continued. "You must know that Krishna is not far from the city. I hope you are ready to greet him. Speak sweet words to him. Give him an attentive ear. Don't be quarrelsome, but be agreeable to his wishes."

Duryodhan looked annoyed. "It seems the noble Vidura had a word with you about this."

Dhritarastra chuckled, "You seem to know everything."

"I have eyes and ears everywhere. You've taught me that, father."

"Listen to me. Krishna is magnanimous and only wants the best for all concerned."

Duryodhan became incensed by this talk. "Why do you hate me so?"

"Please, listen to your father," Gandhari pleaded.

Duryodhan turned away. "The Pandavas have their Krishna to speak up for them. They're practically inseparable. But I have no one to take my side. Not even my own mother and father."

"We love you," Gandhari stroked her son's hair, "and speak for your own welfare. Be satisfied with half the kingdom. Its wealth is more than you'll ever need. My son, when Krishna arrives why don't you be the one to wash his feet? This is a cherished custom."

"That will send the wrong message. Krishna will think I'm washing his feet out of fear."

Dhritarastra offered advice. "My son, don't be like the foolish pilgrim who mistakes the wrong path to be the right one and winds up lost."

But Gandhari offered an alternative. "After his feet are washed, find a moment to take him aside and invite him for dinner."

Word came that Krishna had arrived at the gates of the city.

"Make haste," Dhritarastra commanded. "We must all be off and be ready to greet Krishna when he reaches the palace."

* * * * *

Krishna spent an appropriate amount of time at the reception, receiving gifts, making small talk and joking with the Kurus. When Krishna prepared to leave, Duryodhan, at his mother's prodding, approached him.

"O Krishna, it is good to behold your smiling features. I pray you will accept an invitation to dine at my home this evening."

"I will come after my mission is accomplished," Krishna said.

"But I wanted to honor you for the kind gift of your army you made to me."

"I have a previous engagement."

"Krishna, why do you snub my invitation?"

"I will tell you frankly. Usually, one sits down to dine at another's table either out of affection or because one is compelled by hunger to do so. I'm not in want, nor have you done anything to warrant my affection."

With that, Krishna left the palace. Duryodhan felt angry. He would find some way to get back at Krishna.

* * * * *

When Krishna entered his aunt's quarters, it seemed the luminous sun had entered as well. Kunti felt refreshed upon seeing her nephew and yet, the grief of separation from her sons for so many years weighed heavily upon her. She ran to Krishna and they embraced as tears flowed freely from her eyes.

"O Krishna, how are they? I haven't seen them for over thirteen years. Now they're finally back from their ordeal." Her voice was choked. Her eyes looked to him for reassurance.

"They're quite well, strong and healthy. They send you their undying love."

"They don't deserve this." Kunti wrung her hands as she spoke. "They were precocious children. From the very beginning they have always sought to please their elders. They have always respected the brahmins. They have always spoken truthfully. My heart aches to think of what they've gone through. Their father passed from this world when they were still children. I had to raise them by myself. They became accustomed to hardship from a tender age, and were always so patient and tolerant... And the princess of Panchala?"

"More beautiful than ever."

"And so faithful to my sons. Willing to share their burden. Leaving her children behind. In Panchala she was raised amidst royal comforts, attended by many servants. I still can't believe she had to endure the humility of being dragged before an assembly of nobles and treated so cruelly... And those who should have spoken up for her did not... O Krishna, it's still not over, is it?"

"We'll see. It all depends on Duryodhan."

"I've always treated Dhritarastra's sons as my own. I never made any distinction. But if it depends on Duryodhan, war is inevitable... I don't blame him or his family for my sorrows. When I was a child, my father - your grandfather - took pity on his friend and wife who were childless. I was playing with my ball in the courtyard one morning and they came for me. My father turned me over to them. I was shocked. Abandoned by my own father and mother! How did they expect a child to live with that? But what was worse, as a maiden, I abandoned my firstborn, Karna, whom I bore in secret. Whatever possessed me?... So you see, I blame only myself for my misfortune. The law of Karma unfolds in mysterious ways... I only worry about my boys."

"My dear aunt, there's something peculiar about the human condition. Most people don't mind living humdrum lives. But those who are intelligent are eager to experience the intensity of life: from great suffering to extraordinary adventures and challenges, from the highest of pleasures to the deepest of truths. They're not interested in anything in between. Thus it is for your sons. Fear not. They will be victorious. All will be right in the end."

"Krishna, I know the power of your words, and I take comfort in them. Those who revere your words will perfect their lives."

Lovingly, Krishna gave his aunt a tender kiss on the forehead and honored her by walking around her, and then took his leave.

* * * * *

Bhismadev was furious. "There's no reason why we should not make peace," he told the assembled nobles in the Great Hall. "The Pandavas are strengthening their forces as we speak. But even if that weren't the case, Bhima and Arjuna themselves could consume our armies as easily as a fire would consume the dry grass on the open plains."

Karna could no longer contain himself. "Haven't we all heard this before?... 'The Pandavas are favored by the gods.' 'No one can defeat them'... Why, there's not a soul in the whole damn world who doesn't know of their prowess. But *you* have to go over it again and again and again. Well, let me tell you, I know Duryodhan, and I know he's capable of giving away everything he owns. But he's not going to give anything to anyone because of some threats. If the Pandavas need a place to live, they are always welcome to live under our protection."

Duryodhan beamed with satisfaction over Karna's words.

"Your protection!" Bhismadev was astonished by Karna's arrogance. "Have you so quickly forgotten that our forces were recently battered by Arjuna's arrows in the kingdom of Matsya?"

"Duryodhan is incapable of being kind to his cousins," Drona interjected. "His nature was molded from birth. Our words cannot change him no more than our words can change the nature of a snake."

Dhritarastra's heart ached for his son. He hated to hear the squabbling. He called upon Vidura. "Vidura, you've been silent all this time. Please, speak some sense into my son."

Vidura spoke softly. "I'm at a loss for words, your Majesty. My heart is saddened." He turned toward Duryodhan. "Duryodhan, this I know. I'm not going to mourn over you when you fall dead on the battlefield. Instead, I will mourn for your mother and father. What will they do and where will they go after the dynasty is destroyed? Is this the legacy that you are so willing to leave behind? You're a courageous king and warrior. I'll give you that. But I ask only one small thing of you. Give up your pride, and when Krishna arrives, listen to his good advice."

Gandhari desperately wanted her son to understand this. "My son, heed the words of Vidura. Listen to Krishna. Open your heart to his faultless wisdom. By doing so, you will honor us all. What is the value of war? How can it lead to happiness? Act in moderation and kindness and you will never be the loser."

Trumpets announced Krishna's entrance. He had dined and spent the previous night at Vidura's modest residence. Krishna and Vidura had talked together all night long into the early morning hours, touching upon the sublime aspects of Dharma and Karma. Before dawn, as usual, Krishna bathed, engaged in his morning meditations, and recited mantras. After sunrise, a messenger came to announce the onset of the meeting. But Krishna, as was his habit, leisurely conversed with the brahmins who sought his darshan. He offered them gifts and praises. In no rush, he took his leave, climbed into his waiting chariot, and proceeded to the Great Hall.

Now, as the lotus-eyed Krishna spoke, his words seemed to fill the hall with a calm that enveloped almost all of the nobles. Most were eager for his counsel. Krishna spoke slowly and chose his words carefully.

"Duryodhan, you stem from a famed and exalted dynasty, as do your cousins. You are learned and have excellent qualities, as do your cousins. There's no reason why everyone can't live together amiably. Everyone wants peace for the dynasty. If there's some difficulty, one usually goes to the elders for their good counsel: your father and mother, the Grandsire, Vidura, and Drona. They all want this to be resolved peacefully. The Pandavas also. They bear no grudges and want only to live in peace. They have proven this time and again. Even now, they do not demand the return of their kingdom. But the Pandavas do need some place to live. Duryodhan, you have remarkable power, endurance and valor. You are known to be generous. Find it in your heart to be kind to your cousins."

Krishna paused to allow Duryodhan to feel the gravity of his words and concluded. "Those who are wise tell us that to live honorably we must align the pursuit of Dharma, wealth and happiness. The wise caution us not to abandon Dharma in reckless pursuit of wealth or happiness. It never works. For if we give way to our unrestrained senses, the road we have created will only lead to our destruction. Thus, I implore you, give the Pandavas five villages where they can live in peace."

Duryodhan cast sidelong glances at Krishna. He barely managed to restrain himself as Krishna spoke. When Krishna finished, Duryodhan impulsively leapt from his throne and into the midst of the assembly.

"Why should I give the Pandavas anything? No one forced them to play at dice. Didn't I win their kingdom and wealth in a fair game? And after Yudhisthira foolishly lost everything, didn't I give him a chance to win it all back? Didn't I? So is it my fault that the invincible Pandavas lost their kingdom and were forced to live in the woods? I've never given any trouble to my cousins. So Krishna, I will tell you frankly that as long as I live the Pandavas will get no land from me. I will not even give them so much land as will fit under the head of a pin."

Krishna heard Duryodhan's words patiently. He understood that the only recourse was a fight. "Your words reveal your foolishness," Krishna said, matter-of-factly. "You will destroy yourself along with your dynasty."

Seeing he could do no more, Krishna turned to leave the assembly hall, but Duryodhan was not through. "Krishna, you're no envoy. You're an instigator and have incited everyone against me. I won't allow you to get away with it."

Duryodhan glared at Krishna with unmasked hatred. A glance from Duryodhan signaled Dushasana, Sakuni and Karna to step up beside him to provide support. He also waved for his brothers to surround Krishna. Duryodhan had planned for this moment.

Vidura saw what was happening and stood up, aghast. "What do you think you're doing? You'll all perish like insects flying into a fire."

"Enough talk. Let's take him!" Duryodhan yelled.

Dhritarastra became frantic and cried out in desperation. "Duryodhan, my son! Stop your foolishness. What are you thinking? You can no sooner take hold of Krishna than you could catch the wind."

Others in the assembly also arose in protest.

"Allow me," Krishna said, raising his hand to calm those wanting to come to his aid. And to Duryodhan he said, "Do you think I came here alone?"

Duryodhan was adamant. "I've had enough of your word jugglery. I will see you punished."

Krishna remained unmoved and unconcerned. Dhritarastra and Gandhari feared Krishna would use his chakra against their eldest son. They knew of this deadly weapon of his. Krishna glanced toward Dhritarastra and gave the blind king momentary sight. The king jumped from his chair. "I can see! I can see! The world! The colors!. . . And all these wondrous beings. . . coming out of Krishna himself."

Dhritarastra beheld what everyone in the assembly beheld that day. Krishna had not brandished his chakra weapon, rather, he effortlessly manifested warriors and Celestials. The Pandavas, the Vrishnis, the Andhakas, the Adityas, the Rudras, and the Vasus all emerged from Krishna's being and encircled Krishna to defend him. Numerous rishis, reciting mantras, emerged from Krishna with Brahma at their helm. Next, Shiva emerged dancing and laughing. Streams of fierce Yaksas, Gandharvas and Rakshasas, with upraised weapons, poured forth from Krishna. Krishna had not come alone. Seeing this, Duryodhan's brothers fled in fear, practically falling over each other. In the commotion, Duryodhan hung his head in shame and also slipped away. Dhritarastra saw it all. He trembled, and then his sight was gone.

The meeting was finished. As the nobles left the Great Hall, Dhritarastra summoned Krishna to him. "You see how my son is. He's uncontrollable. I tried to talk to him. I've tried everything I can think of. What more can I do?" The blind king wanted Krishna to console him, to pity him and have mercy upon him and his son.

Krishna, knowing Dhritarastra wasn't as innocent as he made out to be, held his tongue on the matter. "I'm sorry sire. Nothing more can be done," Krishna said. "Now it is left for the armies to decide. With your permission, I take my leave."

* * * * *

Outside the Great Hall Krishna spied Karna in the crowd. Krishna invited him to step onto his chariot and take a ride with him. In silence they drove to a wooded area where they sought the shade of a cluster of trees and sat together.

"I know you've met with sages, scholars and mystics," Krishna remarked. "I know you are a seeker of the truth, and I'll share a truth with you. You are the son of Kunti. You are of noble lineage. Indeed, you are the son of the sun-god and the eldest of the Pandavas. Take your place amongst them and the Pandavas themselves will fall at your feet. They will worship you, as will all kings, as the rightful heir to the throne. You will be the supreme sovereign of the earth."

"Do the Pandavas know of this?"

"No one knows, except for Kunti."

Karna looked at Krishna sheepishly, and quite pleased with himself. "O Krishna, I've already suspected all that you tell me. Surya has come to me in dreams. I know you speak for my welfare and that the Pandavas will do everything you say they will. But in the end I would only disappoint you and my brothers, for if the empire belonged to me, I would gladly turn it over to my dear friend Duryodhan."

Krishna tried to speak, but Karna held up his hand. "Krishna, don't try to dissuade me. I also know that you've come to this world on a mission. I know the ever-growing host of kings and warriors have, for the most part, become like parasites, and are a burden to the Earth. The kshatriyas still have one true principle they can call their own: the glory of battle. This is the wealth of a true kshatriya. So I do not want to deprive them of their wealth nor you of your mission."

Krishna made one last effort. "Karna, is this your decision?"

Karna relished Krishna's perseverance, his unwillingness to give up on him. He replied, "The planets and constellations are aligned. Saturn and Mars are creating trouble. Inauspicious meteors are coming close. The heavens already announce this imminent conflict. In ages to come, the bards will sing of these times."

Krishna added, "And the sages and storytellers will proclaim how all the warriors on both sides ultimately attained to the highest abode, even to that above the celestial kingdom."

"One thing, Krishna. This talk is our little secret. I don't want the Pandavas treating me any differently."

Krishna and Karna embraced, and they drove back in silence.

*****

The next morning Karna stood by the Ganges facing east with arms stretched to the sky. As was his practice every morning, he chanted the ancient hymns in praise of the sun-god. The rays of the rising sun rushed towards him and embraced him. Kunti waited a long time for him to finish his meditations. She trembled in anticipation. But she wouldn't turn back now. She reassured herself he would accept her. He must! When he finally ended his prayers and turned to leave, he saw her.

"What do you want?" Karna asked indifferently.

"Do you know who I am?"

"You are the mother of the Pandavas."

She realized this would not be so easy. Tears were already in her eyes. "I'm your mother. Your father is Surya, the sun-god. I was a frightened young woman when I gave birth to you. I put you in a basket and set you adrift on the river. You must have floated past this spot."

"Now that you mention it, this place does look familiar," he said somewhat sarcastically.

"O my son, please don't go to war with your brothers." The words rushed out of her mouth. "Live together in peace. Work with them rather than against them, and no force on Earth will ever be able to stop you."

A celestial voice emanated from the direction of the sun. "It is I, Surya, your father. Believe your mother. Follow her wishes."

Karna only grew angry. His eyes were locked on Kunti. "Who is my mother? The woman who abandoned me at birth? Or the woman who took me in and gave me her breast to suck that I may live? That woman nourished me and cared for me. She celebrated at my wedding and helped with the birthing of my children. These acts constitute a bond that cannot be broken. A bond greater than any blood bond."

Kunti stood frozen. Hot tears streamed down her face.

"O mother, you have hurt me more than my greatest enemy. And today you come here to tell me what I should or shouldn't do. You come to make a request that is no doubt self-serving. Shame on you. My only purpose in going to war is to fight with Arjuna. One of us will slay the other. But I'll be kind to you. I won't kill any of your other sons. I assure you that at the end of the battle, you'll still have five sons. But it's either Arjuna or me. One of us will be dead."

Strangely, Kunti felt a burden being lifted. She embraced Karna. Although he did not return the embrace, it did not matter. For the first time in a long time she felt calm. She remembered that moment long ago when she put him in the basket and turned him over to Providence. Now, once again, she turned him - and all her sons - over to Providence. "Stay well," she said.

Karna gave a respectful nod and turned away. She watched as he walked along the riverbank and disappeared from view. She could not see the tears welling up in his eyes.

* * * * *

Vidura made one last attempt to stop the war. He went to Dhritarastra's quarters.

"My brother, you've had many good years here in Hastinapura. The people respect you. The bards sing your praises."

Dhritarastra stoically shook his head, knowing what was to come next.

"My brother, how can you let Duryodhan go off to war without saying a word?"

Dhritarastra clutched his cane, unable to speak or move.

"My brother, you must demand that Duryodhan return Yudhisthira's kingdom to him."

Vidura's words were met by silence. Frustrated, he lay hold of the blind king. "Duryodhan is envy personified. Don't be a fool. Why do you ignore your conscience and allow him to usurp the kingdom of your nephews? Please, do what's best for the dynasty. Send him away."

Duryodhan stepped from the shadows. He had been warned of Vidura's visit. "So, what have we here? The son of a servant woman who thinks he can influence the throne. How dare you touch my father the king. No one here is interested in your opinions. You are an enemy in our midst. I should have you beaten within an inch of your life. Leave here at once."

Without hesitation Vidura left. He left the royal palace. He left Hastinapura. He left behind everything he had known and held dear. Internally, he thanked Duryodhan for his insults and for banishing him. Those insults cut the knots of attachment. He was now freed from the politics, intrigues and burdens of aristocratic life. Vidura wandered alone into the forest, beginning his long pilgrimage to the holy places.

Chapter 11

The Cosmic Form

War drums sounded. Armies were on the move. They came from far and wide. Kingdoms were emptied of able-bodied men and it seemed that only the young and old remained behind. The site chosen for the battle was Kurukshetra, an expansive valley, surrounded by rolling hills. It was an ancient place of pilgrimage even at that time. The legendary Emperor Kuru, followed by generations of nobles, had come there to offer oblations and receive blessings from the forefathers or directly from the Celestials. Now it was to become a killing field. Tent camps were set up for many miles: by the rivers, in the forests and on the slopes of the mountains. Veritable cities took shape with millions of inhabitants. The warriors brought their cooks, servants, messengers, physicians, musicians and blacksmiths. Men, animals and provisions continuously poured in for many days. The Pandava forces set up their camp on the western side of the valley, on the slopes of the Asta Hills. The Kauravas set up camp on the eastern side.

The commanders met to establish the rules of engagement. Combat must go on between equals. A warrior who withdraws from the battlefield should not be attacked. Nor one who is without a weapon. Nor one who is off his chariot. Nor one who is wounded. Nor one who is unprepared. Charioteers and their horses should not be attacked. Nor any non-combatant. The fighting should stop at sunset. Attacking in the dark of night is forbidden.

* * * * *

The day of the battle arrived. Arjuna arose before sunrise. He refreshed himself and gathered his quivers and his famed Gandiva bow. He felt confident as he bowed and, on bended knee, recited hymns to Lord Narayana. Yudhisthira also made offerings of fruits, flowers, golden coins and gold-embroidered cloth to the many brahmins who had accompanied him to his camp and who now recited prayers for victory and for the protection of his army. Nakula and Sahadev sat serenely in meditation, and Bhima practiced his club fighting incessantly.

With the coming of dawn, the air was filled with the rustle of horses, elephants, and chariots. Soon conch shells resounded throughout the valley, followed by trumpets and drums. This fanfare enlivened the warriors and called for them to take their places on the front. They strapped coats of mail onto their chests, beautifully crafted golden bands onto their arms and necks, and adorned their heads with golden helmets or silk turbans. They gathered their weapons and moved into position. A splendorous, morning sun peeked over the horizon and greeted millions of warriors kneeling in prayer to the sun-god.

The Pandavas took their positions. Their forces included: Drupada and his two sons Dristadyumna and Sikhandi and their army from Panchala; Virata and his son Bhuminjaya and their army; the charismatic and carefree Abhimanyu; Ghatotkaca, the son of Bhima, who brought with him from the forest regions a powerful force of Rakshasa fighters; Satyaki, the outspoken general of the Yadus who commanded a legion of excellent fighters; and the Pandava's five sons born of Draupadi. Yudhisthira chose the gallant and expert leader Dristadyumna as commander-in-chief of their forces, which totaled seven akshauhini divisions.

On the eastern side of the valley, the Kaurava forces took their places. The unsurpassed Bhismadev, commander-in-chief, took his place in the middle of the line. He was surrounded by: Kripa, a skilled Kuru general and tactician; Duryodhan and his ninety-nine brothers; the expert Drona and his son Ashwattama; King Jayadratha who ruled over the Sindhus; King Salya with his division of warriors from the kingdom of Madra in the foothills of the Himalayas; Sakuni who commanded the horsemen and fierce mountain fighters from Gandhar and Kamboja from the Northwest; the Kalinga clans from the coastal regions of the Southeast; the Samsaptakas, sworn enemies of Arjuna who abandoned happiness and threw caution to the wind, taking a vow to conquer or die; and the Yadu general Kritavarman, commanding Krishna's army. There were also Yavana hordes, along with the giant Rakshasa Alamvashu. In total, the Kaurava ranks consisted of eleven akshauhini divisions. Besides these divisions, both the Kauravas and the Pandavas had countless other warriors that were not part of these divisions.

Bhismadev spoke to his forces in a deep voice, and his message was transmitted from one division to another. "O kshatriyas, hear me. On this day the doors of heaven open for us. To die in the comfort of one's home is a curse for a warrior. So let your hearts rejoice, for on this field you will attain either victory on Earth or the delights of the celestial regions."

The armies were arrayed in a mighty display of force with fighters on elephants, chariot warriors, horse soldiers, bowmen and infantry fighters. Ten thousand elephants stood ready. On top of the elephants, their handlers and several warriors sat comfortably on ornate platforms with canopies to shade them from the sun. On the chariots each fighter had, at arm's length, his favorite weapons, which included bows, swords, spears, clubs and shields of various shapes and sizes. Parts of the chariots were encrusted with gold and silver. A flag fluttered from the top of each chariot bearing the insignia of that warrior so he could be recognized wherever he drove.

* * * * *

Sanjaya sat with the blind king in the royal palace at Hastinapura. "The night is finished. The warriors prepared themselves," Sanjaya said. "They began the day like any other, with cleansing and prayer."

"But this is not any other day."

"O King, I see Arjuna and Krishna, Nara and Narayana, heroic, dazzling and undefeatable. Dharma resides with them and they are always attended by Victory."

"Sanjaya, I'm afraid for my sons."

"Meteors fall from the sky. Today, the earth will drink the blood of many men."

 "How foolish men are. Our intelligence is polluted the moment we chase after selfish interests."

"The armies look like two great oceans."

"Which army is greater?"

"That of your son's, expertly arranged by Bhismadev."

"Then there's hope."

"Numbers are no guarantee of victory. Fifty stout warriors working in unison can defeat an entire army. "

"Soon, the killing will begin. My body is flooded with fear. O Sanjaya, I wish I could abandon the kingdom like Vidura. I would enter the forest this very moment. I would be free."

"Sire, no matter where we are, we cannot live free from fear without giving up worldly attachments."

* * * * *

Again, conches and trumpets resounded across the valley to signal the readiness of both sides. Two massive armies extended to the horizon. Krishna drove Arjuna's chariot and, at his request, Krishna brought him to a place between the two armies where he could view the opposing forces. In the distance, Arjuna beheld his relatives, teachers, friends and elders ready to do battle against him and his brothers. At this sight, Arjuna's eyes filled with tears. His body trembled and his head spun. He struggled for clarity, but to no avail. His mighty Gandiva bow slipped from his hands and fell to the ground. Arjuna sank to his knees.

"What's the good of all this?" Arjuna cried. "How can I kill my kinsmen and teachers for the sake of a kingdom? What would be the value of happiness, or even of life itself? My mind is burning. I don't want to be blinded by the greed and lust that drive my cousins. O Krishna, I will wait here, unarmed. Let them come and kill me, but I will not fight."

"My dear Arjuna, you are a warrior. Others will accuse you of weakness. Give up your lamentation. It does not become you."

"I'd rather live as a beggar than gain a kingdom stained with the blood of my teachers." Tears flowed down Arjuna's face. "I am overcome by waves of grief and confusion. Krishna, you know what is to be done and what is not to be done. You know the intricacies of Dharma and Karma. Please, guide me."

A compassionate smile crossed Krishna's face. "My friend, why do you lament for the body which is destined to perish? You are not the body. You are atma, the true self, the eternal, unchanging, spirit-soul. The body ages from childhood to youth and grows old. At the time of death the soul transmigrates to a new body. The soul is individual, indestructible, miraculous, full of knowledge and joy. Indeed, all of us have always existed, and we will all continue to exist in the future. What is true endures forever, and thus for the self there is neither birth nor death. However, very few understand the nature of the true self. The self is not the doer, but is the observer. Material nature, which is also without a beginning and is constantly changing, has the power to bewilder the soul. Thus, the confused soul strives endlessly for mundane things and becomes lost in maya, illusion."

* * * * *

Arjuna asked, "What are the qualities of one who is in divine consciousness? How does he act?"

Krishna spoke, his voice serene and majestic. "Such a person is not disturbed by the constant changes of this world. He is beyond the dualities of success and failure. Beyond profits and losses. Beyond pleasures and pains. Beyond the constant flow of desires which come and go like the waves of an ocean. He is forever free from fear and anger. His senses are restrained. He eats, speaks, sleeps and works in moderation. He is not attached to the results of his work, but neither does he try to avoid work. He sees that all worldly pleasures, which first appear sweet and alluring, ultimately sour. They have a beginning and an end, and he does not strive for such things.

"Rather, he is situated in the pursuit of transcendence. He is happy from within. He rejoices and is illumined from within. Gradually his heart opens. He sees all beings with equal vision and acts for their welfare. And he sees Me dwelling patiently in the hearts of all as the Companion. He is centered in knowledge, peace and compassion. A person in this consciousness remains fixed, even at the moment of death. Such a rare soul readily attains Vaikuntha, My supreme spiritual abode, free from fears and anxieties, and above heaven itself.

* * * * *

Arjuna asked, "It's confusing. On one hand you encourage me to fight and on the other you tell me to be free from gain and loss. So what is the best course of action?"

"It's true. Those who become entangled in the pursuit of worldly opulence and pleasures are bewildered as to the real goal of life. In this state of being they are frustrated life after life and continually chase after the fleeting pleasures of this world. They give up the search for the true self. On one hand, work binds you, but on the other hand, you should not abstain from work. That will not bring you to enlightenment. No one can stop from being active. Everyone must work according to their nature. Thus, it's best when you perform your work as a sacrifice, an offering, to the One Supreme Lord. Seeing your actions, even the gods in the heavens will be pleased with you and give you their blessings. Ultimately, freedom from lust, greed and anger, and from all worldly entanglements is found through acts of self-sacrifice. Therefore, whatever you do, whatever you eat, whatever you give in charity or whatever acts of kindness you perform, do it as a sacrifice for Me."

* * * * *

Arjuna asked, "O Krishna, what is your origin?"

"I *am* the Origin. I am the One who countless ages ago imparted these teachings to the sun-god, who in turn spoke them to Manu, the father of humankind. Manu gave the teachings to his son Iksvaku, first of the earthly kings. In this way these principles of yoga were understood and transmitted through a succession of spiritual teachers and upheld by the saintly kings. But over the ages, the teachings were lost. Now, I share these same teachings with you because of your devotion and friendship."

"How is it that you instructed the teachings to the sun-god in times long forgotten?"

"My friend, both you and I have gone through many births. Whereas you have forgotten, I remember all things and births and times, for I am the Lord of all beings. Whenever Dharma is corrupted, I descend to set it right. I also appear in this world, time and again, to protect the virtuous and to curb the demoniac. The foolish mock Me when they hear of My appearance in this world, but the wise who know Me as the source of all things open their hearts to Me, serve Me in love, and delight in always speaking and hearing of Me."

* * * * *

Arjuna asked, "My Lord, You are inscrutable, and I am no yogi. How can I meditate upon You for my purification?"
"O Arjuna, numerous are the ways to meditate upon Me.
I am the life in all life and the ability of all beings,
I am the beginning, the middle, and the end,
I am the father, the mother, the laws of the universe,
I am the guide and the goal,
I am sound, I am taste,
I am the sweet fragrance of the earth,
And the wish-fulfilling cow,
And the bountiful herbs that cure,
I bring or withhold the rain,
Of offerings, I am the chanting of My sacred names,
I am the Om vibration, I am the Vedas,
And of poetry, I am Brahma's primeval prayer.
I am the vast ocean and the mighty wind,
I am the luminous sun and the soothing moon,
I am the seed of life and the vibrant spring,
Sowing great renewal across the land.
Of rivers, I am the sacred Ganges and of trees, the banyan,
And of that which cannot be moved, the mighty Himalayas.
In living beings, I am consciousness,
I am achievement and wondrous adventure,
I am the strength of the determined,
The wisdom for which knowledge seekers long,
The source of all things yet to come,
And the breath of life flowing in and out.

I am silence, I am unceasing time,
I am death who brings all to an end,
And yet, I am seated in the hearts of all,
I am their shelter and their most dear friend."

* * * * *

Arjuna said, "Krishna, if You are who You say You are, and if it pleases You, I humbly request that You kindly show me Your Cosmic Being."

Krishna smiled serenely, and He gave Arjuna divine sight as the cosmic, mystical, multi-featured form became manifest in all directions simultaneously. Majestic forms, faces, mouths, and eyes unfolded before Arjuna without limit, all decorated with crowns, emeralds, garlands, and holding an array of auspicious symbols and lethal weapons. It seemed to Arjuna that thousands of suns appeared in the sky. Arjuna trembled and his hairs stood on end. Past and future lost their meaning. It was impossible for him to grasp the enormity of these unlimited forms. Myriads of indescribable colors streamed forth without beginning or end. Arjuna saw Celestials emanating from the Cosmic Being. He saw Asuras, vicious, threatening and grabbing plunder. He saw hosts of warriors in full battle regalia. He saw bearded, long-haired rishis reciting Vedic hymns, offering prayers of peace, and asking for divine protection, crying "shanti, shanti, shanti, – peace, peace, peace." Bursts of fire emanated from the many mouths of the Cosmic Being. Arjuna saw all the warriors at Kurukshetra being devoured, flying into His mouths as if they were moths flying into a blazing fire. Arjuna saw them helplessly ground up by His teeth. He saw multitudes evaporated by nuclear rays.

Stricken with fear and desperation, Arjuna cried out, "O Supreme Refuge, I bow before You again and again. Tell me, what is Your purpose?"

And the Cosmic Personality answered from all directions, "Time I am. Destroying all worlds. No one can oppose me. I give you this cosmic vision. Never has it been seen before. You are here to assist in My mission. Thus, fight."

The Cosmic Being was both wonderful and horrific, both giving and consuming. He was beauty and terror woven seamlessly together; all the mysteries of the universe in one place, all a great whirl of motion, and yet, almost motionless. Simultaneous creation and devastation. Timelessness.

Arjuna's mind unraveled. He felt stunned and fearful, thrilled and exhausted. He heard himself call out to Krishna again and again. His call echoed into infinity. He'd seen enough of this cosmic vision. He wanted Krishna Himself to return. He wanted his eyes to bathe in Krishna's soothing human-like form. At Arjuna's request the Cosmic Being melted away, revealing Lord Vishnu. Vishnu's four-armed form held His four eternal symbols of the lotus, conch, mace, and the razor-sharp chakra. Vishnu appeared formidable and infallible. Waves of ecstasy overcame Arjuna. Krishna relished teasing him by still withholding Himself, making Arjuna long for Him all the more. Finally, Krishna returned to His original two-armed form, and Arjuna breathed a sigh of relief, happy to see his friend again.

Krishna told him, "My dear Arjuna, the form you now see before you is My most sublime and intimate form. One cannot understand Me by knowledge, nor by giving in charity, nor by performing pious acts, nor by great austerities. Only by pure, unmotivated loving service can one truly come to understand Me. Such a person sees Me everywhere and sees everything in Me. I have come to help you and guide you, for you are without envy. You are My friend for you seek to be a friend to all."

Arjuna felt his strength and poise returning, along with his resolve. He picked up his Gandiva bow and held it firmly to his chest. "O Krishna, O Lord of lords, by Your mercy my confusion is dispelled, and my knowledge is reawakened. Come what may, I am prepared to act."

Chapter 12

On The Battlefield

Yudhisthira had one last thing to do before he would allow the battle to begin. Bhismadev gazed upon him as he crossed the field on foot and unarmed. *Such a noble figure,* he thought. *The Pandavas did not deserve such hardship.* Since his youth Bhismadev had done everything in his power to ensure the preservation of the Kuru dynasty. But now, it had come to this.

Duryodhan and his friends snickered at the sight of Yudhisthira. Someone asked, "What type of kshatriya is this?" The others made unflattering remarks, but as Yudhisthira drew closer, they fell silent.

When Yudhisthira approached Bhismadev, he beheld a faint smile behind the Grandsire's beard. He knew that smile and he remembered Bhismadev's unbounded affection for him and his brothers. Yudhisthira bowed before him. "O Grandsire, I come on behalf of my brothers and myself. We are nothing without you. From the time we were children, when we first came to Hastinapura with our mother, you always sought after our welfare. You were like a father to us. Please give us permission to fight you. If you do not, my brothers and I will simply lay down our bodies and die right here."

"My son, you have pleased me very much. May you achieve victory in all that you do. How can I help you?"

"O Grandsire, if you deem it fit, tell me how we can defeat you who are undefeatable?"

Bhismadev smiled at the question. "I will reveal it in due course."

Yudhisthira bowed to Bhismadev and turned to Drona and Kripa. He honored them and asked for their blessings.

Drona told Yudhisthira, "I would have cursed you if you had not come to offer your respects. But now I bless you. May you be victorious. But I must warn you that I cannot be vanquished in battle, that is, unless I hear an unpalatable truth which causes me to lay down my weapons."

Kripa told Yudhisthira, "All my life I have lived at the beck and call of the Kurus. All my life I have served wealth and power. The common knowledge is that wealth and contentment abide together. But I've learned that they seldom do. I envy you, for you have no illusions about such things. You don't need my blessings. I need yours."

With tears in his eyes Yudhisthira bowed before them and returned to his chariot.

Karna impulsively grabbed the reins from the driver of his chariot and brought the vehicle forward. Seeing the exchange between Bhismadev and Yudhisthira made his blood boil and he had to speak. "Since the Grandsire sympathizes with the enemy, I will not follow him into battle." He looked sternly over to Bhismadev. "You've practically turned your back on Duryodhan, our king. I cannot accept you as commander of our forces. I'll only fight when you are finished fighting."

Karna circled his chariot before the leaders and, raising dust, he sped down the line of warriors and disappeared from sight.

* * * * *

In the heavens, Siddhas, Gandharvas, and Charanas gathered to watch the battle below. A moment of silent anticipation descended upon Kurukshetra, a moment which hung heavy, a moment of waiting, of postponing death a little while longer, and then drums and bugles sounded and warriors blew their conch shells, and Time once again ground forward as battle cries arose from the ranks of the armies and rolled across the valley, and like a great beast stirring from its slumber, the warriors shook their weapons and rushed at one another and collided together with a thunderous force.

Krishna, at the reins, guided Arjuna's chariot toward Bhismadev, who stood firm and unopposed like a Himalayan peak. Arjuna and the Grandsire initially sent forth bursts of arrows at one another. Bhismadev tried to gain the upper hand by shooting a relentless barrage of arrows toward Arjuna. But Arjuna easily cut down the arrows that descended upon him. They fought steadily, each displaying a mastery of bow and arrow, but neither could outdo the other.

The field was dry, and the dust raised by the movement of the armies made it difficult for the combatants to see clearly. Arjuna and Bhismadev lost each other in the melee. Bhismadev turned his attention to destroying the Pandava army. The shadow of death fell upon whomever he turned his weapons toward.

The movement of troop formations looked like the mighty waves of an ocean coming one after another, and as the day wore on the fighting grew more intense and desperate. Some men had one or both arms cut off and wandered forlorn on the battlefield. Some who were wounded endured their pain and continued fighting. Other wounded men sat down, but were not attacked since they had lost both their weapons and their will to fight. Some called out for their loved ones. Some fighters had their heads cut off, and their bodies fell lifelessly on the ground. Some were trampled by elephants.

No one wanted to be near the lines of elephants when they came charging forward to crush warriors underfoot. The elephants gored oncoming steeds with their tusks and used their trunks to topple chariots. Opposing elephants tore at each other. The elephants were well-guarded, but some enemy warriors found a way through their defense and hacked at the elephants with their battleaxes, and the elephants fell to the ground, shrieking in agony and bleeding profusely. Covered with that blood, the warriors continued fighting in the midst of the carnage.

Destruction swirled around Bhismadev like a whirlwind. At a moment of grief and torment for many warriors, he cheerfully roamed the battlefield. Bhismadev's chariot carried numerous celestial weapons he kept close at hand. He was in fine form. Even in his old age, Bhismadev could not be vanquished by Celestials nor by the most powerful Rakshasas. Duryodhan, Dushasana, and Ashwattama gathered around the Grandsire who was the unequalled tiger amongst warriors. Bhismadev could do more damage than all of them combined. They knew it and wanted simply to protect him from all directions and let him, with the ease and grace of a dancer, careen across the battlefield and annihilate the enemy. To Bhismadev, however, these men appeared like little cubs, wanting not to protect, but to seek his protection.

Duryodhan watched Bhismadev with fascination. He had never seen anyone wreak such havoc. Wildly elated, Duryodhan called to Ashwattama, "Look at him. He's glorious. Bhismadev is devouring our foes like fire devours grass. The Pandavas don't have a chance. This will be all over by tomorrow."

* * * * *

The roar of untold Kalinga horsemen resounded across the valley like a raging ocean. That roar was like music to Duryodhan's ears. He had ordered Bhima to be slain. With the mightiest Pandava eliminated, a Kaurava victory would undoubtedly be close at hand.

The Kalinga's were up to the task and descended upon Bhima with the force of a tsunami. When Bhima saw them approaching, a smile appeared on his lips. This was exactly what he hoped for. He had started out on his chariot early that morning, leaving his brothers and allies behind. Now he was alone on the battlefield and the fierce Kalinga warriors saw it as their opportunity to destroy him. Releasing a thousand shafts from their bows, the Kalingas killed the four swift horses that drew Bhima's chariot. Bhima was furious at the death of his favorite animals, but he restrained himself for he knew that uncontrolled anger blinds a fighter and makes him do foolish things.

One after another, Bhima hurled a dozen lances that dropped as many oncoming horsemen. He grabbed his mighty club as he abandoned his chariot. Bhima already had his imposing double-edged sword strapped on his back. He boldly met the Kalinga ranks, smashing their skulls and faces, their chests and backs. An elephant charged down upon him. Bhima ran toward it and jumped up, and with one swift blow from his club smashed the elephant fatally on the head. He did that with another and another. All around him, dying elephants shrieked in pain. Falling over, they crushed the soldiers and horses beside them. The ground was littered with mangled corpses and broken and bloodied men, moaning and dying. Bhima did not care if they attacked him on foot or on horse or on elephant. He continually summoned for them to continue their attack and fought them with all the skills at his command.

After a time Bhima grew tired of using his club and put it aside. He reached behind and drew his thick, sterling sword that he swung with both hands as he continued to level Kalinga warriors. Flesh ripped. Sinews snapped. Bones cracked. Bodies piled up and served as an embankment to protect Bhima. His enemies rained arrows upon him, but Bhima quickly picked up a shield lying nearby and held it over himself. A band of enemy warriors flew at him and he sent the shield spinning toward them and severed their heads. At that moment, he let out a deafening roar that seemed to fill the sky. The remaining warriors stopped in their tracks. They had only to look around at the piles of dead to realize the futility of their efforts. Bhima was covered with the blood of their kinsmen. The ground everywhere was soaked with it. The remaining Kalingas saw him as an apparition of Death, and they ran away in fear for their lives.

* * * * *

Day after day the slaughter on both sides continued. On the fourth day a thousand furious elephants attacked Bhima. He fought them off, aided by Abhimanyu, Nakula and Sahadev who, with their long bows, struck down the warriors on the large mammals' backs. Bhima drove the remaining elephants back into the Kaurava ranks where they trampled many men. Later that day Bhima slew eight of Dhritarastra's sons and many more on subsequent days.

On the fifth day Bhismadev relentlessly attacked the Pandavas and exacted a heavy toll. On the sixth day Dristadyumna saw Bhima on the battlefield, stranded and wounded, surrounded by the enemy, and whisked him to safety on his chariot. Later that day Duryodhan had to be rescued after being wounded by the rejuvenated Bhima. The next day, Duryodhan complained that his wounds still caused him great discomfort, and Bhismadev, who was expert in all things, took herbs from his pouch to mitigate the king's pain. Each day Bhismadev and Dristadyumna tried to outdo one another by arranging deadly military formations. But neither commander could gain the upper hand.

* * * * *

Eight long days of fighting made Duryodhan incensed. The battle had taken far too long for his liking. Bhismadev had slain thousands upon thousands of Pandava fighters, but he had not killed any of the five brothers. The next morning Duryodhan hurriedly approached the Grandsire.

"Arjuna and Bhima wreak destruction upon our forces. Everyday they throw our army into chaos. Our men flee whenever their chariots speed toward them. Yesterday Bhima came upon me like a thunderbolt. I barely escaped with my life. I am your king! What are you going to do about this?"

Bhismadev tried to be patient. "O King, I'm making every effort for you, as are our generals: Drona, Kripa, Kritavarma, Sakuni, and so many others. We are all ready to die for you."

"But why the setbacks? Our warriors are more capable. We have superior numbers, and have you at the helm. Yet, we have failed to vanquish the Pandavas."

"Listen to me, " Bhismadev countered, "the Pandavas cannot be defeated even by the Celestials led by Indra."

"How can that be? You and Drona are both fighting on our behalf? The Pandavas are no match for either one of you. You have never been defeated."

"What is ordained by Providence cannot be otherwise."

"You disappoint me. Karna was right. He saw this coming. In your heart you favor the Pandavas. If you wanted, you could strike them down, but you're holding back."

"The Pandavas are protected by Krishna."

"So? Are you ready to give up and abandon me?"

Bhismadev took a breath. "Duryodhan, I assure you, today I will kill Arjuna. Or he will kill me."

Duryodhan smiled. "I know you can do it. Just give up your sentimental attachment for him."

"I'll show you my full prowess before the day is done."

* * * * *

That day Bhismadev's chariot roamed the battlefield like a shark in the ocean, leaving a sea of dead in his wake. Hosts of

Pandava warriors scattered in all directions as he sliced through their ranks. After a time, Arjuna heard of Bhismadev's unrelenting attacks, and he gradually made his way across the valley. When Bhismadev beheld Arjuna's chariot in the distance, he headed straight for him. The Grandsire unleashed a cascade of arrows striking all around Arjuna and Krishna, with some even piercing their armor. Bent on victory, Bhismadev attacked them with the strength of a maddened elephant.

Arjuna held back. Krishna observed how timidly he responded to the challenge. Krishna understood that Arjuna and his brothers looked upon the Grandsire like a father. But Krishna would have none of it. He sprang from the chariot like an enraged lion and charged Bhismadev on foot. Krishna spied a nearby wheel from a smashed chariot. He swept it up and, using it as an impromptu weapon, held it above his head.

Bhismadev looked on in wondrous surprise. His hair stood on end at the sight of Krishna's anger. "Come, O Lord of the Universe. I welcome death at your hands." He spread out his arms. "To protect your friend, you have broken your vow to refrain from battle. This moment will be sung for ages to come."

Arjuna cast aside his bow and rushed after Krishna. "Krishna! No! Don't do it." he yelled, desperately trying to catch hold of him. Arjuna lunged forward and threw his arms around Krishna. But Krishna would not be stopped, and he dragged Arjuna behind him. Arjuna finally slowed Krishna down by grabbing his legs.

Arjuna breathed heavily, his energy spent. "Krishna, what do you think you're doing? You promised not to fight."

"I'm fighting to protect you," Krishna yelled. "To compensate for your lackluster attempt."

"I beg you, don't break your promise on my account. From now on, I won't hold back again. This I promise you."

"Let's go." Krishna seemed unconvinced and headed back to their chariot. At this moment the sun set and the day's fighting came to an end.

And Bhismadev felt happy in his heart to see this exchange between Krishna and Arjuna.

* * * * *

That evening the five Pandava brothers, along with Krishna, visited Bhismadev in his regal tent amidst the Kuru encampment. The visitations of opposing warriors during the evening hours was not uncommon. Bhismadev fondly welcomed the group as they bowed before him.

"Come, sit down. What brings you here? It would be my great pleasure to serve you in whatever way I can."

"O Grandsire," Yudhisthira began hesitatingly after they were comfortably seated, "you are like the sun whose scorching rays are unbearable in the noon hour. Your arrows are inexhaustible and you cannot be vanquished. During the day you roam across the battlefield and you do not give us a moments reprieve. My army is on the verge of exhaustion. What must we do to turn the tide of this war in our favor?"

"As long as I am alive you can't win. Your only hope is to kill me."

"We can't do that," Sahadev pleaded, almost jumping up from his seat. His brothers were also taken aback.

"But I give you my permission." The Grandsire tossed out the words casually and with a smile on his face. "It's all right."

"We won't do it," insisted Nakula.

Bhismadev became serious. "There is, however, someone in your camp who is very eager to slay me, and can be the instrument of my death."

Yudhisthira leaned cautiously forward. "What do you mean?"

Bhismadev leaned back in his seat and told the story of Amba, one of the sisters he had kidnapped years ago:

"Amba was outraged. She felt that I had ruined her life and she wanted me punished. She went to the forest to perform austerities. I

felt badly for her and consulted with both Vyasa and Narada Muni. They told me to remain true to the vow of celibacy I had made, and that she must work through her own Karma. Eventually, out of compassion, Shiva came to Amba and assured her that her desires would be fulfilled. She went to her death with the words, 'I want to see Bhismadev destroyed.'

In due course, Shiva appeared to a king in a dream who was eager to have a male child. Shiva told him, 'You will beget a female child, but you and your wife must raise her as if she were a male.' After the child was born, they raised her as a male, telling no one otherwise, dressing her in male clothing and even training her in the military arts. The girl remembered her purpose, and all the while wondered why she inhabited a female body. That was not part of her plan. So one day she entered the deep forest, and went to the manor of a solitary Yaksha wizard by the name of Sthuna. He was deformed and hardly received visitors because of the many hurtful rumors that circulated about him.

Able to see through her disguise and surprised by her presence, he asked, 'My dear maiden, why have you come here?'

'I've heard you are a sorcerer. I need your help to achieve my mission.'

The maiden's courage touched his heart. 'Ask from me whatever you desire,' he said. 'I can help you ward off evil spirits, cure diseases, solve riddles, or gain riches.'

'What I have come for is not as easy as that.'

'My dear girl, I can accomplish things that cannot be accomplished. Just tell me what you want.'

'I want to become a man.'

Sthuna paused. 'You're right. That's not so easily done . . . But there is a way. You'll have to find someone who is willing to trade sexes with you.'

Her heart sank. It seemed all was lost. Wherever would she find someone?

'I'll do it,' offered Sthuna without even her asking. 'But once you've attained your goal, we'll revert back to our original sexes.'

When the maiden heard this, she threw her arms around Sthuna and thanked him profusely. At last she felt she would achieve her purpose."

The Grandsire concluded, "That woman was Amba in her previous life. Now she is a warrior in your army by the name of Sikhandi, the daughter of Drupada."

"But he's a man," Yudhisthira protested.

"He was born a woman, so I still consider him one," Bhismadev explained. "Under no circumstances will I harm a woman. It's immoral. I won't lift a finger to defend myself against her. So tomorrow, have Sikhandi advance towards me. Arjuna should take cover behind her and strike me when he gets close enough."

"I couldn't do that," Arjuna protested, his face already contorted with shame at the thought of such an act.

"No. It doesn't sound very valiant," Bhismadev admitted. "But an extended war like this wears down the soul. It makes men desperate. So that's exactly what I would do if I were in your place and get it over with as quickly as possible."

A stillness permeated the tent. The Pandavas' thoughts returned to their childhood memories of Bhismadev. He, along with Vidura, watched over them. He guided them. The brothers fondly remembered the many wonderful stories Bhismadev told them. They would never have come back from their exile had they known it would lead to this. The brothers, crestfallen, looked at Krishna for an answer.

Krishna spoke softly. "It is destined."

The Pandavas accepted the inevitability of Krishna's words, and one by one they embraced Bhismadev and departed into the night.

* * * * *

On the tenth day of battle, the Pandavas cast off their weariness from the long days of fighting and spilled onto the killing field with a purpose. Dristadyumna instructed one section of the army to attack Bhismadev. As they charged at him with a roar, Bhismadev tossed them off as if they were playthings. For a long time he roamed at will between the two vast armies, and again, to the delight of the Kurus, the Grandsire tore like a scythe through the Pandava ranks. He quickly dispatched anyone who opposed him.

Krishna urged Arjuna to take action. "There!" Krishna pointed. "He's destroying our line of defense." As Krishna steered their chariot into the fray, Arjuna unleashed a cascade of arrows upon the Grandsire. Bhismadev, in turn, sent forth a wall of arrows to nullify Arjuna's efforts. A host of chariot warriors descended to aid Arjuna: Bhima, Nakula, Sahadeva, the Kaikaya brothers, Satyaki, Ghatotkaca, Draupadi's five sons, Dristadyumna, and the valiant Abhimanyu. From within their midst, Sikhandi's chariot stealthily moved into place at the fore, right in front of Arjuna. Bhismadev noticed his advance, but disregarded him.

The Grandsire's chariot had become a vortex. Everyone rushed toward him. The plan unfolded perfectly. From various directions, a thousand arrows were released at Bhismadev. His coat of mail could not withstand them all, and dozens of arrows pierced his flesh. Bhismadev was made of stern mettle for he showed no pain and his faculties remained intact. He was supremely happy now, for he knew he would soon pass from this world. *This is a good day to die*, he thought while releasing several choice arrows that each struck Arjuna, Bhima and Dristadyumna. The arrows' sharp bites announced to his adversaries that the old man was still someone to be reckoned with.

Sikhandi pushed forward as Arjuna took cover behind him. Sikhandi had waited for this moment for a long time. Whatever might happen after this did not matter, but today would be his day. From a distance Drona, Jayadratha, Dushasana, Salya, and

Bhagadatta rushed to aid the Grandsire. But it was too late. Sikhandi drew within range and destroyed Bhismadev's bow. He also pierced him with several arrows and killed his charioteer. Before Bhismadev could reach for another bow, Arjuna, coming from behind Sikhandi, released a continuous stream of arrows that coursed into the Grandsire. The moment froze in time. Everyone looked toward Bhismadev's chariot. When no more arrows emanated from his bow, a cry of victory rose from the Pandava forces and their conch shells resounded across the valley. The Kauravas beheld their leader pummeled full of arrows. But they had no time to lament. The Pandavas released countless shafts from their bows, darkening the skies as their enemies fled.

Only Dushasana drew his chariot alongside Bhismadev's. The Grandsire turned to him and smiled serenely as the last of Arjuna's arrows ripped into his mangled body "These arrows are like thunderbolts from heaven. I accept them gladly. . . Look, the sun is descending. The day is almost done." And with that, Bhismadev fell backwards to the ground. So many arrows covered his body that the Grandsire did not touch the ground at all. Still, he lived. Dushasana gave one last look at Bhismadev before he too retreated. The sight of the Grandsire was so riveting that he could not tear himself away. At the same time, he was confused by what he saw. It seemed to him, that while lying on a bed of arrows, the Grandsire reclined comfortably and appeared almost relieved.

* * * * *

High on a Himalayan plateau there lived a group of rishis. Ages ago they had assumed the form of swans and now spent their time by the tranquil waters and lush gardens of Lake Manasa, surrounded by snow covered peaks. Gangadevi came to them.

"It's my son," she said. That's all they needed to know. They bowed to her and in their own way reassured her. They lifted their wings in unison and flew in the direction of the setting sun.

Drona had seen Bhismadev fall to the ground and he felt faint. He held tightly to the guardrail of his chariot so as not to fall. Goals and men and sounds seemed so far off, so futile. Time hung suspended. Drona heard himself call for a ceasefire and sank into the seat on his chariot.

Horsemen galloped along the battlefront to spread word: "Stop the battle. The Grandsire has fallen." It was beyond comprehension. The warriors from both sides let their weapons slip from their hands. Tears welled in their eyes as they understood the magnitude of what had happened. Facing the Grandsire's chariot, they all stood forlorn. That most magnanimous soul, who had guided the Kuru dynasty for as long as anyone could remember, had now fallen. An eerie stillness settled upon the battlefield.

And then the warriors saw them. The swans, with wings spread, descending from the sky. The warriors looked on in wonderment as the swans touched down before the Grandsire and circled him with respect, and began talking among themselves in their own language. Only Bhismadev could understand them.

-All glories unto this exalted soul who lies before us-

-The Celestials are astonished by his activities-

-And his mother has sent us here-

-She thinks of him often-

-It seems that he is now preparing to die-

-He's been waiting for this moment since the time he arrived on Earth-

-He looks forward to it with great joy in his heart-

-This is seen in his eyes-

-But the sun is in the southern solstice-

-The time is not right for him to leave-

Bhismadev addressed them, "Thank you, my friends. Thank you for reminding me. I am indeed anxious to depart from this world, but I realize now that for me to attain my cherished abode, the sun must be in the northern solstice. My father blessed me that I can choose the moment of my death, and so I will stay a while longer until the sun and stars align to make an easy journey for me to return to the heavens."

The swans bowed to him and once more took flight and disappeared into the evening sky. Bhismadev knew that for the time being, he couldn't go anywhere. He rested on his bed of arrows and called for a pillow. Court physicians who were expert in extracting arrows came with royal pillows and with herbs and potions, ready to attend to his many wounds. But Bhismadev dismissed them, and instead asked Arjuna to provide him with a pillow. Arjuna promptly shot arrows, crisscross, into the ground under Bhismadev's head. With a smile on his face, Bhismadev laid his head comfortably on the arrows.

*****

Karna came alone in the dead of night. Torches were staked around the Grandsire and several men attended to him.

"Who approaches?" Bhismadev inquired.

"One whom you look upon with disgust," Karna answered.

"Come closer and let me see you."

Karna stepped into the light. "I've been a thorn in your side."

"You're no worse than anyone of these arrows in me," Bhismadev affectionately chided him.

"I'm sorry that you hate me."

"I have no animosity toward you. You're courageous, respectful of brahmins, and unsurpassed in gift-giving, but your pride holds you back. I've chastised you on occasion simply to smash that pride."

"I'm sorry I've been so obstinate."

The Grandsire's voice softened. "Karna, there has been enough killing. If you call a truce with the Pandavas you can end it now."

"I cannot turn my back on Duryodhan. I have come only to beg your forgiveness for any offenses I have made against you. And to receive your blessing."

"My son, it is yours, unequivocally. That you have come here shows great character. So be it. Ride into battle. Use all of your skills. A true kshatriya has no greater happiness than an honorable fight and a noble death."

Karna bowed reverentially before Bhismadev and departed into the night.

* * * * *

By sunrise a host of Pandava and Kaurava warriors gathered before the fallen Grandsire. They mingled together and many embraced one another and spoke together in friendly voices. When the Grandsire called for water, everyone became attentive. An ornamented vessel, along with a silver chalice, were brought to him. Bhismadev frowned. With a slight movement of his hand he waved them away. Again he called for Arjuna to assist him. "My body burns with pain. I feel faint and my mouth is dry."

Arjuna stretched the Gandiva bow to its limits and sent an arrow deep into the ground near the Grandsire's head. At once, a fountain of water gushed forth and flowed into Bhismadev's mouth. Everyone was struck by Arjuna's amazing feat, and the Grandsire drank long and heartily until the water subsided. He looked into the faces of the many warriors. "I'm done with fine pillows and silver cups and regal encumbrances."

The weight of his words sent a shiver of admiration through all who heard them. One by one, warriors took off their turbans and spun the cloth round and round over their heads, and they filled the valley with their cheers which rose into one great shout of affirmation, as if to say, "Yes! This is the way one should boldly meet death!"

* * * * *

Later that day Karna rode into the battle. Duryodhan was elated. He always felt Bhismadev had been too soft on the Pandavas. Certainly now the tide would turn in his favor. After consulting Karna, Duryodhan placed Drona as the new commander-in-chief of the Kaurava forces. Although advanced in years, Drona fought with the vigor of a young man. The Pandava forces scattered before him like dried leaves in the wind and many of them were slain.

The next day, Dristadyumna, backed by Satyaki, Abhimanyu and Ghatotkaca, led the Pandava forces into battle. Renewing their efforts, they killed thousands of Kaurava warriors. Elsewhere on the battlefield Arjuna killed Sakuni's two brothers right before his eyes. Sakuni shook with rage. He cast a spell that sent a myriad of wild animals to threaten the Pandava prince. Darkness enveloped the battlefield, followed by a seemingly endless deluge of rain. Countless snakes crawled in the mud. Foot soldiers went scrambling, spooking the horses around them. Arjuna knew this was all an illusory device to create chaos among the Pandava ranks. Thus, Arjuna released his celestial weapons to counteract these threats and turned the day's battle decidedly in their favor.

That evening the Kauravas returned to their camp disheartened. Duryodhan confronted Drona. "I gave you command of my forces hopeful that things would change."

"The Pandavas are very skilled in combat," Drona said. "It will take time."

"Yes, you taught them very well. And just like Bhismadev, you hold back. You're reluctant to attack them with full force."

"That's not true. I've seen you watching me on the battlefield. You see how I fight. No one fights with more prowess than I. Admit it!"

"Yes, that may be true. So why aren't we winning?"

"Duryodhan, tomorrow I will show you something the likes of which you have never beheld. I will place our forces in the chakra vyuha formation. It is impenetrable and unstoppable."

That night Duryodhan slept soundly.

* * * * *

The next morning the tide of the battle turned against the Pandavas. Thousands of their troops lay slaughtered. Drona, an expert tactician, had arranged the Kaurava forces in the chakra vyuha, a wheel-shaped, enigmatic formation that proved to be deadly. This great 'wheel' rotated forward as sharp blades, protruding from behind a wall of shields, took down everyone in its path.

Yudhisthira was in a conundrum. Arjuna and Krishna were off fighting in the distant, southern end of Kurukshetra and were unreachable. Although surrounded by many stalwart warriors, Yudhisthira's hopes now rested on a sixteen-year-old youth – Abhimanyu. From an early age, Abhimanyu had been trained in the military arts and the dynamics of leadership. Yudhisthira called for him to attend an impromptu battlefield council of commanders. But when the youth arrived, Yudhisthira wondered if he should burden him with this predicament.

"I don't know who else to ask," Yudhisthira began. "Apart from your father and Krishna, you're the only one who knows the secret of penetrating the chakra vyuha. We need to stop it before it chews up our entire army."

"My dear uncle, do not doubt my prowess. My father taught me how to break into the formation. Inside is a complex maze. But he hasn't yet taught me how to break out of it."

Yudhisthira paused to gauge the consequences of the plan, but Bhima spoke up first. "My boy, there'll be no need to break out. You lead the way. Dristadyumna, Satyaki and myself, and our forces will be right behind you. Once it's smashed open, no one can stop us."

That's what Abhimanyu wanted to hear. A grin crossed his face. "Then it's done."

Yudhisthira saw how eager Abhimanyu was. "Well... if Bhima is going to be right behind you, we have nothing to worry about." All the commanders shouted in agreement, "So be it!"

At Abhimanyu's prompting, his charioteer urged the horses into motion. Abhimanyu playfully shouted to the others, "Keep up with me if you can!"

Trumpets sounded the call forward. A thousand chariots stirred and followed the youth. Warriors, tightening the grips on their weapons, braced themselves for a fierce encounter. Yudhisthira, a few chariots behind Abhimanyu, hoped that this was the right course of action to take. He knew, for better or worse, it was the only course.

Across the valley, Drona stood on a moving platform in the center of the chakra vyuha. He couldn't believe his eyes. Rather than retreating, the Pandava forces led by Abhimanyu hurtled toward them like a mighty wave. *This is madness,* Drona thought. *A desperate act. My forces will annihilate them. . . But perhaps their desperation is a thing in itself to be feared.*

"Steady. . ." Drona shouted, drawing the word out and letting it fall heavily on the ears of his men. The pounding of horse hoofs and the clatter of chariot wheels drew closer and closer. "Steady. . ." Ten thousand archers drew back their bows. "Fire!" They let sail their arrows toward the oncoming enemy. The Pandavas, undeterred, put their shields skyward and, with hearts pounding, released a war cry meant to shatter the will of the Kauravas.

At the right moment and the right place, Abhimanyu's chariot slipped into the chakra vyuha. He looked back, expecting the Pandava forces to be there behind him, but saw instead Jayadratha's chariot cutting off his kinsmen and creating a great commotion. Jayadratha stood fast and, with arrows flying, refused to give them entry. For an instant, Abhimanyu beheld a forlorn look on Yudhisthira's face.

Then the chakra vyuha closed in on itself.

Mahabharata: The Eternal Quest

* * * * *

Alone, Abhimanyu fought his way through the Kaurava ranks. An incessant stream of arrows from his bow left hordes of dead in his wake. Many others, their limbs severed, lay dying, and their eyes rolled and their bodies shook in agony as their blood spilled forth and soaked the ground. Abhimanyu soon rode into the clearing at the center of the chakra vyuha. There, Duryodhan and eminent Kaurava warriors awaited him. They all smiled and regarded him as already dead. Dushasana raised his hand for the others to hold off as his chariot alone sped forward to attack the Pandava youth. Abhimanyu's sharp arrows quickly found their mark. Dushasana collapsed in his chariot, and his driver whisked him off to safety. Karna next attacked and they exchanged a volley of arrows. But in a short time, Karna also made a hasty retreat after being wounded.

At a gesture from Duryodhan, a hundred chariots pressed forward, each carrying a noble youth from the finest families and wearing the finest silks. As they approached, Abhimanyu invoked a celestial weapon his father had given him, and it appeared to his enemies that a hundred Abhimanyus came in all directions, releasing their shafts everywhere. The nobles became bewildered. They screamed and shot their arrows frantically and drove their chariots helter-skelter. It seemed Abhimanyu was all around them. Many mistakenly shot their own friends and kin. Soon, their lifeless bodies littered the field.

Duryodhan was blinded with rage. His son lay among the dead. He called for Drona, and other maharatha warriors. "Abhimanyu must be stopped. Only our unified attack will defeat him."

Karna felt uncomfortable with this plan. "The rule of battle is that many lesser warriors can attack one maharatha. But to maintain the honor of our positions, great warriors amongst themselves must fight one on one. We just have to find Abhimanyu's weakness."

"He doesn't seem to have one." Drona interjected. "His armor is impenetrable. He releases his arrows with lightening speed and deadly precision."

Smarting from his wounds, Karna agreed. "I'd rather not fight him," he said, not wanting to employ Indra's deadly weapon on the son of his enemy, "but I will because it's my duty as a warrior."

Duryodhan was annoyed with this talk. "Forget the rules. Enough is enough. Kill him now. Do whatever it takes."

Together, the Kauravas set their might upon Abhimanyu. Six maharatha warriors rushed him at once: Drona, Ashwattama, Kripa, Karna, Kritavarma, and Sakuni. One destroyed his bow. Another felled his horses. A third killed his chariot driver. Others smashed his chariot.

Abhimanyu grabbed his sword, spear and a shield bedecked with jewels, and leapt from the ruined vehicle. "Come. I'm ready. I'll fight you one at a time."

Drona and Karna responded with a deluge of arrows that deprived the Pandava youth of his remaining weapons. He picked up a chariot wheel to defend himself, but the Kauravas quickly cut that to pieces. Undeterred, Abhimanyu picked up a club from the ground and rushed at Ashwattama's chariot. Without a thought of defending himself, Ashwattama jumped from the car and ran off. In the open field Abhimanyu was repeatedly struck by the shafts of these battle hardened warriors. Blood flowed from his wounds. He felt dazed. His limbs grew heavy. He could hardly take another step. His long, flowing hair, stained with blood, waved in the breeze. Surrounded by foes who unleashed arrows from every direction, Abhimanyu looked up into the clear sky and found comfort.

Dushasana sent his son into the fray. With his club raised high, he ran towards this lone Pandava warrior who had single-handedly brought the chakra vyuha to a grinding halt. He gave Abhimanyu a blow on the head, and the bright-faced youth fell to the earth like the moon falling from the sky. From all directions, screeching wildly like jackals, Kaurava warriors descended upon his dead body.

* * * * *

That night was cruel for the Pandavas.

Arjuna and Krishna leisurely made their way back to the camp, recounting all the while their hard-fought battle in the south against the stalwart Samsaptakas. Krishna and Arjuna reveled in their victory. Krishna slapped Arjuna on the back again and again. But as they approached the Pandava camp, a cloudless sky gave out a thunderclap. Arjuna saw this as an ill omen and immediately knew something was amiss. At the camp, they entered a somber world. No musicians played tunes to soothe weary warriors at day's end. A silence hung over the regal tents like a tomb. Everywhere they looked, warriors sat plunged in grief. Usually Abhimanyu was the first to greet his father. Now, no one greeted him. Men only turned their eyes from him.

Arjuna jumped from his chariot and ran toward the royal tent. He found Yudhisthira sitting, staring into space, surrounded by Bhima, Nakula, Sahadev and other leaders. He scanned their agonized faces.

"Where's. . . Abhimanyu?" Arjuna could hardly get out the words. His tongue weighed heavy in his mouth. His mind ceased. He felt encased in a soundless, motionless landscape. Then he heard himself scream, "Where is my son?"

Painfully, Yudhisthira explained the events that led up to Abhimanyu's death. He told how Jayadratha cut them off, and how Abhimanyu alone entered the chakra vyuha, and how, in the final moment, he was outnumbered by many maharathas, and how they all attacked him at once.

Arjuna was beside himself. "Jayadratha! That wretch! When we lived in exile, he slipped into our forest hermitage one day and tried to kidnap Draupadi. We captured him. We forgave his trespasses and spared his life. And this is how he repays us. . . And you, my brothers, where was your resolve? And where were your weapons? Were they drawn? Or do you keep them only to impress others?. . . Perhaps I am the foolish one. I thought you were all able warriors. Why else would I leave my son in your care?. . . O my son, my son of sweet words and smiling eyes. You were always at ease with yourself. My child, I would go to the court of Death for you." Hot tears streamed from Arjuna's eyes. "Krishna, you know everything. Why didn't you tell me my son needed my help?

Krishna was silent.

Arjuna sank to the ground, sobbing uncontrollably. "If I had only known. If I had only known. I would have gone to him in an instant."

"My friend," Krishna began slowly, "this is the way of a warrior. You cannot expect otherwise. Your son died a glorious death, saving many lives in the process. He will attain the highest celestial regions meant for heroes who do not retreat in the face of adversity." Krishna's words overflowed with love for Arjuna.

Arjuna did not speak for a long moment. He took a deep breath and found the resolve to go on. "That may be, my friend. But I promise you this. Tomorrow, before the sun sets, I will slay Jayadratha. If he's alive at day's end I have no right to be called a kshatriya. If I do not achieve my goal, I will gladly enter fire and I will curse myself to attain the hellish regions reserved for those who slay their own mothers or fathers; or for those who envy the kindhearted; or for those who are betrayers of trust, or speak falsehoods, or accept bribes; or for those who are vile and wicked, or who insult the godly. This is my vow. Let it be known to one and all."

* * * * *

The next morning a headless horseman holding a mace emerged from the rising sun and rode across the sky. The warriors on the battlefield shivered upon seeing the apparition.

The Kauravas were on the defensive. They simply had to hold out until the end of day. Then Arjuna would have to eat his words and enter fire. The battle wore on tediously. In the afternoon the sun blazed. The fighting subsided and warriors rested as vultures feasted on their dead comrades nearby. With Krishna driving the chariot, Arjuna had fought his way through enemy ranks. Now, Krishna also stopped to rest, water and groom the horses. But water was scarce. Arjuna paced about, searching the ground. He stopped abruptly and shot arrows into the earth, bringing forth water, creating a pond replete with lotuses, fish and swans. Next, with his arrows, Arjuna created a domed hall to safely contain the pond. And there, Krishna lounged as if he were at a resort rather than on a battlefield. The Kauravas looked on with mounting envy and, after much bickering, launched an attack. Arjuna fought them off until Krishna finished his nap and readied the horses and chariot.

After a time, the sun made its western descent, down toward the Asta Hills. Jayadratha had been anxious all day long even though Duryodhan had placed a thousand warriors as his personal guards. Jayadratha would only find solace when the day was done.

Arjuna's chariot again moved through a landscape littered with the bodies of warriors, horses, and elephants. They passed broken chariots bedecked with jewels and fineries its owners would never use again. On all sides, Kaurava warriors closed in. But Arjuna and Krishna were intent on slaying Jayadratha, and they penetrated deeper behind enemy lines. The attacks against them grew fiercer and their faces and clothes were caked with dust raised from the movements of men and animals. Yudhisthira, Bhima, Satyaki and their troops maneuvered in place to support Arjuna as Krishna steered their chariot through many encounters.

The sun descended quickly. It practically touched the mountain peaks and Jayadratha's heart pounded in hopes of eluding Arjuna's wrath. Jayadratha felt that surely he was now safe. But he did not know Krishna's potency. Krishna, that supreme magician, conjured up an illusion by covering the sun while at the same time creating a false sun which immediately set beneath the mountains.

A cheer arose from the Kaurava ranks. Wildly ecstatic and waving their turbans, they fearlessly ran toward Arjuna, dancing and shouting. Jayadratha joined the jubilation. A sense of relief coursed through him and he danced for joy. Arjuna would now have to enter fire.

Krishna leaned back in the chariot and reassured Arjuna and told him to be vigilant. Krishna cautioned him. "Cut off his head, but don't let it touch the ground." And he told Arjuna why: "*At Jayadratha's birth, a Celestial warned his father that his son would die by having his head cut off. Naturally, his father was disturbed by the son's fate. The father was not only a king, but a great mystic as well. So he crafted a curse. 'That man who causes my son's head to fall on the ground will immediately have his own head cracked into a thousand pieces.' Later, his father gave Jayadratha the throne and repaired to a forest ashram not far from here where he sits today in meditation.*"

With the nod of his head, Krishna dismissed the false sun, and the real sunset reappeared. The sun's upper rim still protruded from the mountains. The warriors were stunned and confused. They all tried to rush Arjuna. At this crucial moment Arjuna released Shiva's powerful Pasupata weapon, which severed his enemy's head. The last thing Jayadratha saw was that last sunray lingering above the mountains. Sending one arrow after another, Arjuna shot the head out of the valley and sent it flying into the lap of Jayadratha's father, sitting deep in meditation at his ashram. The father was startled and frightened by the bloody ball in his lap. He frantically knocked it to the ground. At that moment, the poor man's head burst into a thousand pieces.

Mahabharata: The Eternal Quest

* * * * *

Consumed with fury, the impassioned warriors continued fighting after sunset, against tradition and the rules of engagement. When darkness fell, thousands of torches sparkled throughout the valley. Ghatotkaca had waited for this opportunity, for a Rakshasas' strength increased at night. He made his way across the battlefield toward Karna whose arrows rained havoc on the Pandava forces. Ghatotkaca's head was a coppery hue, with deep, blood-red eyes, a thick nose, and pointed ears. Like all Rakshasas, his mouth curved around his face from ear to ear. He wore an ornate headdress with gold lacing that hung down the back of his broad shoulders. The Rakshasa driver of his chariot looked equally fierce, and bloodthirsty vultures perched on the chariot's roof. Its rumbling wheels sounded like a death knell and warriors trembled at the sight of its approach.

But not Karna. His keen gaze followed the chariot as it came across the valley. Karna waited eagerly. Duryodhan, however, felt uneasy. He saw the threat to Karna, and decided to pit Rakshasa against Rakshasa. Duryodhan called for Alamvashu, a demon Rakshasa he kept in reserve. The demon sprang forth, smashing all the Pandava chariots in his path, and headed straight for Ghatotkaca. Many warriors melted into the night to avoid him.

Alamvashu was a giant of a Rakshasa and loomed over Ghatotkaca. Warriors gathered and held their torches high to witness the fight. The Kauravas chuckled and gave one another assuring glances. The Rakshasas struck each other with an array of weapons. They moved effortlessly across the land and sky as they conjured up many forms and illusions to deceive one another. They could even change their own forms. A spectacle unfolded. One became a wild fire; the other became a towering wave. One became a gathering of sinister clouds; the other, a whirlwind to push the clouds away. One became thunder; the other, an impenetrable mountain. One became the sun; the other an eclipse.

Ghatotkaca suddenly stretched his arms forward across the sky to reach past the illusions. He seized Alamvashu by the neck and threw him to the ground. Ghatotkaca pounded the demon's chest with his foot, knocking the breath from his lungs, and in one swift motion, he severed the demon's head with his razor-sharp scimitar. Roaring in victory, Ghatotkaca hurled his opponent's head, dripping with blood, toward Duryodhan's chariot. The Kauravas were panic-stricken.

Ghatotkaca again turned his attention toward Karna. The time had reached the midnight hour when Rakshasas were most powerful. But Karna was ready for him. He drew his bow back to its fullest extent and sent forth a stream of arrows. But the arrows barely pierced the Rakshasa's thick skin. Ghatotkaca let fly his own arrows, one of which struck Karna, who, without interrupting his attack, ripped the arrow from his shoulder. They fought on, circling one another, looking for the other's weaknesses. Ghatotkaca hurled clubs, battleaxes, and wheels from smashed chariots at Karna. Karna easily deflected them with his arrows. Neither one of them could gain the upper hand.

With a constant stream of arrows, Karna shot Ghatotkaca's horses dead and destroyed his chariot and struck the Rakshasa prince again and again. Ghatotkaca fled into the sky, his body so riddled with arrows that he looked like a bizarre, flying porcupine. But still, the Rakshasa's terrible laugher sent shivers of fear through all who heard it. "I'll be back," he cried out.

*****

Duryodhan heard a commotion behind him. He looked back as his forces stepped aside and gravely opened up a path for a troop of strange visitors. From out of the dark, the cannibals arrived at the battlefield riding mangy horses, and led by their Rakshasa chieftain, Alayudha. He wore a shimmering crown, and a long furry coat with bones hanging on all sides that clattered as he moved. Alayudha was intrigued by this battle raging on at such an ungodly hour. Unlike Rakshasas, humans did not usually fight in the dark since they did not have the eyes for it. To Duryodhan's surprise, the Rakshasa chieftain offered his services to the Kauravas.

"I have a bone to pick with the Pandavas," Alayudha explained with a raw, aching voice. "Years ago, Bhima and his brothers killed my dear friend Hidimba after they invaded his land. And Ghatotkaca, Hidimbi's half-breed, with his high morals, is a blight on us Rakshasas. Our people become confused whenever that rogue spouts his profanities about kindness and compassion, taught to him by the Pandavas. He even tries to change our nature. The sooner he is dispatched to hell the better. So tell your warriors to stand down. We night raiders will finish them off."

Duryodhan was thrilled. It would all soon be over for the Pandavas. Looking at these ghastly cannibals, he almost felt sorry for his cousins. But he wouldn't allow himself to miss out on the action.

"All of our warriors will fight together to defeat the Pandavas."

"So be it! And soon enough, we'll gorge on their fresh corpses and drink it down with the blood from their severed heads," added Alayudha. "Will you join us?"

Duryodhan graciously declined.

In the meantime, Bhima, accompanied by Dristadyumna, Nakula, Sahadev and the Panchala warriors, stealthily took their positions. Their spies had earlier warned them of the approaching Rakshasas, giving the Pandavas a brief time to plan an action. Now, as the Rakshasa troop started across the valley, their horses snorting the cold night air, Bhima catapulted into their midst and began to unceremoniously smash their brains in with his club. Panchala bowmen, who had lain hidden among the dead, rose up and unleashed a fury of arrows into their ranks. Ghatotkaca and his band of Rakshasas descended from the sky like bats out of hell.

Twirling his scimitar above his head, Ghatotkaca further decimated the enemy. He sought out Alayudha and cut off his horse's head with one clean stroke. Alayudha stared uncomprehendingly at his headless horse, and he also lost his head as the horse collapsed in a heap to the ground. The last blow came when Nakula and Sahadev lead a charge of horsemen. Their swords ran with blood. Bedlam permeated the battlefield. The startled Rakshasa troop hardly had time to respond before many of them lay dead. The remainder cried piteously and melted into the night.

Once again a severed head landed abruptly before Duryodhan. It was the second gift Ghatotkaca had sent him that night.

In the end, all of Alayudha's boasting didn't amount to much.

* * * * *

Earlier, Duryodhan had been certain about the outcome of the battle; certain he and his brothers would enjoy a long life. Now he dreaded the night and cursed it under his breath. He looked up. Countless stars blanketed a silky sky. The universe displayed itself, majestic and serene. Beneath the stars the armies struggled; an ebb and flow of warriors in a frenzied desire for victory. Forces pressed against each other, grinding each other down. On both sides, the toll was horrific.

Once again Ghatotkaca turned his attention toward Karna. But as the two fought neither of them prevailed over the other. Changing his strategy and employing his mystic powers, the Rakshasa prince vanished from sight. No one knew from where he would strike next. With lightning speed, Karna shot an incessant flow of arrows upward in all directions. The Kauravas prayed that Karna, with his prowess and cunning, could escape the Rakshasa's wrath.

An ominous, red cloud suddenly appeared over the Kaurava forces. Before anyone could determine its purpose, the cloud poured down spears, swords, clubs, axes and stones. Men, horses and elephants dropped where they stood. Where a moment before they surged with energy, bodies lay lifeless, weapons lodged in their backs, their heads bashed in, and limbs broken. Streams of blood flowed everywhere. Others, barely alive, lay wailing in agony, and jackals howled their response from the distant mountains.

Karna remained focused, shooting his arrows one after another, smashing weapons as they descended from the sky. He saw no other recourse than to reach for his most cherished weapon, Indra's celestial Vasavi. This weapon could easily track down its prey. No one could escape it. Karna had been saving it to use on Arjuna, but to halt this carnage from Ghatotkaca, he had to use it at once. A chilling wind began to blow and lightening streaked across the sky. When Ghatotkaca spied the Vasavi glowing in Karna's hand, he felt fear for the first time. He tried to flee further into the sky, but it was too late. Karna released the weapon that went straight through Ghatotkaca's heart. The Rakshasa and all his creations were instantly vanquished in a cataclysmic burst of light above the valley. Ghatotkaca, in his last conscious effort, expanded himself into an immense form and crushed thousands of Kaurava warriors upon falling to the earth.

* * * * *

Seeing the Rakshasa prince lying dead, the Kauravas let out shouts of joy. But Duryodhan felt extremely irritated. It was a dear price to pay. Duryodhan had expected another outcome. He'd been telling Karna for the last few days to use Indra's dart against Arjuna or even send it against Krishna. Each time, Karna had promised to use it the next day. But on the next day, either the opportunity never presented itself or the promise he had made slipped from his mind. Or perhaps Karna found comfort in simply possessing the weapon. In any event, Duryodhan suspected Krishna's trickery at play, just as he had fabricated the false sunset to kill Jayadratha. If Karna had only used it on Arjuna, he could have swayed the battle.

Now, the opportunity was lost, but at least Karna was alive. With his skill in combat, he alone could still defeat the Pandavas. Duryodhan reassured himself that he had nothing to worry about.

The Pandavas were grief stricken at Ghatotkaca's death. The inscrutable Krishna, however, declared, "This is a wonderful turn of events."

Arjuna, dumbfounded, looked at him. "Wonderful? Krishna, do you hear what you're saying? Ghatotkaca was such a dear friend and family member. He assisted us in many ways."

"Now he's assisted you again."

"Look at our men. Without Ghatotkaca our troops are trembling. They've lost their will to go on."

"My dear Arjuna, please hear me. Don't be morose. Ghatotkaca made a glorious sacrifice. To kill him, Karna spent his greatest weapon. A weapon that made him undefeatable. Now, we no longer live under its threat."

And Krishna began to dance joyfully.

* * * * *

The fighting was far from over. The armies continued to batter one another into the night. Warriors' bodies ached from fatigue. Many could hardly lift their weapons. Some, driven mad by the long and horrible hours of combat, attacked friend and foe alike. Arjuna took compassion on all the warriors and called upon them to stop fighting and rest awhile until the moon came up. His order went up and down the line. Even the Kaurava warriors were relieved and praised Arjuna for his thoughtfulness. They all knew he could very well do without sleep. The battlefield became eerily silent save for a horse's whinny or the distant cry of a jackal. Men slept in their chariots or on their elephants, or horses, or on the cold ground. Men who were on opposing sides now practically slept next to one another.

But the reprieve lasted only a few hours. In the dark of the early morning before sunrise, a full moon rose in the eastern sky. Duryodhan, wanting to get the upper hand, planned to strike first. He approached Drona who sat serenely in his chariot deep in meditation.

"It's time to take up our weapons." Drona did not stir, but Duryodhan knew he was listening. "Drona, just a word. You've been too lenient on the Pandavas. No one can match your prowess. You are the foremost of warriors. All of our men look up to you. You must forget the Pandavas were ever your students. You must set the example and show them no mercy." For good measure he added, "Your old enemy Drupada, is on this side of the valley. You can start with him."

Drona understood that Duryodhan wanted to incite his anger. "In our youth we were friends once," Drona recalled. "I, the son of a poor brahmin and he, heir to a kingdom. But he became intoxicated with power and later he turned his back on our friendship. When my son was first born, I struggled to provide for my family. I went to his palace to beg milk and food. He wouldn't even see me. All these years I could never forgive him."

Duryodhan smiled. He would have his way. He felt the anger surge in the old fighter.

Drona stood up and glared at Duryodhan. "Your greed is the cause of all this."

Duryodhan countered, "My family has maintained you for years. This is your duty to me. I only want what is rightfully mine."

"Then let the battle commence," Drona ordered, his chariot already in motion.

* * * * *

The sun came up without warning. Sounds of conches and bugles stirred the men from their slumber. Before many of them were even cognizant of where they were, the warriors found themselves in the thick of battle. Drona's chariot made its way across the field. His bloodthirsty arrows flew across the sky.

In the midst of fighting, warriors realized they had neglected their morning meditations. They stopped, faced east, and offered prayers on bended knees. A stillness blanketed the valley, and, briefly, the sun and moon, like friendly rivals, together occupied the eastern sky until gradually the moon faded from view.

Once again, the clashing sounds of battle pervaded the air and blood saturated the ground. Drona's arrows consistently found their marks and cut down countless warriors. Among them, Drupada, riddled with shafts, fell to the earth, as well as his three grandsons, Dristadyumna's sons, in the bloom of youth. Dead.

Drona circled back to pay his respects, saddened that it had to end this way.

* * * * *

Dristadyumna received the news from Nakula and Sahadev. He sank down into the seat on his chariot and buried his head in his hands. His father and all his sons, gone. It was too much to bear. His grief gave way to rage and he commanded the charioteer to drive forward, towards Drona. Nakula and Sahadev followed in their chariots on either side, sending forth arrows to protect Dristadyumna. But no one could stop Drona's rampage and the Pandavas were driven back by the constant flow of arrows from his bow. Yudhisthira, Bhima and Arjuna pulled over to Dristadyumna and the twins for a quick conference.

"I'm very sorry," Yudhisthira said of Dristadyumna's loss.

Dristadyumna ignored the condolence and asked, "What are we going to do about Drona? He won't let up. No one can stop him."

"Arjuna's the only one who can take him down," Nakula stated.

"No. I can't do it," Arjuna shot back. "I won't go up against my teacher."

"So, it's hopeless?" Sahadev countered.

"Listen to me," Krishna spoke up, and they turned toward him. "In one sense it *is* hopeless. As a warrior, Drona is unsurpassed. No one can defeat him. That is unless Drona, on his own, lays aside his weapons."

Nakula was curious. "Why would he do that?"

"The only way he'll give up the fight is when he hears his son is dead," said Krishna.

"But he's not dead," Yudhisthira interjected.

 "No. He's miles away, fighting at the far end of the valley. But if you declare that Ashwattama is dead, Drona will accept it as an unequivocal truth."

"I cannot speak a falsehood!" Yudhisthira insisted.

"You must. To speak a lie in order to save yourselves from annihilation is no sin."

The others heartily approved of Krishna's plan. Yudhisthira remained reluctant, even as he remembered Drona's blessing to him on the first day of battle: *I cannot be vanquished in battle, that is, unless I hear an unpalatable truth which causes me to lay down my weapons.* "It's still not right to do such a thing," Yudhisthira reflected.

But no one was listening.

Bhima took the initiative and immediately killed an elephant named Ashwattama and wandered across the battlefield brazenly declaring, "Ashwattama is dead. Ashwattama is dead."

When this news reached Drona's ears, he searched out Yudhisthira who was surrounded by his brothers and Dristadyumna. With his heart pounding wildly, Drona called out, "Yudhisthira, I want to hear it from your lips. Tell me. Is it true?"

Krishna gave Yudhisthira a hard look.

Yudhisthira answered, "Yes, it's true. Ashwattama. . . is dead." But while loudly saying the name Ashwattama, he had whispered beneath his breath, "the elephant."

Hearing of his son's death from Yudhisthira, Drona tossed aside his weapons and sat down in his chariot. He thought, *Why continue the fight? What is the value of comforts or fame or happiness.* Now, he wanted only to abandon this world. He closed his eyes in yogic meditation and he evoked Brahman by uttering the sacred syllable OM. Celestial melodies and hymns resounded in the sky to honor Drona and proclaim his glories.

Seeing Drona resigned to his fate, Dristadyumna seized the moment. He reached for his sword and ran toward Drona's chariot. Krishna, Yudhisthira, and Arjuna called out to him in desperation. "Dristadyumna. No." "Don't touch him." "It's not becoming of you."

But Dristadyumna did not hear their pleas. Thirsting for revenge, he rushed forward, knocking Kauravas out of his way. He grabbed Drona by the hair, and with one swift motion of his sword, cut off his head. Yudhisthira and Arjuna watched in horror as their teacher's body slumped to the ground, his blood overflowed upon the earth.

Krishna told Yudhisthira and Arjuna, "Drona had himself already given up his own life, and his spirit- soul flew from his body, even before Dristadyumna's sword touched him."

* * * * *

Tears of rage streamed down Ashwattama's face. His breathing was heavy and his mind swirled in disbelief. His father was killed because of Yudhisthira's ignoble words and Dristadyumna's heinous act. He thought, *How could they live with themselves? Why don't their bodies burn to ashes from their lie?* Ashwattama raised his hand to get the attention of the Kaurava warriors. "Today I will avenge my father's murder. Today I'll smite down those whose lives are rotting from the inside out. No one can stand in my way. Today the Pandava forces will fall before my might like a forest of trees."

The Kauravas roared in approval, a roar that swept across the valley like rolling thunder. Ashwattama calmed himself. He freed his mind from any malicious thoughts and touched his fingertips to water as he invoked his most powerful weapon, the Narayana; a weapon to be used only with clarity of mind lest it destroy its wielder; a weapon that would annihilate even those who appeared to be invincible; a weapon granted him by his father who received it as a boon from Lord Narayana. No one in its path would survive.

Violent winds blew. The earth and mountains trembled. Rivers flowed upstream. Clouds rumbled. And within this cacophony, the distinct and eerie neighing of a horse.

'That's Ashwattama,' Krishna told Arjuna in a whisper. "At birth he made that sound."

The Pandava forces readied themselves in whatever way they thought they could. The sky darkened as many thousands of arrows, spears, battleaxes, razor-sharp discs and iron balls gathered high above the valley. Slowly, in one motion, this arsenal descended upon the Pandava ranks. Warriors did not know which way to turn. Should they flee or stand and fight? Their breathing ceased. Their hearts pounded. Their senses became numbed. Many warriors shivered uncontrollably.

"We had better retreat," one warrior said.

"Retreat? We might as well enter a funeral pyre," Yudhisthira replied. He blamed himself for having tricked Drona into giving up the fight.

Bhima boldly held up his mace and shouted. "A warrior fights to the death."

Krishna called from Arjuna's chariot. "We will neither retreat nor enter fire nor fight until death."

"So then what?" challenged Bhima.

Krishna explained the secret. "If you run, the Narayana weapon will cut you down. If you resist, it only grows stronger. The only way to come out of this unscathed is to lay down your weapons and fall flat on the ground to honor this great force."

Krishna's instructions went up and down the line: the Narayana, intended only for warriors, and not for their animals nor chariots nor non-combatants, could only be pacified with humility.

Searing lights emanated from the Narayana's sharp blades, searching out its intended targets. The weapon picked up speed as it approached the earth and hurled toward the Pandavas. The warriors fell to their knees and embraced the earth, murmuring prayers as never before.

Furious with Krishna's command, Bhima stood his ground and lifted his club. "Why should I submit. With my mace, I can crush mountains. I am imbued with the strength of ten thousand elephants from the rasakund given to me by the Nagas. I alone will stand in opposition to the Narayana."

A strange, unbearable force preceded the Narayana weapons. Bhima began to shake as the force surrounded him, but still, the mighty Pandava held his ground. Seeing his stubbornness, both Arjuna and Krishna defied the Narayana and ran at Bhima, tackling him to the ground.

Krishna looked Bhima in the eyes. "Give up your pride. Be still. Don't even think about resisting. The Narayana will detect it and hunt you down."

The multitude of weapons swarmed over the battlefield again and again, looking for a challenger, but found none. Finally, the Narayana departed and the Pandava warriors jumped to their feet, ready for battle.

Duryodhan shouted to Ashwattama. "Call back the Narayana. Now we have them."

Ashwattama looked cheerless. "Once it's gone I can't call it back."

* * * * *

Hours before Drona had been killed, Dushasana and Sahadev had engaged intensely in combat. Sahadev had sent a torrent of arrows toward Dushasana, but his charioteer intercepted the shafts and fell dead. Without a driver, the horses and chariot sped recklessly across the field. Dushasana could barely retrieve the reins. He dropped his bow and sweat poured down his face as he grabbed the reins and brought his steeds under control. Sahadev was close behind and would not give him a moment's rest. Dushasana clearly glimpsed his opponent's thirst for victory. He felt like a hunted animal. Death breathed down his neck. He wanted it all to go away. In the last moment, Karna appeared out of nowhere and miraculously intervened and drove Sahadev off.

Dushasana had been drenched in sweat. If that wasn't enough, then came the death of Drona, his beloved teacher. Several days earlier, the Grandsire had fallen before his very eyes. Dushasana's mind screamed. His own mortality stared him in the face. He couldn't shake it. His will cracked. He hastily fled the battlefield so no one could see his fear, and his body trembled uncontrollably for a long time. Duryodhan found him, and only after much urging did he return to the fight.

* * * * *

The day after Drona's death, Duryodhan made Karna commander of the Kaurava forces. Karna fell at Duryodhan's feet and swore his undying allegiance. Immediately, Karna jumped into action. He sent the remaining thirty thousand Samsaptakas against Arjuna to kill him, or at least weaken him enough so that he may kill Arjuna himself. Karna also sent thousands of warriors against Bhima. He knew Arjuna and Bhima were the only ones who stood in their path toward victory. They must be stopped at all costs.

On the morning of the seventeenth day Arjuna and Bhima were still alive. Arjuna killed Karna's son in battle. Karna raged against the death of his dear boy. He wanted revenge. "Where is Arjuna?" he demanded to know. "I'll give a hundred villages to the man who leads me to him."

But Karna didn't have to look far. His army scattered as Arjuna fast approached with arrows flying. Karna held his ground against the Pandava prince. Their chariots were almost identical: both were drawn by four white horses; the floor and seat of both were covered with the skins of tigers they each had killed; both were arrayed with the most extraordinary weapons. At long last, Arjuna and Karna confronted one another, and, just as quickly, lost one another in a cloud of dust raised by horses and chariots.

Emerging from the dust cloud, Karna found Yudhisthira instead, and ferociously attacked him, sending him all of his anger and forcing him to flee the battlefield. Shaken, Yudhisthira returned to his tent at the Pandava camp. He remembered when he first laid eyes on Karna so many years ago. He had sensed the grave and formidable threat that lurked in that warrior. All that time he had harbored an irrational fear of Karna. He never told anyone. Now, his fear had indeed become a reality. Karna had killed Ghatotkaca. It seemed he was unstoppable. Yudhisthira closed his eyes to shut out the world. But his quiet was interrupted when Arjuna and Krishna entered. He was relieved to see them. He felt his brother had come to save him from his obsession. He rushed to Arjuna. "Is Karna dead?"

"Why would you think that?"

"Then what are you doing back here?" asked Yudhisthira, almost challengingly.

"I came to ask you that very same question."

"You must kill Karna without delay."

"You ran from the battlefield! You're in no position to tell me what to do."

"Yes, I am afraid of Karna, but so are you. You're afraid to fight with him. You might as well give your magnificent Gandiva bow to someone else or throw it into the fire."

"I should kill you for saying that."

"You're an expert killer, aren't you?"

"That may be. But not on my account. I've practically killed half the Kaurava ranks for your sake. Even today, thousands are dying because of you, you who so foolishly lost our kingdom in a game of dice."

Yudhisthira fell silent, stunned by the harsh truth of it. He came to a decision and a loving gaze appeared on his face. "Arjuna, I don't deserve your loyalty. Your words give me resolve. There's nothing more for me here. I'm going to the forest to live in seclusion. I will spend the rest of my life fasting and praying for forgiveness. Let Bhima rule the kingdom. It's best you forget I exist."

As Yudhisthira tried to remove his protective mail, Krishna took his hand. "O King, please listen to me. You are the personification of Dharma. I know your only desire is to live a life of virtue. You are so noble you didn't even want to speak a lie to gain the upper hand. You understand that even to kill or harm an animal is a sin, let alone to kill another human being. I must confess, this is all my doing. I have engaged you and your brothers in my mission to destroy those who are drunk on power. Because of their unlimited greed, they have become a heavy burden to Mother Earth. The Earth shall replenish herself by drinking the blood of these miscreants. Take heart. Finish what you've started."

Arjuna fell to the ground and touched his head to his brother's feet. "I'm sorry for the way I spoke, that I threatened to kill you."

Yudhisthira took Arjuna by the shoulders and raised him up. "You said what needed to be said."

With tears in their eyes they embraced each other.

"My brother, my King." Arjuna's eyes sparkled through the tears.

"I'm ready," said Yudhisthira.

Krishna was already waiting for them by the chariots.

* * * * *

That day, Bhima found Dushasana and smashed him with his mace and threw him from his chariot. His foot pressed down on Dushasana's throat. The Kaurava gasped desperately for air and Bhima laughed mightily. Dushasana could hear nothing else, for Bhima's horrible laughter drowned out the din of battle.

"Remember my vow to you on the day of that evil dice match?" asked Bhima. He grabbed Dushasana's right arm. "You used this arm to drag Draupadi by the hair into the Great Hall that night, didn't you? You piece of filth!" Bhima violently ripped the arm from its socket and thrashed its owner with it, yelling all the while, "I've killed most of your brothers and soon I'll kill the rest."

Dushasana convulsed in agony. Finally, Bhima stabbed him in the heart and ripped open his chest. As Dushasana slipped from this world, Bhima drank the blood that gushed from his heart. When he finished, Bhima looked at the inert body. "So you've taken shelter of Death," he observed. "It's a shame I can't do anything more to you."

* * * * *

Arjuna and Karna were like rays of light, searching each other out, speeding toward one another. Each with an insatiable thirst for victory. Each confident of their own prowess. Each releasing showers of arrows. But as the day wore on neither could outdo the other. Karna's chariot weaved across the battlefield. Suddenly, to his dismay, it came to an abrupt halt. One of his wheels was mired in the blood-soaked earth. Karna wondered why this was happening now at this crucial moment. He had always been righteous, and does not Righteousness protect the righteous? Arjuna's shafts whizzed past his head. It seemed like a dream. Karna had no time to lose. He jumped down and tried desperately to extract his wheel.

Krishna observed Karna's plight. "Mother Earth has grabbed hold of his wheel and won't let go. Arjuna, this is the moment. Strike him down."

Krishna turned the chariot hard and Arjuna readied his bow. Karna looked on, incredulous. "Arjuna, what are you doing? Wait! We can resume our combat when I get my wheel out of the mud. You know the rules of battle. What you are doing is against the code of a warrior."

"What is this that I hear?" Krishna asked coyly. "When it suits you, you adamantly oppose an unjust act against yourself or against your friends. But you do not speak up against the injustice of others. Where was your sense of justice when the Pandavas were cheated out of their kingdom? Or when Draupadi was dragged into the assembly by her hair? Or when six warriors surrounded Abhimanyu and cut him down? No my friend, you'll be treated the way you have allowed others to be treated."

Karna had no reply for Krishna. But he was ever diligent and seized the moment. By the use of a mantra, Karna invoked the deadly Brahmastra weapon. Seeing this, Arjuna invoked Agni's celestial weapon, which resembled fire, to immediately overwhelm the Brahmastra. Karna countered with a powerful water weapon. He also released another weapon that shrouded the land in darkness and caused fierce winds to blow and confusion to reign. Time enough for his shaft to strike Arjuna in the chest. Arjuna reeled back. All the warriors on the battlefield looked on with baited breath. Each side hoping their warrior would prevail. Arjuna made a supreme effort to collect his faculties. He let fly his Anjalika weapon which flashed like thunder and shook the earth so violently animals everywhere cried out in horror. Even the holy rishis trembled in fear. Arjuna's dreadful weapon descended upon Karna with the force of a hurricane and ripped off his head. All the warriors stood riveted as Karna's splendorous soul ascended into the sky and disappeared into the noonday sun overhead. Karna's father was waiting to greet him.

The remaining Kaurava warriors fled. There was no hope left for them. The Pandava warriors rejoiced. Victory was in sight.

* * * * *

On the eighteenth day, a thick pall of smoke hung over the battlefield. The Kaurava forces numbered in the hundreds of thousands, many times more than the Pandavas. But after Karna's death, they were dejected and powerless. Somehow or other, Duryodhan was still confident. Sakuni, more cautious, surrounded himself with ten thousand expert horse riders from Gandhar. They sought desperately to protect their master. They were renowned for fighting on horseback and their maneuvers astonished their enemies. Unfortunately, they allowed themselves to be caught amid the arrows of the Pandavas and soon their bodies littered the battlefield. Sakuni took an arrow from Sahadev through the neck. With arms flailing, he stepped forward and fell from his chariot. The Kaurava warriors panicked at the sight. Duryodhan tried to rally them for a charge, but to no avail. Whether attacking or fleeing, they did not go very far before they were all slaughtered by the long bows of the Pandava forces.

In the melee, Duryodhan's horse had been shot out from under him. He fled on foot and, carrying his weapons with him, he skirted past dead and dying warriors. The ground was soaked in blood and slippery. All around, chariots burned, the targets of flaming arrows. Vultures descended from the sky to claim corpses. Duryodhan's eyes darted here and there, seeking an escape from this inferno. His every muscle ached. The world that had been his was no more, and his spirit was shattered.

Duryodhan walked for several miles until he came upon a lake. There, he hid in the tall reeds. He tried to relax, but something was amiss. Then it struck him. The silence all around pressed upon him like a great weight. His head throbbed. Then he heard the braying of a donkey. Two men passed nearby with their animal.

Knowing a little of the mystic arts, Duryodhan created a cocoon for himself and sank beneath the waters and settled in. Hopefully, he wasn't seen. Within the lake Duryodhan felt secure. He allowed his thoughts to wander. His mind flashed over the events of the last eighteen days. This was no pleasure, this war. He had been warned many times. If he had only listened to his elders, it would have been different. Or he could have just been more focused and tried harder to achieve his goal. But the trick was to not blame himself. *What could I do if Destiny was against me? And that scoundrel Krishna, he ruined everything. Krishna will have to pay for his misdeeds.* Duryodhan was at peace. He felt relieved. He had done the best he could.

* * * * *

Yudhisthira and his brothers scanned the horizon for Duryodhan. Only debris and dead bodies. Vultures and jackals moving about. In the distance, they saw two men pulling a donkey with a great load on its back. The men were heading right toward them. Every so often, they tugged at the donkey even though he was moving briskly along.

"Should we tell them what we saw?" said one man to the other.

"Of course. It's a piece of information I'm sure they're eager to get their hands on."

"But he looked so pitiable scurrying off into the water."

"What we saw is worth something. I'm sure Yudhisthira will reward us kindly."

"It seems strange to get payment just for some information."

"You're a dullard. You only know how to work hard like this ass we're pulling. To make a living by your brain, rather than your brawn, is gentlemen's work."

"Listen, what I do is honest work. And I don't think it's gentlemanly to put someone into trouble."

"Duryodhan has made a career out of putting the Pandavas into trouble. He deserves everything that's coming to him. If we can be the better off for it, I say, why not? Now keep your mouth shut and let me do the talking."

The Pandavas were overjoyed by the news the men supplied. Yudhisthira removed two gold bands from his arms and gave one to each of them.

* * * * *

The Pandavas and their remaining forces stood by the shores of the lake.

Yudhisthira called out, "Duryodhan, why are you hiding? This is not at all becoming a kshatriya. Come out and meet us in combat."

Duryodhan hesitated for a long moment. "I'm not hiding. I'm exhausted. I've come here to rest. Leave me alone for now and after a while I will fight all of you in battle."

"We're ready to fight now, confident that whoever dies on this hallowed ground of Kurukshetra will attain heaven. Come out and fight for the kingdom."

"My brothers and my friends are all gone. What need have I for a kingdom now? You can have it. Enjoy yourself."

Yudhisthira was annoyed by his offer. "Duryodhan, you're in no position to give anything away. Come before me now and defeat me in battle."

Duryodhan sprang out of the water like a lion. "I'll give you a fight, if that's what you want. I'll fight with each of you brothers one at a time."

"My dear King," Yudhisthira admonished him, "you didn't give Abhimanyu that chance when he asked for it. But we'll be more accommodating. Choose the weapon, and choose any one of us to fight with. If you win you can have your kingdom."

Krishna groaned. "Yudhisthira, are you ready to throw away your hard-earned victory with such a casual offer? This is the height of folly. Duryodhan may yet snatch the kingdom away."

Everyone noticed that Duryodhan's bodily vigor and luster became restored by this opportunity to defeat his lifelong rivals. Duryodhan reached for the mace he hid in the reeds. "This is my choice of weapons. None of you are equal to me in use of the mace except perhaps for Bhima. Therefore, I will only fight with him. What do you say Bhima? Are you ready to die today?"

"I say to my brothers and all of our warriors - stand back and do not lift a finger. Duryodhan, it will give me great pleasure to personally kill you today. My mace has helped me slay thousands of warriors in this battle. It will not be difficult to slay one more."

While they readied themselves, Krishna approached Bhima. "Duryodhan possesses great skill in the use of the mace. Be careful, he is very powerful."

"More powerful than I?" Bhima asked, agitated by Krishna's statement.

"Don't underestimate him," Krishna cautioned. "Duryodhan has a secret. Before he came to Kurukshetra, his mother attempted to make him invincible. She lifted her blindfold and glanced upon him. Because she had kept her eyes bound for so many years, her glance had great power, and that brief glance of hers made his body like iron. His thighs, however, are vulnerable, for they were covered when Gandhari looked upon him."

"To strike a blow beneath the belt is against kshatriya principles."

"That may be, but remember your vow at the dice match. It's your only chance to succeed."

"My aim is to defeat Duryodhan fairly in this fight."

Duryodhan and Bhima ran at each other. They looked like two storm clouds colliding, two maddened elephants, two raging oceans, two furious winds, two blazing suns, two insurmountable mountain heights, and two graceful dancers, each swinging his mace. They were two warriors exquisitely matched. Each felt a supreme satisfaction, having found a worthy opponent in the other. Their maces clashed together, sounding like thunderbolts. Each longed for victory. But neither could find it.

Krishna told Arjuna, "Duryodhan is like a cornered animal who will fight like anything to snatch victory away from you. He has to be put down."

Arjuna felt the same way and tapped his thigh conspicuously to remind Bhima.

Bhima had stopped fighting to taunt Duryodhan. "Is this all you have? Come on. What are you waiting for? I've killed everyone of your brothers. I sought them out and struck them down. You're the last one."

"What's the value of your boasting? Is that supposed to make me afraid of you?"

They lunged at each other, striking and dodging.

Bhima continued his taunting. "Remember how you treated Draupadi in the Great Hall? How your bunch tried to strip her naked? Remember the vow that I made?"

Before he knew it, Bhima was struck forcefully on the chest. He was stunned and he did all he could to dodge another blow, but Duryodhan's mace still caught him on the side of his forehead. Bhima scrambled for his life. He realized he could not hesitate for a moment, least his enemy gain the upper hand. He put all his weight behind his swing and landed a blow that sent Duryodhan hurtling to the ground. At that moment, Bhima intentionally let down his guard. Duryodhan, seeing a likely opportunity, charged towards him, whirling his mace. The trap was set. In the last second, Duryodhan saw the ruse and rolled head over heels to avoid the blow from Bhima's mace. Those titanic warriors circled one another. Bhima searched for a weakness or an opening, but found none. Duryodhan laughed. The Kaurava King rushed forward and flew high into the air, intending to land a fatal blow on his opponent's head using the full force of gravity. In an instant, Bhima brought up his mace and smashed Duryodhan between the thighs, and the last of Dhritarastra's sons came crashing to the ground.

The earth rumbled. Jackals howled. The day was ending and the battle was done. Victory had been secured. Silhouetted against the twilight, myriad headless creatures danced a strange jig. The vast sky vibrated with murmuring voices, and the Pandava forces trembled.

The Pandavas were about to leave. Duryodhan still clung to life. Lying on the ground, tormented with pain, he managed to raise up his head and shoulders and call out to Krishna. "So this is who you really are. You, who are supposed to be so noble and wise. Have you no shame?"

Krishna turned back to him. He was happy to see that Duryodhan still had some fight left in him.

Duryodhan continued. "You told Bhima how to defeat me, didn't you? And you urged Arjuna to attack Karna while he was trying desperately to get his chariot wheel out of the mud. You insisted that the righteous Yudhisthira tell a lie. You created a false sunset which caused Jayadratha to be killed. You encouraged the Pandavas to violate the rules of engagement. And though you vowed not to fight, you still attacked Bhismadev. I know all about your tricks and machinations. You could never have won if you fought by virtuous means."

Krishna looked surprised. "Duryodhan, I'm sure you are well acquainted with virtue, you who are deluded by greed and pride. But this war, after all, was of your choosing. So don't be angry with me. I am not the cause of your misfortune. I'm only holding up a mirror to reflect your cheating and conniving over so many long years, including on this battlefield. When you live by deceit you will be vanquished by deceit. So if you feel misfortune has overtaken you, you should look within yourself for the reason." Krishna turned to the Pandavas. "Let's go."

Yudhisthira saw Duryodhan shivering and in pain. "We can't leave him here like this."

Duryodhan spoke up. "Yudhisthira, don't worry about me. You'll face your own death soon enough. Each of us must die."

And Krishna added, "Yet, each man dies in his own way."

* * * * *

After the Pandava forces left, Ashwattama, Kripa and Kritavarma, walking their horses, made their way to where Duryodhan lay dying. They were all that remained of the once mighty Kaurava forces. Ashwattama cried out in grief at the sight of his king, bloodied, in great pain, and trembling uncontrollably.

Duryodhan tried to console him. "My friend, don't worry about me. My suffering will be over this very night. Shortly, I will be welcomed into that exalted, celestial region reserved for warriors who die on the battlefield."

In tears, Ashwattama fell to the ground and, holding Duryodhan tenderly, spoke into his ear. "My King, let me do one last thing for you. Tonight, I'll kill that wretch Dristadyumna. I'll kill the Pandavas. Tonight, I will wipe their clan from the face of the earth. This will be my gift to you."

Duryodhan, in the midst of his pain, released a smile. "Let it be so."

The three warriors climbed on their horses and headed for the Pandava camp, as Duryodhan steeled himself against cold death.

Chapter 13

The Night Raid

The Pandavas, Satyaki and Krishna rode to the Kaurava camp to survey the spoils of war. Although his brothers were impressed with the abundance of wealth they found, to Yudhisthira these spoils were just so many things of no particular value.

"Let's return to our camp," said Bhima, weary from his fight with Duryodhan.

"We're not going back tonight," Krishna told the Pandavas.

"What! Why not?" Bhima was afraid he would be deprived of his evening meal, and his fear proved to be true.

"Duryodhan was right. You couldn't have won if you had not repeatedly applied my tactics to confound the enemy," Krishna admitted. "You won by unfair means."

"We won," Bhima said flatly, "and that's all that counts."

"That's true. Even the Celestials, when greatly outnumbered, use duplicitous means to defeat their enemies. Nevertheless, we will proceed to the banks of the Oghavati River to perform penance, to fast and meditate throughout the night."

Bhima was exasperated. "Krishna, can't we do that tomorrow?"

"There's no time to lose," Krishna replied, ignoring Bhima's question.

When they arrived at the Oghavati, the sun had already set and soon the last light faded from the western sky. Without any blankets or comforts, the cold night surrounded the small group and chilled them to the bone.

And Bhima's belly rumbled.

* * * * *

Ashwattama could barely put one foot in front of the other. His body ached, but he had to go on. He had promised Duryodhan. He pushed forward by sheer willpower. Kripa and Kritavarma were reluctant to go with him. They wanted no part in this immoral night attack. Ashwattama continued alone and, under the cloak of darkness, stole past the sentries and entered the sprawling camp of his enemy. The remnant of Pandava warriors still alive were exhausted and buried in sleep. Ashwattama had nothing to worry about from the few animal tenders, cooks and servants who were finishing their duties at a long day's end.

He entered Dristadyumna's tent and beheld him asleep in his comfortable bed, oblivious of the vengeance he was about to receive. Ashwattama savored the moment. He reached for his dagger, but then put it back in its sheath. *A dagger would be too good for this murderer. Dristadyumna is a dog and he should die a dog's death.* Instead, Ashwattama grabbed him forcefully by the hair and dragged him from his bed, and rubbed his face into the ground. Steeped in slumber, Dristadyumna could hardly defend himself as Ashwattama kicked him relentlessly in his face, neck, stomach and groin.

Dristadyumna was barely conscious. "Please, not like this," he pleaded. "Kill me with a weapon so I may die a warrior's death."

Ashwattama pulled him up by the hair and looked into his terror-stricken eyes. "You don't deserve any better than this. Go to hell!" And he kicked him in the head repeatedly, passionately, until Dristadyumna's body lay lifeless.

Ashwattama reached for his sword and stalked into one tent after another, gleefully butchering the sleeping warriors. Soon he came upon the Pandavas' tent. The Pandavas' five youthful sons were sound asleep. Ashwattama stabbed them to death where they lay. Somewhere, a warning bell sounded danger and men hurriedly jumped up from their slumber. Ashwattama strolled through the camp, slaughtering men, whether they were awake or asleep. Sikhandi came rushing out of one tent and into the blade of Ashwattama's sword. Sikhandi dropped to his knees, gushing blood and unable to speak. Ashwattama pushed him away with his foot and moved on, bathed in the blood of his victims.

A thousand warriors were up and armed. But none could tell friend from foe, and men desperately fought one another. Horses and elephants became frightened and ran wild, crushing everyone in their path. Kripa and Kritavarma heard the commotion and crept closer. Emboldened, they felled anyone who tried to flee the camp. In the night's confusion, Ashwattama continued to wreak havoc. By daybreak, all those who had survived the eighteen days of intense warfare lay dead.

* * * * *

Patches of morning mist lay scattered across the valley.

The three returned to Duryodhan to bring him news of the night. Duryodhan had been vomiting blood, and its smell attracted jackals and vultures who gathered nearby. The jackals became especially aggressive, snapping at Duryodhan's feet. He kept them at bay with great difficulty. When he arrived, Ashwattama pelted them with rocks and they scampered off.

"So what news do you have for me?" Duryodhan made a supreme effort to control his pain.

"It's done," Ashwattama boasted. "I killed Dristadyumna, Sikhandi and thousands more. I didn't see the Pandavas, but I killed their five sons."

Duryodhan seemed to come alive. "You did this for me. This is the best news. My friends, I look forward to that time when the four of us will be together in the celestial kingdom, where warriors who die on the battlefield reside." He looked contentedly upon the three survivors and thought on what they had achieved that night. "I would have loved to have been there. To see you cut them down."

"My King" Ashwattama explained in wide-eyed delirium, "the Pandava youths were already down, and I didn't want to disturb them from their sleep." And he laid a bag before Duryodhan. "Their heads." He took out one to show his master. "My gift to you."

Duryodhan was perplexed. "You. . . killed them as they slept?"

Ashwattama nodded, a contorted grin on his face.

Duryodhan looked at him in disbelief. He pushed the bag away. "Go. Go and take this far away from me. I want nothing to do with this heinous act."

Dejected, Ashwattama picked up the bag and turned to leave. He stopped and looked back. He deserved some recognition for risking his life and acting so boldly.

"Go!" shouted Duryodhan, and he breathed his last.

* * * * *

At the palace, Dhritarastra heard of Duryodhan's death and fell into Sanjay's arms. "Sanjaya, I am undone. I've lost my sons. . . What am I to do now? Ultimately, everyone will blame me for what has happened. People will treat me with contempt. It's not always easy to understand what is to be done and what is not to be done. Sanjaya, you must tell them, I never wanted this war. I never wanted any of this. I tried to save my boys. I tried to treat my brother's sons as I would my own. I tried to dissuade Duryodhan from his course, but he was strong-willed and would not listen to me. Not even to the advice and warnings of his mother. Years back, when news came that the Pandavas had escaped the flames of Varanavat, and that Arjuna had pierced the fish and won the hand of Draupadi,

I had no hope to save my sons. And when the Pandavas were cheated at dice and Draupadi was dishonored in the Great Hall, I had no hope to save my sons. And when the Pandavas returned from their years in exile with Krishna at their side, I had no hope to save my sons. Because of my blindness, I have been surrounded all my life by darkness, and now that darkness has turned into despair."

Tears flowed freely down Dhritarastra's cheeks as he pressed his face against Sanjaya's shoulder. Sanjaya held him and tried to comfort him. "My dear King, do not lament. You tried your best, as did the Grandsire and Drona and your brother Vidura. All this was ordained by Providence. Neither men nor gods can stop what Providence wills. Providence is but eternal Time. Time is the inexhaustible force at the root of all things in this world. Time is forever vigilant. Eventually, Time crushes all plans and things and creatures. So my dear King, please do not become bewildered by the workings of eternal Time."

* * * * *

When Draupadi heard of the murder of her sons, the ground came rushing up at her, almost to embrace her as she fell. She could not speak. She could not cry. Her dear, precious sons were gone. Her world flashed before her. Nothing made sense. The long years in exile. All the austerities she suffered through. All the prayers she had offered. What did anything mean? Her life had been chewed up by cruel fate. She wanted to rage against it all, and when she saw Yudhisthira standing helplessly before her, she sent her anger toward him.

"So *this* is the victory you so long sought after. Now, the Earth and all her riches are yours. Are you happy now?" Yudhisthira dared not move nor speak as a torrent of words flowed from Draupadi. "I am burning up with grief. Why does my heart not break into a thousand pieces? The wealth of my labor has been plundered by Ashwattama. I want him slain. Do you hear me? I want his head cut off. I know the jewel on his head is like none other in this world. It gives him great power. Bring it to me, along with his head. "

* * * * *

Ashwattama left the valley of Kurukshetra. He turned east onto a road that led through the forest toward the Ganges River. He rode on relentlessly and after some time his horse became exhausted. He abandoned the animal and, in a frenzy, threw away his garments and weapons. He assumed the guise of a humble ascetic and continued on foot until he came to the Ganges where hundreds of brahmins and rishis gathered to hear the illustrious Vyasa, along with his guru, Narada Muni. Ashwattama marveled at his good fortune. This was a perfect place to hide and, just like the rishis, he smeared his body with the mud of the Ganges and mingled amongst the crowd to remain undetected.

Bhima surged ahead of his brothers and Krishna, and he arrived at the Ganges shortly after Ashwattama. Bhima came to a spot overlooking the site of the gathering. There, he saw Vyasa and Narada Muni surrounded by rishis who all sat in rapt attention, listening to their teachings. Some of the ascetics were mere youths, while others were hundreds of years old with long beards and tanned complexions, still looking youthful themselves. Bhima's keen eyes spotted a jewel on someone's head reflecting the sunlight. *It's Ashwattama*, he thought. *No ascetic would wear a jewel.*

Ashwattama also spied Bhima with bow in hand. The son of Drona realized it was futile to hide. He plucked a blade of grass from the earth and infused it with mantras. The crowd of sages quickly scattered in all directions as they felt the great energy of the Brahmastra weapon in their midst. The blade of grass burned and quickly assumed an extraordinary brilliance.

The Brahmastra was the most remarkable of all weapons. It could devastate the landscape, or destroy precise targets, while leaving all others unscathed. To wield the Brahmastra required great self-restraint, since a warrior could not release it in anger. It had been obvious to Ashwattama that his father had hesitated to give him the Brahmastra when he asked for it long ago. He felt angry and neglected when his father had taught its use to Arjuna, but not to his own flesh and blood. Drona had known well Ashwattama's impetuous and selfish nature. He had feared that, in his son's hands, the weapon would be used inappropriately. Drona eventually relinquished its secrets to his persistent son. He had instructed him to only release the weapon against the likes of Rakshasas or supernatural creatures. Under no circumstances should he use it against human beings. Now, Ashwattama released the weapon, sending it toward the five Pandavas to annihilate them.

When Arjuna and Krishna arrived and saw what was happening, Krishna urged Arjuna to deploy his own Brahmastra. Arjuna calmed himself and touched water. He honored the Celestials of the four directions, and uttering mantras, invoked his Brahmastra. Arjuna did not mean to destroy Aswattama, but only to counteract his weapon.

The two Brahmastras clashed overhead. They appeared like colossal balls of fire, and hung suspended over the Earth, surcharged and sending deadly streaks across the sky in all directions. Billows of smoke covered the sun, countless meteors rained down upon the Earth, and the oceans receded. The thunderous sound of the Brahmastras grew ever louder. Even a thousand miles away, lions and elephants roared and living beings trembled in fear. Vyasa and Narada themselves feared the Brahmastras would destroy all life on Earth, and, summoning all their psychic powers, they gradually contained the weapons.

Narada and Vyasa were enraged by this unprecedented recklessness. "Withdraw your weapons now," they demanded. "You should never use a Brahmastra, even if it's to protect your own life.

The region where a Brahmastra is released suffers a drought for twelve years or more. This is totally irresponsible."

Possessing great self-control, Arjuna completely pacified his weapon. Vyasa again called upon Ashwattama to withdraw his weapon. But although he tried, Ashwattama could not.

Vyasa grew irate. "You're the greatest fool. You have no ability to control your senses and neither can you control the Brahmastra."

Ashwattama was furious by such an insult. No, he could not stop the Brahmastra, but he could redirect it. He yelled at them. "I have a destination for my Brahmastra." And as he guided it, he revealed where. "Into the wombs of all the Pandava women, and especially Uttara who is quick with Abhimanyu's child. That child in her womb will be burned up alive. All the Pandava women will be barren. Their dynasty will cease to be."

Everyone who heard his vicious words was aghast. Narada and Vyasa pleaded with him to stop. Ashwattama only laughed fiendishly. As the Brahmastra blazed forth, the child felt its terrific intensity and died. But only for an instant. Krishna, that Soul of souls, appeared in the womb of Uttara. He embraced the fetus and brought the child back to life. The child opened his eyes and beheld Krishna's wondrous smile. He would never forget it, and all his life he would always search for that divine person who had revived him.

After redirecting the weapon, Ashwattama dropped to the ground spent, unable to move a muscle. The Pandavas immediately fell upon him and bound him tightly with ropes. Draupadi soon arrived with her entourage. She had a change of heart and anxiously called out, "Stop! Stop! Don't hurt him!"

Bhima couldn't believe his ears. "What are you saying? You begged us to bring you his head."

"Now I'm begging you to let him go. So many women mourn the deaths of their sons and husbands. It's senseless to continue the killing. You must spare him."

"No! Never!" Bhima turned to Arjuna who was holding Ashwattama. "Arjuna, kill him and send his soul to hell." When Arjuna hesitated Bhima scolded him. "Arjuna, do I have to remind you that you wanted him dead. We all wanted him dead."

Yudhisthira spoke up. "Draupadi's right. There's been enough killing. Ashwattama is the son of our illustrious teacher who died in a horrible manner. As a result Ashwattama became maddened and lost his senses. We must deal with him kindly."

Bhima was dumbfounded. "Ashwattama is the slayer of our sons. He must be punished. Is it not the duty of a kshatriya to administer justice in this world?"

When no one responded, Bhima turned his blazing eyes to Krishna for support.

And Krishna gave it. "Ashwattama has murdered sleeping men and boys. He even tried to kill the child within Uttara's womb. He must be punished."

At that moment Arjuna took out his sword and swung it, not at Ashwattama's neck, but at the gem on his head. He whacked off most of the culprit's hair along with the gem that gave him so much power. Energy drained from Ashwattama's body. Krishna and the other Pandavas felt at peace. Arjuna had found the right solution. Being robbed of his hair and gem was both killing him and not killing him at the same time. Ashwattama slumped helplessly to the ground.

"Don't worry," Krishna assured Ashwattama, "you'll live. And the child in Uttara's womb, whom you so wickedly tried to kill, is also alive. That child will become a wise and just king. He will rule for sixty years and he will be renowned both on the Earth and in the heavens. As for you, no glory awaits you. Because of your ignoble deeds you will wander the Earth alone and abandoned for three thousand years. Your body will always be racked by disease and pain. No one will speak to you or listen to your pleas or give you comfort. After this punishment, if you are repentant, you can enter the heavens."

Ashwattama looked at Draupadi and the Pandavas. He saw the affection between them. How palatable it was. They had each other. They had Krishna. What more did they need? Now, they even had his jewel. Ashwattama was certain that his father and all of his friends had attained the heavens. He felt abandoned. The world he knew was gone. He turned away and wandered into the wilderness alone.

Chapter 14

Grandsire's Story

The tears had ceased. The blind king lingered on his throne, stunned. His hundred sons, dead. As with all the tribulations throughout his life, Vidura was by his side. For a long time Dhritarastra sat motionless. He did not speak. Finally, he uttered, "It's too much to bear."

"Grief is like a hot coal that burns the heart," Vidura said. "Do not let it fester inside you. Dispel grief through reflection upon Dharma."

"How can I go on? My sons were everything to me. How is it that I am still alive when my sons are dead? It's not supposed to be this way."

"Your sons died like warriors. There is no better way to enter into Indra's heavenly court than by death on the battlefield. Know that all things must pass. Death awaits even the Celestials."

"We are all part of Death's caravan," mused the king. "You have been a true friend, Vidura. You tried to warn me from the very beginning when Duryodhan was born. You told me to send him away. Bhismadev tried to warn me, and Drona as well. I could have had my kingdom, along with ninety-nine sons. But I would not listen."

"It was Providence," Vidura replied. "Duryodhan brought about his own destruction. He was arrogant. He could not control his own senses and yet he sought to rule a great kingdom."

* * * * *

The royal coach carrying Dhritarastra and Gandhari moved slowly along the road to Kurukshetra amid thousands of grieving citizens. A river of humanity. Women weeping for their loved ones pleaded to the four directions. "Who will protect us now? Who will protect our children and our children's children?" The earth, devoid of its kshatriyas, remained eerily silent.

Riding in his chariot, Yudhisthira met them on the road as they came toward the blood-soaked battlefield. He had not turned from his grief, nor would he turn from theirs. Yudhisthira, his brothers, and Krishna rode silently through the throng. Women stretched their arms out to Yudhisthira. Some cursed him for the death of their fathers, brothers, husbands and sons, while others praised and appealed to him for protection. Yudhisthira rode on, tears streaming from his eyes.

Nothing prepared the women for what they would encounter. The sight was unfathomable. When they came upon the battlefield and beheld the carnage and saw beasts of prey feeding upon the dead, they lost their senses and threw themselves on the ground, inconsolable, beating their heads and breasts. Severed limbs and heads were strewn everywhere. The women could hardly walk without stepping on a body. Bodies as far as the eye could see. Their piteous shrieks rivaled the shrieks of the crows. They wandered, forlorn, across the killing fields, searching out their loved ones.

Some distance down the road, Yudhisthira's group came upon the royal coach. Dhritarastra and Gandhari, with Sanjaya's help, got down from their coach and proceeded on foot. Since the king and queen could not see them, the Pandavas each came before them and announced themselves by name.

Gandhari trembled when she heard Bhima speak. "The killer of my one hundred sons! You had to kill all of them? You couldn't leave one alive for me? I should curse you. I should curse all of you."

Yudhisthira, his brothers, and Krishna all remained motionless as Gandhari's scathing words washed over them.

"Come closer. Do not fear, " the blind king petitioned the Pandavas. "My sons are gone. You are my sons now. I want to embrace each of you."

One by one they came forward. Seeing his brothers each receive an affectionate embrace from Dhritarastra, Bhima felt reassured. Krishna suspected otherwise. As Bhima stepped forward, Krishna stopped him and pulled out of Bhima's being a virtual replica and placed it before the king. Dhritarastra promptly grabbed hold of it in his arms and squeezed the form with titanic strength. Spending every ounce of his energy, he crushed it, thinking it to be Bhima.

"Is he dead?" the king asked.

Krishna spoke gently. "You only crushed an image of Bhima."

The king started to cry. "It was my pure anger," was all he could say.

Vyasa appeared before them at the speed of the mind. Vyasa embraced his son, the king, as well as his daughter-in-law, and spoke pleasing words to them. He studied their faces and noticed that the king and queen had aged considerably, and looked much older than he did. Vyasa understood their hearts and spoke what was on his mind.

"Give up your anger. The Pandavas are not at fault. My Lady," he addressed Gandhari, "you often told your son Duryodhan, 'Victory goes to the righteous.' And so it has. You are well-known for your kindheartedness. Therefore, I implore you to forgive the Pandavas for the death of your sons and let your heart be at peace."

"Duryodhan could not be killed in a fair fight," Gandhari responded, not yet ready to forgive.

Yudhisthira stepped forward. "Curse me. It's all my fault."

Gandhari peeked out from underneath her blindfold and scorched Yudhisthira's foot with her glance. Yudhisthira grabbed his foot and fell backwards, trying to stop the pain. The other Pandavas moved back, fearful of her power.

Krishna stepped forward. "It's my fault. I encouraged Bhima to strike your son where he was most vulnerable. That's the only way we could win."

Gandhari shared this account with them.

"Before the battle, I told Duryodhan to come before me with no clothes on. When I lifted my blindfold, I sought to make him invincible by looking once over his body. My eyes had gained powers through my long years of austerity. I had been saving this great feat, this one glance, for my son. But to my dismay, Duryodhan had a loincloth covering his waist and thighs. 'Why didn't you follow my instructions?' I asked him. 'Krishna was in the hallway,' he said, 'and he told me it was inappropriate to come before you completely naked. So I threw this cloth around my waist.'

"I knew then that I could not save my son. I knew that Krishna's plan could not be thwarted." Gandhari paused and gave a faint cry. "My sons' bodies are now scattered across this battlefield. What am I to do?" And she turned to the one who was responsible for all this. "Krishna, this is all your fault. You could have stopped this if you so desired. But you didn't. Thus, I curse you. Your dynasty and your family will not remain unscathed in this tragedy. Thirty-six years from now your kinsmen will turn upon each other and slaughter each other until there is not one left alive. And your women will beat their breasts and weep with abandon, just as the Kuru women have wept."

Krishna smiled that smile of his. "I've had this troubling thought. My Yadu clan is unconquerable and future generations, claiming to be my descendants, would become very arrogant. How could I leave the Earth with such a burden? So, my dear lady, I thank you for your curse. You have provided me with a fitting end to the story of my clan. It will keep them humble and keep others perplexed."

* * * * *

Great funeral pyres blazed for days and nights. Each of the Pandava and Kaurava dead were wrapped in fine silk cloth. Other warriors were burned en masse, according to their kingdom. Vast amounts of ghee and wood kept the fires burning steadily. Much of the wood came from the abandoned and smashed chariots which littered the battlefield.

The Pandavas privately performed a ceremony, making offerings for their dead family members: Abhimanyu, Draupadi's five sons, and Ghatotkaca. As they finished, Kunti erupted into tears, shaking uncontrollably.

"What have I done! What have I done!" She fell to the ground and called out helplessly, tormented by her neglect of her first born. "My son! My son!"

Yudhisthira and his brothers rushed to their mother's side, surrounding her as if to protect her. "Mother, we're all here," Yudhisthira explained, trying to comfort her. "This must be upsetting for you. Come away."

"You don't understand," she told them. "This ceremony is not yet finished. It cannot be finished until you perform oblations to Karna, your eldest brother. He was born of Surya, before I met your father." Her words burst forth in anger. Angry at herself for her long-kept silence. Telling her sons would have made all the difference.

The Pandavas were shocked by her admission. They had unknowingly fought against their elder brother in battle. They had cursed his ability to elude death in those last days as he skillfully commanded the enemy forces.

"If I had only known," Yudhisthira uttered in disbelief, "this terrible destruction would not have happened."

In the distance, brahmins chanted mantras, their bodies almost black from the fires, performing last rites for the warriors. Millions of dead burned as the smoke and the mantras rose heavenward.

* * * * *

Yudhisthira went through the motions, as if in a dream. His eyes were guided upwards by the streams of regal banners hanging down from the high ceiling in the Great Hall at Hastinapura. For generations the Kurus had ruled Bharata-varsa from this hall, and now the coronation for Yudhisthira was ready. His brothers were happy for him, but he felt empty and unworthy. Yudhisthira sat on the balcony of the royal quarters surrounded by his brothers and Krishna. He gazed for a long time upon the distant mountains.

He finally spoke. "What is the value of all this? I should shave my head, go back to the forest and live as a mendicant. I will simply depend on the kindness of others. I will eat fruits, herbs and roots. I will abandon the worldly life for good. I will give up all desires and cheerfully accept whatever may come. I will let myself grow thin. I will endure hunger and thirst, heat and cold. I will be happy with the music of the birds and the glistening waters of the clear streams. I will befriend the trees and sleep beneath their branches. I will be at peace with all beings. Do you remember? We lived like that once before. What more do I need?"

Yudhisthira felt obliged to his brothers and the citizens. He duly attended the coronation and allowed the brahmins to place a golden crown on his head. But after the ceremony his condition only grew worse. He had nightmares. He blamed himself for all the deaths at Kurukshetra. He charged himself guilty, and he could never forgive himself. He confided in Krishna, Vyasa, and his brothers.

"I have seen many years filled with adventure. But now the days that remain to me are empty. People will look at me and wonder, 'What kind of fool sits on a throne attained at such a price?' Because of me, the Grandsire, our teacher Drona, our elder brother Karna, and Abhimanyu, the youthful flower of our family, have all been killed. To gain a kingdom I have abandoned morality. I am a sinful man. Millions have died on my account. The wealth and power I have gained are of no solace. The Earth is desolate. The great heroes are gone, and my heart burns. What can I do to amend the injustices I have perpetrated?"

Vyasa spoke to him, and Krishna also tried, but to no avail. Krishna saw how inconsolable Yudhisthira was and offered another course of action. "My dear Yudhisthira, there is only one person I know who can dispel your grief. The Grandsire. He was like a father to you. He is a veritable reservoir of knowledge, both physical and metaphysical. When he leaves this world much of that knowledge will leave with him. You must go to him."

They brought Yudhisthira to Bhismadev, where he still lay at Kurukshetra.

* * * * *

Bhismadev had lain patiently on the bed of arrows for many weeks after the battle had ended. The group now came before him in great reverence, as if entering the presence of a holy man, and sat down around him. Bhismadev appeared serene and he smiled upon them.

Krishna was the first to speak. "O Grandsire, you are astonishing. I've never seen anything like this before, that you have maintained your poise and elegance under these circumstances."

Bhismadev smiled. "O Krishna, lotus-eyed one, I have been lying here meditating only upon you."

Krishna spoke lovingly. "And I in turn have been meditating on you. We have returned to you in your last days to hear your words of enlightenment. Yudhisthira is especially here to seek your guidance."

Yudhisthira leaned forward and asked, "O Grandsire, the responsibilities of leadership are a heavy burden to bear. What is the course for a king or leader, who in difficult times, becomes confused about his duty?"

Bhismadev spoke. "At all times, the king must uphold Dharma. He must be devoted to the truth. He must protect and cherish the brahmins and seek their guidance. He must seek the guidance of elders and those conversant in various fields. With good counsel the king can proceed in clarity."

Yudhisthira asked, "What should be the proper mood of a king or leader? What skills must he have?"

"He must execute his authority in humility. He must be of good behavior and show self-restraint. The king should not lose his composure or be overwhelmed by grief or anger if his efforts do not meet with success. If the king is too mild he will not be taken seriously, but if he is too heavy-handed the citizens will become troubled. He must extract taxes, but not burden the citizens with too many taxes. In peaceful times he may take up to twenty-five percent. The king should not be greedy and he should not usurp the wealth of others. He must understand diplomacy and be attentive to the smallest details. He should offer gifts, speak kind words, and be respectful to all. The king must be powerful enough to protect the kingdom from threats, miscreants and thieves. He must also be conversant in the use of weapons and skilled in warfare. He must be a man of action.

"His foremost concern, however, is for the happiness of his citizens. The king must always act in a way to benefit and protect them. He should also tend to the needy, the widows, and the elderly. The peoples' well-being is his constant duty. If he does nothing else, by this act alone he will attain the merit of all pious activities. Indeed, anyone who gives protection to others for just one day will reside in the heavens for ten thousand celestial years."

"O Grandsire, please describe the symptoms of a kingdom wherein the king is just."

"The citizens live without fear. They can speak candidly. They don't have to hide their wealth. The citizens are considerate of one another. Everyone can find employment and they engage wholeheartedly in their duties. The citizens understand what is to be done and what is not to be done. They are forever loyal to their king. In a society devoid of cheating, envy and wickedness, the king and its leaders are eternally benefited. In such a kingdom, a king's chariot will easily glide across rivers and lakes, and the mountains will gave way. His path will never be obstructed, for good always begets good."

"Please speak more about our relationship with the brahmins."

"True brahmins are our friends, for they look after our eternal welfare, and in turn we must be friends with them. The best way to enjoy wealth is to give in charity to deserving brahmins. They are peaceful, honest, pure in mind and without envy. They always act for the benefit of all, shining upon us the light of Dharma. Follow the Dharma and live in peace, free from fear, grief and lamentation. Whoever is a king, leader, guide or protector of others must abide by the principles I have explained to you."

At the end of their talks, Bhismadev came to the story of how he, as one of the eight Vasus, had once shamefully transgressed Dharma:

"Once upon a time in the Heavens, at my wife's insistence, my brothers and I stole Vasistha's wish-fulfilling cow. And when the sage cursed us to take birth on Earth, we Vasus were beside ourselves. We appealed to the goddess Gangadevi.

'You have to help us.'

'We've been cursed to be born as mere men.'

'If you don't help we'll be stuck on Earth.'

'What would you have me do?' she inquired, sympathetic to our plight.

'O beautiful lady, there is a young and virtuous king amongst men who warrants your love and affection.'

'His name is Santanu. He is handsome, heroic and his fame will spread throughout the world.'

'Go to him. Entice him.'

'And one by one we can be born as your children.'

'That sounds like a delightful idea,' She pondered.

'The only thing is, you'll have to kill us all.'

'What!' Gangadevi was horrified. She shivered. 'No one in the history of the world has ever entertained such a thought.'

'Do it for us.'

'That's the whole idea.'

'Right after we're born you must throw us into the Ganges River.'

'And we'll drown.'

'We quickly fulfill the dictates of the curse...'

'And we're back in the heavens.'

To ease their burden, Gangadevi agreed to the plan. She paused to consider it more thoroughly. 'To have children is the proper and rightful fruit of every marriage. The joy of every parent is to nourish the child, watch the child grow, and revel in the child's newfound abilities. And you would deprive me of that?'

'No, no, of course not.'

'You can have all that.'

'Dyu is cursed to live a long life.'

'You can enjoy raising him.'

'And we'll all invest part of ourselves in Dyu.'

'Yes. That way you'll get the best of all of us.'

In this way Gangadevi was reassured. And so it came to pass.

One day, she emerged from beneath the waters of the Ganges. Her clothes, dripping wet, clung to her body. Santanu happened to be walking in solitude by the river which flowed nearby his palace. When they came upon one another, he was struck by her beauty. Nothing else mattered. He saw nothing else. He knew nothing else. He had to have her. She agreed, but under one condition.

'I'll be your wife,' she said. 'I'll love you and satisfy your every wish. But you can never be unkind to me or question anything I do, whether you understand it or not. I will leave you the moment you transgress that rule.'

The king, my father-to-be, didn't think it an unreasonable request at the time and happily agreed. Every year a male child was born to them. After each child was born, Gangadevi carried the baby down to the river and dropped him into the water. Each time, Santanu had followed her, and, in silence, witnessed this seemingly heinous act. He did not protest nor did he try to stop her, knowing that if he did she would leave him immediately. But the sight of his helpless children being drowned festered in his heart. I was their eighth child. As she carried me to the river, Santanu confronted her. He was furious.

'How can you do this? Why? It all seems like a bad dream. You're perfect in every way, but after you give birth you become a monster. This is the greatest sin! And you've made me part of it. I can't allow you to kill another child.'

He broke down in tears. And she calmly explained to him the entire story. How we Vasus were cursed and how we had appealed to her for help. She wasn't going to the Ganges to drown me, but rather to take me with her to the celestial kingdom where I would be raised and have a proper education.

"People say that I've been fortunate to live a long and illustrious life. But for me, this long life has been a curse. The ways of the Earth are crude and not fit for a gentleman. Even the so-called pleasures, comforts and glories of this world are shallow consolations. Men become blind in pursuing material wealth. They will do almost anything to achieve their petty goals. Earthly pleasures, however, are nothing compared to the heavens. But ultimately, even life in the heavens is temporary."

Bhismadev fixed his eyes on Krishna and addressed him. "My sojourn on Earth has finally come to an end. The curse of a long life has turned into a blessing because with my own eyes I have beheld your beautiful features. I was fortunate to play a part in your story and assist you in your mission. Now you, the dear-most friend of all, are graciously present before me in my final hour. I cannot ask for a greater gift."

To the Pandavas the Grandsire said, "My sons, know that every action Krishna takes is rooted in love. He cannot do otherwise. We are all his eternal servants. So my dear Yudhisthira, do not lament, for Krishna has blessed all the warriors who have died on this battlefield. They will soon meet one last time here on Earth to enjoy one another's company by the riverside."

Bhismadev became silent. He and Krishna looked at one another for a long time. Tears of love flowed from their eyes. The sun set in the west. Bhismadev stopped breathing and left this world.

*****

In Hastinapura Krishna sought out Kunti before he left for Dwaraka. "Didn't I tell you everything would work out well for your family?"

Kunti was awed by Krishna's concern for them. "O Krishna, you are the refuge of all. You have kindly come to this world just to alleviate the Earth's burdens. Although you casually appear in the midst of human society, very few indeed know who you really are. It's a wonder to behold. It seems you are invisible, beyond the range of their senses."

Krishna laughed gently at her observation, and Kunti joined in. Again, she turned solemn. "My Lord, you have been kind upon my sons and me. Even though we have endured so many tribulations, we would do it all over again in an instant, for we have been blessed with your love and shelter. I have only one wish. Grant that my consciousness always flows to you, just as the Ganges naturally flows into the ocean."

"Dearest Kunti, you and your sons have allowed me to dwell in your hearts, and thus, you will always dwell in mine. You will never lose sight of me, nor will I ever lose sight of you."

Krishna boarded his chariot and slowly made his way along the broad avenues of Hastinapura. It would be the last time the citizens would see him.

Chapter 15

The Omens

Krishna's chariot left Hastinapura traveling as swift as the wind. On his way, he passed through a barren, mountainous land. There, an ascetic by the name of Utanka spent his days in a cave, deep in meditation. In his trance, the ascetic had a vision of Krishna fast approaching. Having not seen him for many years and eager to get his darshan, Utanka hastened from his cave, leaving a trail of dust flying from his robes, and went to the lonely road that passed through that region and waited.

When Krishna saw the sage he stopped his chariot and bowed and offered words of respect. "O holy one, how can I be of service to you?"

Beholding Krishna's form, Utanka felt waves of ecstasy inundate his being. "O Lord of the Universe, I am here to serve you. It gives me great joy to look upon your transcendental features. It is my good fortune to meet you again."

As he spoke, Utanka's thoughts turned to Krishna's friends and relatives, the Pandavas. He lived in seclusion and had not spoken to anyone for years, and now he wanted to find out about them.

"Tell me, years ago I heard of some tension between the Pandavas and their cousins, the Kauravas. I am eager to hear of what transpired between them. Surely, you must have interceded and, carried by your wisdom, their dynasty is now united in peace."

"O holy one, I tried my best to bring about an amicable result. Even Grandsire Bhismadev, as well as Drona and the noble Vidura, offered the sons of Dhritarastra good counsel. But unfortunately none of us could sway the hand of Providence. The forces of the Pandavas and the Kauravas met on the field of Kurukshetra and after eighteen days of battle only the five brothers and several others emerged alive. The hundred sons of Dhritarastra are gone. The Grandsire and Drona are gone. The allies of both parties are all gone."

Utanka could not believe his ears. He could only imagine the carnage that took place. As Krishna's words still hung heavy in the ether, Utanka felt his heart uncontrollably swell with anger. "Krishna, how could you allow this?"

Krishna remained calm in face of these challenging words. "People have free will."

Utanka surprised himself as words of rebuke flowed from his mouth. "Krishna, all beings spring from you. You are the Soul of souls, within the hearts of all. Not a blade of grass moves without your sanction. You could have changed their minds. You could have prevented this destruction. What will happen now? Who will protect the citizens? Who will protect the wives of the great warriors who are left alone without husbands? Who will give shelter to the brahmins and protect Dharma?"

"I understand your concern, but I can't force men to act against their will. Besides, I've descended to this mortal world to play the role of a human being."

"Krishna, this didn't have to happen." Hot tears streamed down Utanka's face and wet his beard. "I should curse you, Krishna. I should curse you."

Krishna smiled upon the ascetic. "My dear Utanka, you have spoken well. The essence of a brahmin lies in his compassion for all creatures. But you must also know a brahmin's strength lies in his ability to forgive. So don't waste your energy on me. Besides," Krishna declared quite proudly, "I've already been cursed by Queen Gandhari."

Utanka composed himself. "My Lord, you are very kind upon this fallen soul who is so quick to anger, not understanding the mysterious ways of your divine will. But one other thing concerns me. The Kali-yuga is fast approaching. People will need you more than ever. Please stay to guide them."

"Don't worry. I'll be back. But in a different way. A sublime way. In the Kali-yuga they can call out my name and I'll be there for them."

Utanka's eyes widened. He could not believe his ears. He trembled and the hairs on his body stood on end. "Simply by calling out your name? But yogis and rishis strive long years, performing severe austerities and meditations to behold your divine nature."

"And very often their pride in their austerities prevents them from seeing me."

"But in the Kali-yuga..."

"In the Kali-yuga they can have me for a song and a dance," Krishna said rather nonchalantly.

Utanka could not speak. He could not move. He thought, *Krishna, as he always does, will bring about something wonderful.* Utanka saw that all around Krishna, above him and below him, everywhere, appeared unending manifestations of Krishna's unlimited forms. Utanka was unable to maintain his equilibrium. He closed his eyes and sank slowly to his knees. He bowed again and again and again, constantly murmuring "Krishna, Krishna, Krishna."

* * * * *

One day, just as the sun peeked over the eastern horizon, Vidura returned to the capital of the Kuru kings. Before the battle at Kurukshetra, Vidura had left Hastinapura to go on pilgrimage. Now, fifteen years later, Yudhisthira and the members of the royal household were overwhelmed with joy to welcome him back. Vidura gave the Pandava family freely of his time. Vidura observed them. They were well situated and didn't need his guidance. Besides, he was finished with palace life and planned to stay only briefly. He had come back for only one thing.

After the initial greetings, Vidura sought out the solitary Dhritarastra in his quarters. As was his habit, Dhritarastra sat on the balcony, looking towards the eastern horizon, when Vidura called his name. Vidura had to call again loudly to get Dhritarastra's attention.

Dhritarastra turned. "Yudhisthira?"

"Now do I sound anything like Yudhisthira?"

Dhritarastra now recognized the voice. "My dear brother!" The blind king felt a mixture of elation and melancholy as they embraced. "Vidura, how is this possible? Is it really you?"

Vidura spoke into his ear. "My brother. It's been a long time."

"So long. So many years…" Dhritarastra's mind wandered for a moment. He struggled with what to say next. "Vidura, I returned it all to the Pandavas. Everything they lost in that silly dice game. I tried to right the wrong done to them. Do you remember, Vidura?"

"Yes, yes, I remember."

"But what could I do? Duryodhan would not listen to me. . ." Dhritarastra paused. He had relived this moment a thousand times. Why had he allowed it to happen? "Duryodhan was insistent. He always had to have his way."

"That's all done with. We can't bring it back."

"Where has the time gone?. . . It seems like yesterday. . . Vidura, where have you been?"

"Traveling on pilgrimage to the holy sites. It's my life now."

"You sound robust. The pilgrim's life suits you well."

"My brother, I've come back for one reason only."

"And what would that be?"

"For you?"

"What?"

"We have both grown old. Our time is over. Time takes us and carries us along just like the clouds are carried by the wind. It's time for you to leave this place. Get out now. Throw off the shackles of worldly life. You are not this body."

"This body is all I've known."

"My brother, without understanding who we are, we will only betray ourselves. Open yourself up to the final journey that each of us must take."

"Vidura," Dhritarastra seemed to clutch his name like a lifeline. "Vidura, I can't. . . I'm afraid."

Vidura laughed out loud. "My dear brother, by all means be afraid. Be afraid of Time. It's unconquerable. Be afraid of maya, illusion. It batters us like playthings. Be afraid of the material world which is a constant source of anxiety. This is all the more reason to leave. In the end we are all forced to give up our comforts. Our wealth. Our pride. Our life's breath. Our everything. Learn to simply depend on that Soul of souls who is residing within the heart, waiting for us to turn to Him. He has been waiting patiently for years. . . for lifetimes. Find the resolve to get out now."

Dhritarastra considered Vidura's words. Vidura had always given him good advice. He took his brother's hand. "Yes. Of course. Help me, Vidura. Guide me."

* * * * *

Vyasa saw that many still grieved for their loved ones who died in the battle, especially Dhritarastra, Gandhari and Kunti. At Vidura's urging, the three of them planned to retire to the forest. But Vyasa didn't want them to leave like this, still burdened with the past. He took them, along with Hastinapura's many other families of the departed, to the banks of the sacred Ganges. There he entered waist deep into the water. With arms upraised and chanting hymns, Vyasa summoned back all who had died at Kurukshetra. Bhismadev, Drona, Karna and Drupada led legions of warriors from beneath the waters. They surged onto the land. Their cheers resounded throughout the valley. Exuberantly, they threw their arms around one another and their loved ones, crying and laughing in great delight.

Many warriors had descended from the celestial races, while some came from the Rakshasas or Danavas or other races of demons. They had fought fiercely. Now, their animosities were washed away and they met one another with joyous hearts. Thousands of campfires shone brightly all along the riverside, and lights and lanterns encircled the open air tents. It all appeared like a wonderful carnival. The warriors continually embraced wives and sons and daughters. They and their families sang, danced, and feasted to their hearts content. Their reminiscences, joking words and laughter drifted into the night sky. That night, peace was upon all the world.

For the occasion, Vyasa bestowed sight upon Dhritarastra, and Gandhari removed her blindfold. The royal couple shed tears of joy as their eyes bathed in the sight of their one hundred sons. The Pandavas heartily embraced their brother Karna along with their cousins. Everyone passed the night in unbounded happiness.

When the dawn came, they bid one another farewell and the deceased entered again into the river. Some went to the region of Uttarakuru, a paradise where they would sport for ten thousand years. Others went to reside in the mansions of Kuvera, the lord of wealth. Others attained the higher celestial regions and the planets of particular gods, while some entered the rapture of Brahmaloka, the highest material realm. A few went yet higher to merge into the ego free, stillness of Brahman. All, in time, would attain Vaikuntha, the eternal abode of Vishnu.

Vyasa beckoned the wives of the warriors. "Ladies, you have an opportunity now. If you want to join your husbands, cast aside any fear or apprehension. Enter the waters, end these lives, and proceed to the higher regions. It is your choice." Vyasa, that giver of boons, proclaimed, "May all your wishes be fulfilled, both here and in the next life."

Many of the women took up his offer and entered the deep waters and gave up their material bodies. Soon, thousands of celestial chariots descended from the heavens. The women emerged from the Ganges in their heavenly forms, adorned with fragrant garlands and priceless jewels. They each stepped onto a luminous chariot that slowly lifted upwards and transported them into the heavens.

Shivers went up and down the spines of all the onlookers standing by the riverside. They waved their goodbyes and cheered the women. They would never forget this night, or this dawn.

* * * * *

Dhritarastra, Gandhari, and Kunti retired to the forest. With Vidura's help they journeyed to the North country and he brought them to the region called Saptasrota, where the Ganges River separates into seven branches. He spent time with them, built a fire, helped them to adjust to the austere life, and prepared to leave.

Dhritarastra thanked him. "Vidura, I feel alive again."

"Life is a constant, on-going miracle. But our time in these bodies is drawing to a close. We must cut our attachments to worldly things."

"Vidura, you yourself are a place of pilgrimage, for the brilliance of the Divine shines through you. Farewell Vidura."

"And fare thee well, my brother."

Vidura embraced Dhritarastra, Gandhari, and Kunti, and then he was gone.

The three offered oblations into the fire. In the early morning, at midday and in the evening, they bathed in the rushing waters of the river. They subsisted only by drinking that clear, fresh water. The blind king, however, took on more severe austerities for himself. He sat silently in meditation, facing east, recognizing himself distinct from his body, senses and mind. Sitting day after day, he grew indifferent to the heat of the noonday sun which hung heavily upon his skin. Indifferent to the torment of wind and rain. Indifferent to the dead of night when temperatures dropped to a freezing cold. He kept pebbles in his mouth to prevent him from eating, speaking or sleeping. The taste of the pebbles somehow sustained him. The air, mixed with forest aromas, nourished him. And he continued to sit even when a forest fire suddenly flared up nearby and threatened them. Dhritarastra would not budge. Nor did Gandhari and Kunti run away in fear. They gathered by his side to meet the encroaching flames together.

But those flames never touched them. Instead, Dhritarastra ignited the flames of the mystical fire that burns within each being. Those flames were more fierce than any mundane fire, and, as they sat unmoving, their bodies were consumed and turned to ashes, and the ashes were carried away by the wind.

* * * * *

Yudhisthira ruled for thirty-six years after the battle. Then came a day when he realized how uneasy he felt. He'd been feeling like this for a long time, but never acknowledged it. Some strange, inexplicable mood had settled upon the kingdom. He wanted to see for himself the mood of the citizens. He left the palace in the guise of a laborer and wandered through the streets, unnoticed. What he found sent chills up his spine. In the market place, dealings were corrupted. People cheated one another. They no longer kept their word. He found people greedy for wealth and power. People were quick to anger. Quarrels erupted between friends and relatives. Strain between brothers. Between husband and wife. Even between parent and child.

Yudhisthira was astonished. *How could this be? These things rarely happened. But now, so often.* As he continued, dogs growled at him, and owls and crows shrieked overhead. Something was amiss.

It seemed the course of Time had changed. Nothing would remain the same as before. The Celestials appeared in the distance and faded away. Yudhisthira saw a cow, the symbol of Mother Earth, with tears in her eyes, grieving, even as her calf sucked on her teat. She had no milk to give.

He understood. The Kali-yuga had begun. The age of quarrel and destruction was upon them. Yudhisthira could feel it. He could smell it. His left arm trembled - *an ill omen*. Out of the corner of his eye, he glimpsed several large birds descending fast upon him. Their wings against the sky, ready to lash out. . . shrieking. . . horrific. . . like agents of Death. Yudhisthira made a hasty retreat. Somewhere, a jackal howled at the sun. The sunshine withdrew. The earth pulsated. The rivers shook. Severe winds blew, scattering debris everywhere. And the sound of thunder rippled across the land. Suddenly, lightning struck nearby, and clouds rained blood.

"What is this time?" Yudhisthira yelled into the wind. "People are confused. The world is devoid of happiness. What is coming?"

Yudhisthira was the last of his generation to behold the Celestials. He heard the Earth weeping. The sorrow, the grief, the anxiety were palpable. The Kali-yuga was upon them and would last for thousands upon thousands of years, until finally the greed of man would spend itself, and violence destroy itself, and lust ravish itself. Only then, after a long, long time, could Mother Earth ever so gradually recover and replenish herself.

*****

In Dwaraka ill omens appeared across the land and sky. The Sun became shrouded in mist. The skies became murky. The horizons were obscured. Meteors showered the Earth and rivers flowed upstream. Suddenly, one day, an ominous stranger stalked the streets and a chilling wind drove the citizens to the safety of their homes. This went on for days. At times the stranger lingered in front of a home, and when the inhabitants rushed out to confront him, he was gone. Sometimes archers shot at him, but their arrows went right through him as if he were thin air. It seemed the stranger had unleashed a swarm of rodents upon the city. Flocks of birds came from all directions and forever circled the skies, as their intolerable shrieking confounded the human ear. Men gave way to lust and anger. Women wailed piteously as an unseen curse descended upon Dwaraka. Then the darkness came.

* * * * *

In Hastinapura the people felt forlorn and depressed. However hard they tried, they couldn't shake their despondency. When they heard the news of how the Yadus had suddenly lashed out at one another and, in a blind rage, fought and slaughtered themselves, their hearts sank. While Arjuna hastened to Dwaraka, they waited with trepidation for any word of their beloved Krishna. No one could believe that the Yadus were gone and that their mighty Dwaraka lay abandoned.

* * * * *

Krishna went into the solitary forest, sat down beneath a tree and entered into meditation. After a time a hunter came along and, mistaking Krishna for a deer, released an arrow. Upon reaching the spot, the hunter saw the arrow lodged in Krishna's heel.

The hunter cried out, "What have I done? Please forgive me."

"There's nothing to forgive," said Krishna calmly.

The hunter chided himself. "Why did I shoot without getting a clear vision of my target? I have acted just like Pandu! How stupid of me! By shooting you I have condemned myself to the darkest regions of hell."

"Please, don't be alarmed." Krishna reassured him. "This is my opportunity to pass from this world of men and Celestials and return to my own abode."

And as Krishna ascended into the heavens, illuminating all directions, his Dwaraka was claimed by the sea and sank beneath its waters.

Chapter 16

The Final Journey

A sullen mood permeated the palace. Yudhisthira wondered if he could ever find happiness again. Krishna, the anchor of his heart and his world, was gone. Arjuna returned from Dwaraka and brought back the news of the Yadus' demise. Krishna's departure left a gaping void in the life of the Pandavas. Yudhisthira felt drained and weary from carrying so long the burden of power. *Was it not time for a new generation of leaders to step forward?* he pondered. And so, he enthroned the young and able Pariksit as king.

Yudhisthira put aside his crown and scepter. He gave up the garments of the royal order and dressed himself in simple cloth. He carried a plain wooden staff for support. He stopped speaking and eating. He neglected visitors and envoys from distant lands. His hair became matted. In a profound stillness, he sometimes sat, sometimes walked, and sometimes stood watching the sunset. Yudhisthira wandered about the palace like one who is deaf and dumb. One night he quietly left everything behind and journeyed on foot into the North country.

His brothers had been observant. They watched him as he left his chambers. They followed him, and Draupadi, their queen, also followed. And a stray dog also followed them. The Pandavas willingly shed the city life and the lights of the great metropolis gradually faded into the night. The dog stubbornly followed them as they roamed across rivers and through forests. Together, they journeyed to the Himalayas, treading the same path they had taken years before; indeed, the path their ancestors had taken generations before them. The kings of old were not ones to die in the comfort of their chambers. And so too, the Pandavas journeyed into the barren wilds. Behind them, the Kali-yuga tightened its grip upon the world.

They came to where the Ganges emerged from the mountains. There they stood for a long time in prayer to Mother Ganges. Before they moved on, Arjuna removed the bow and quivers that were never far from his side. He weighed them in his hands, reflecting upon them one last time. They were of no use to him any more. He had nothing left to protect. No one to conquer. He cast them into the river and they were taken under by the current.

On their journey, they fasted and prayed. To sustain themselves the brothers and Draupadi breathed deeply the fresh mountain air. It gave them the strength to go on. Yudhisthira led the way and they followed one behind the other. They journeyed together and yet alone. Each of them alone in the solitude of the vast mountains. Their hearts and minds became absorbed in constant thought of Krishna.

Yudhisthira felt his legs walking, felt his eyes seeing, his ears hearing, his lungs breathing and his body moving. He felt himself both within and beyond his body. He was happy and undisturbed. He felt himself perpetually prostrated in service to Krishna.

Arjuna remembered his friend's playful words and laughter. He was awed. *Krishna treated me like an ordinary friend! How on earth did I allow him to serve me as my charioteer? What was I thinking? Yet, I could not have confronted that ocean of warriors without him. He drove me into battle as casually as if going out for a morning stroll.* Arjuna remembered how Krishna watered his horses and lounged on the battlefield as if he were at a resort. *Krishna is remarkable,* he thought. *That's all there is to it.*

Bhima had freed himself from the pleasures of eating. Indeed, he stopped eating altogether. It wasn't as difficult as he thought it would be. He knew now that it was Krishna who gave him the strength to do what he did. He trembled when he thought about Krishna's kindness toward him. *With Krishna at my side nothing was impossible.* He remembered how waves of ecstasy overcame him when Krishna tackled him as he so foolishly tried to face-off the Narayana weapon. And this brought tears to his eyes.

Nakula and Sahadev remembered Krishna's kindness to the animals. *Krishna loved all creatures so, and they naturally loved him.* They both meditated on Krishna's lotus feet.

Draupadi remembered the dice match in the Great Hall. She remembered how Krishna supplied her with unlimited cloth. She remembered the many times Krishna came to help her and her husbands, never asking for anything in return. Just helping for the sheer joy of helping his friends. Despite all their misfortunes, she had nothing to complain about. Her life was perfect.

The high country, however, proved harsh and desolate. It was bitter cold. Draupadi was so fragile. She was the first to give up her life. Then Nakula and Sahadev, the calm and tender twins, left this mortal world. Next Arjuna, the great bowman. He could go no further. He fell to the ground. Finally, Bhima, of colossal strength, sat down. He too passed into Eternity.

Only Yudhisthira and the dog remained.

The dog kept him company, at times watchful and protective, always loyal to his master and eager to please him. Together Yudhisthira and the dog journeyed through valleys and over mountain heights. Vast mountain ranges stretched out before them as far as the eye could see.

One day, Yudhisthira beheld a shimmering light in the distant sky. It approached him at a great speed. As it came closer, Yudhisthira saw the form of a golden chariot drawn by four pure white horses. Thunder cracked in the sky all around. Indra announced himself. It was he driving the chariot. It circled the mountain peaks and descended, coming to a halt before Yudhisthira and hovering slightly above the ground.

King Indra beckoned him, "Come, climb onto my chariot. Come with me to the heavens."

Yudhisthira shook his head. "I have no desire to enter the heavens without my brothers and without Draupadi."

"Well, hurry," said Indra, "for they have already reached the celestial abode and are waiting for you at this very moment."

Upon hearing this, Yudhisthira joyfully mounted the chariot. The dog also tried to jump on, but Indra looked upon the creature with disdain and blocked his way.

"A dog is an unclean animal. Get away!"

"But he has been my constant companion," said Yudhisthira "I cannot leave him behind."

"There is no place in heaven for a dog," Indra scoffed.

"If the dog cannot go, I will not go either," Yudhisthira proclaimed and stepped down from Indra's magnificent chariot.

"What! You are willing to give up the splendors and comforts of heaven for a dog? Have you lost your mind?" Indra stood in disbelief.

"This dog has been a faithful friend," said Yudhisthira, "and to abandon a friend is infinitely sinful. I will not go without him."

No sooner did Yudhisthira speak these words when the dog shed its gross form and revealed himself as Dharmaraj, the lord of justice.

"I have arranged this test just for you," he said, smiling upon Yudhisthira. "You are truly noble and compassionate. An act of kindness is far greater than performing a thousand ceremonies. You and your brothers and chaste queen will certainly attain the highest abode."

Together they mounted Indra's chariot. The horses stirred, and carried them up, higher and higher to the celestial kingdom.

* * * * *

Yudhisthira entered the celestial realms to sounds of music and singing which overwhelmed his mind and senses and made the hair on his back stand on end. The countryside was bedecked with pristine lakes and gardens. Marble pillars with sacred inscriptions rose in all directions and spread across the horizon. The mountaintops glittered with gold. A myriad of Siddhas, Caranas, and other celestial denizens lined the way to greet Yudhisthira. But the singing stopped abruptly, and a great murmur arose from the Celestials. They could not believe their eyes. Yudhisthira had attained their realm in his own human body. No one had ever done this before at the time of death.

Yudhisthira's eyes searched eagerly among the crowd for Draupadi and for his brothers. That's all he wanted to know. "Where are they?" he inquired of Indra when he could not find them.

Indra's mood seemed to change. "Yudhisthira, don't be attached to human relations and affections. Forget the past. Stay here and enjoy yourself to your heart's content."

Indra's chariot halted before a mansion. There, Duryodhan, without a blemish and in ideal health and humor, relaxed on the patio, surrounded by many admirers.

When Yudhisthira saw Duryodhan being lavished with such attention, anger welled up in his heart. "What's he doing here? His greed and envy destroyed a dynasty, and he achieves this in return?"

"Yudhisthira, I'm surprised by your speech. Here in the celestial kingdom no enmity should exist. Duryodhan has attained heaven because he died a warrior's death."

"I do not see Karna, or Bhima. I do not see Arjuna, nor Nakula and Sahadev. Where are those great warriors?"

"They have gone elsewhere."

"Then why should I want to remain here? This place will not satisfy me if I do not have my brothers and Draupadi. I wish to go where they have gone."

Indra beckoned a messenger to take Yudhisthira to his brothers. The messenger proceeded quickly on foot, and Yudhisthira followed behind.

The skies darkened and the path sloped down past jagged cliffs. The messenger led Yudhisthira into a lifeless, smoke-filled valley with lakes of boiling oil and putrid smells. Corpses and bones lay scattered across the landscape. The ground was soaked with blood. From deep within the fog that surrounded Yudhisthira, a cacophony of moans and cries assaulted his ears. Yudhisthira glimpsed vultures as they swooped down and ripped at the flesh of depraved and tortured souls. Yudhisthira thought, *Surely, this is a place where the sinful are brought to be punished.*

The messenger stopped abruptly. "This is as far as I go. You can return with me or you're welcome to go on alone."

Anguish enveloped Yudhisthira. His muscles ached as never before. He wanted to go on, but the stench and cries were unbearable.

"Let's go back," he said as he turned to leave. Voices called out to him. Familiar voices.

"Please help us."

"Brother, show us compassion."

"Don't go. Stay awhile."

"Your presence relieves our pain."

"All of us are here."

And they each identified themselves by name. "Karna..." "Bhima..." "Arjuna..." "Nakula..." "Sahadev..." And a frail voice. "O my lord, it is your good wife Draupadi."

Yudhisthira, in disbelief, fell to his knees and hot tears streamed down his face. Moment by moment, his grief turned into rage.

"What type of perverse joke is this? How has Destiny so twisted the laws of Karma? My head is spinning. Am I walking through a dream? Have the gods forgotten what is righteous and just?" Yudhisthira turned to the messenger. "I will not leave these great souls. Go back without me. Tell your master his 'heaven' is a sham and his blessings are useless. I will stay here to comfort my wife and brothers."

And as Yuhisthira's tears soaked the ground, Indra, Dharma, along with the various gods of universal affairs descended upon that spot. All of Yudhisthira's terrible visions disappeared. The skies became illuminated and the landscape became lush and full of life. Opulent palaces meant for the Pandavas appeared nearby where the sacred Ganges serenely flowed.

Indra spoke. "O Yudhisthira the Wise, we welcome you and your wife and brothers into the celestial regions. Stay here for a time and grace us with your presence, before you continue your journey home to the Eternal Abode."

Dharma smiled upon Yudhisthira. "This was my third and final test for you. To see if you would endure hell for the sake of the people you love. Indeed, this type of human love will be rare in the Kali-yuga."

Indra explained, "The vision of hell you experienced was but a brief illusion. Kings perform both good and bad deeds. And this is the rule: if one's sins outweigh the good, he goes to heaven for some time and later must suffer in hell. But when the good deeds are greater, he will experience hell first and afterwards is free to enjoy heavenly pleasures continuously. The only blemish on your deeds is that you lied to Drona to make him think his son was dead. For this reason you had to experience hell briefly."

"My dear Indra," Dharma interjected, "I think you have missed the point. Krishna *told* him to lie. Yudhisthira only lied to save the lives of his men. There is no sin in that."

"But is not a lie under any circumstances still a lie?"

"My friend, I am but the judge who upholds Dharma. The answer to your question lies with Krishna who is the actual author of Dharma, of what is truth and what is just. And so, in the battle at Kurukshetra, it was Krishna's will to settle misdeeds with the use of misdeeds."

"My dear Dharma, I think these points will be discussed for millennia to come."

"So it will be, Indra. So it will be. This great history of the Pandavas and their friendship with Krishna will be told again and again for as long as the heart holds even a drop of virtue. Indeed, anyone who hears this sacred epic and keeps it in their home will attain their heart's desires. One who seeks prosperity will prosper. A woman bearing a child will get a son or daughter of blessed nature. One who desires victory will achieve victory. One who seeks heaven will attain heaven. I declare that the bards who share these stories should be lavished with gifts. By reciting or listening to the stories of Mahabharata, one benefits both the ancestors and the generations to come. Those who especially hear with faith and devotion will purify their hearts. And like the virtuous Pandavas, they too will attain Vaikuntha, the Eternal Abode, where Sri Krishna is forever engaged in loving exchanges with His devotees."

Epilogue

Vyasa and Ganesh

Once Vyasa approached Ganesh, the one with the elephant's head and the scribe of the Celestials.

"Ganesh, I need your help," Vyasa said. "I have compiled the Mahabharata, the history of our time. I need it written out. It's 100,000 verses and I want to preserve the story for future generations in the age to come. For them, it will be more important than the original Vedas. The Mahabharata will be the fifth Veda. The whole account of human nature will be found herein, and what is not here will be found nowhere else. This history will capture people's hearts and give them spiritual awareness. Anyone who speaks it or hears it or reads it will receive great blessings."

"But only 100,000 verses?" inquired Ganesh, rather surprised at the request. "It should be easy enough for people to commit to memory."

Vyasa frowned. "Ganesh, you don't understand. The Kali-yuga will soon weigh heavily upon us. It's the age of iron, quarrel and hypocrisy, the age of forgetfulness and confusion. But the Mahabharata will contain everything to help people cross over this age of darkness. In the Kali-yuga people are condemned to short lives and even shorter memories. No one will remember all the details of such a lengthy story. Ganesh, I have the entire story in my mind's eye, but it would be too daunting a task for me to write it all down. I need your help."

"It will be my great honor to assist you. I'll write it all down for you. But it must be done all at once. You must tell me the entire story without pausing even for a moment."

"Yes, of course, I agree," said Vyasa, "and in turn you must only write what you fully understand. If you find any detail of my story vague, anything that's ill-defined, you must let me know so I can explain it properly."

"Then let us proceed," said Ganesh as he removed one of his tusks to serve as a quill.

And Vyasa began.

Vedic Worldview

The Mahabharata unfolds within the scope of these Vedic concepts:

1) Vedic Pantheon

God, the Supreme Lord, resides in Vaikuntha, the spiritual world (aka the Kingdom of God, the Eternal Abode). Vaikuntha means the place free from anxiety and fear. Innumerable names of God are found throughout the world, especially in the Vedic tradition. In Sanskrit, Vishnu, Narayana, and Krishna are His predominant names (see these names in the glossary). There are also innumerable expansions of the Godhead, including His Brahman (divine light).

Three Lords, Brahma, Vishnu, and Shiva, preside over the material world. Brahma, the topmost of Celestials, is the Creator of the innumerable planets and stars which make up the upper, middle and lower regions of the material universe. Vishnu presides as the Maintainer who provides Brahma with the ingredients to create. Shiva, the Destroyer, is the lord of the Bhuttas (ghosts, goblins and otherworldly beings). Even though Shiva once drank poison to save the world, his dance of destruction brings the universe to an end.

The Devas - Celestials - reside in the heavenly, or upper, regions. The predominant Celestials, the gods (aka the gods of universal affairs or demigods), have extraordinary powers. Traditionally, people might appeal to them for their blessings just as Catholics appeal to the Patron Saints. The Celestial races are the Charanas, Siddhas, and Gandharvas, among others.

The Asuras - demons - reside in the lower regions. Their races include the Daityas, Danavas, and Rakshasas. The Asuras are constant adversaries of the Celestials and the Supreme Lord, and vie for control of the middle regions of the universe, which include the Earth.

2) The Four Ages (Yugas)

There are four great ages which are cyclical like the four seasons of a year:

The Satya-yuga (Krita-yuga) - the age of goodness, lasts 1,728,000 years. In this age there is no need of governments or kings or law enforcement since everyone lives a virtuous life

The Treta-yuga - virtue declines by 25% and it lasts for 1,296,000 years

Mahabharata: The Eternal Quest

The Dvapara-yuga - there is further decline of virtue and it lasts 864,000 years

The Kali-yuga - the present age (not to be confused with the goddess Kali) is the most degraded age and lasts 432,000 years.

The Kali-yuga, the last of the four ages, began approximately 5000 years ago. It is characterized by quarrel & hypocrisy, the cheaters and the cheated. In this dark age, people are less intelligent and have a decreased duration of life, and are inclined to be more materialistic, always impatient for sensual pleasures which ultimately leave them unsatisfied. In the advanced stages of the Kali-yuga people will hardly live 25 years.

1000 cycles of these four yugas equals one day of Brahma & another 1000 cycles is the night of Brahma. 360 such days and nights equals one year of Brahma. Brahma, along with the universe, exists for 100 of his years.

3) Bharata-varṣa

Bharata-varṣa, (named after King Bharata of ancient times) refers to both the Earth (aka Ilāvṛta-varṣa) and specifically to greater India (the center of Vedic culture), the region spanning from Iran to Cambodia and Indonesia. The Vedic culture at one time flourished all over the world. Ancient cultures throughout especially worshipped, or petitioned, gods and goddesses, if not the Supreme Lord directly. Although the Earth contained innumerable kingdoms and peoples who all abided by the Vedic culture, over time, and influenced by the Kali-yuga, many of their practices become perverted. One of the principle concerns of Vedic culture is to uphold Dharma. In the Bhagavad Gita, it's stated that Krishna appears time and again to reestablish the Dharma whenever there is a decline in spiritual practice.

4) The Dharma

This Sanskrit term has no equal in any other language. Its multiple meanings include: universal law, morality, religion, justice, one's duty to society & family, one's calling or life's purpose, the Path (i.e. Sanatana Dharma- the Eternal Path; Yuga Dharma – the path, or means of liberation, for a particular age).

The four pillars of Dharma are: **Compassion, Truthfulness, Cleanliness, Austerity**.

The essential teaching of the Dharma is that we are all spiritual beings involved in an evolutionary process to reawaken our relationship with the Godhead, and that human life is meant to undertake austerities in order to advance in our spiritual growth and realizations.

Dharma also refers to the inherent characteristics of someone or something (i.e. the heat & light of fire, the sweetness of sugar).

Upholding justice, governance, and protection of the populace were the responsibilities of the king. According to Vedic literatures, the rule of the king/leader was subject to the guidance and counsel of the brahmanas and the people. The Vedic culture contained democratic and republican principles and was by no means feudal, or simply prone to the whims of a monarch. Everyone abided by the Dharma.

In the Vedic culture, an Aryan is described as one who is noble & truthful & always abides in the Dharma, knowing the importance of spiritual realization. (a common misconception is that Aryan refers to a race).

5) <u>The Vedas</u>

Veda means knowledge. Originally there was only one Veda. About 5000 years ago Vyasa divided the teachings into four principle Vedas: *Sama, Atharva, Rig, Yajur*. Written in Sanskrit, the Vedic literatures explain different levels of spiritual understanding and also deal with worldly matters and laws. There are also 108 *Upanishads*, the *Vedanta Sutras*, the *Brahma Samhita*, and *Manu Samhita*. The Vedic literatures and scriptures meant for spiritual guidance and inspiration in the Kali-yuga are the *Mahabharata, Ramayana*, & the *Puranas*, especially the *Bhagavat Purana* (aka *Srimad Bhagavatam*). The *Bhagavad Gita*, the Song of God, spoken by Krishna to Arjuna (an abbreviated version in this book - Chapter 11: The Cosmic Form), is the culmination of all Vedic teachings. *The Mahabharata*, according to the astrological occurrences mentioned in its text, is calculated to have taken place over 5000 years ago.

6) <u>Social Orders: Varna-ashram</u>

For centuries, there has been a gross misunderstanding on the part of many Hindus who think that the social order, or caste system, is based on birth. Although birth (janma) at times might be a factor, it is not the underlining principle of the social order. Krishna explains in the *Bhagavad-Gita* (18:41) that the four varnas (the classes of society) are distinguished not by birth, but by the work (Karma) one performs, and that work is derived from one's inherent propensities (svabhava). So even if one is born in a so-called low class, one should be free to pursue one's propensities, be it in scholarship, business, agriculture, etc.

The social structure is compared to the body, and the four classes of society are likened to different parts of the body. One part of our body does not exploit another part of the body, but all parts function for the well being of the whole. Likewise, one social class should not exploit another. In a healthy functioning society, all the social parts function in tandem for the well-being of the whole body.

Varna (occupation):

Brahmins (likened to the head of the social body) are those inclined as priests, scholars, researchers, teachers, doctors, and act in peacefulness, truthfulness, self control, and knowledge. Traditionally brahmins did not take a salary but received donations for the services they offered.
Kshatriyas (likened to the arms) are administrators, warriors, protectors of society, and act with courage and resourcefulness.
Vaisyas (likened to the stomach) are inclined toward the independent enterprises of banking, manufacturing, selling of goods, agriculture, and cow protection.
Sudras (likened to the legs) comprise the working class and are employed by the other three classes.

Ashram (living situation):

Brahmacari- single, celibate student
Grhasta - householder engaged in family life and following the path of Dharma (as opposed to Grhamedhi, householder who does not follow the Dharma and is engaged in illicit – adharmik - activities)
Vanaprasta – husband and wife retire from family and worldly activities, entering the forest (vana) together
Sannyasa – strict order of monkhood, celibate life

7) Duhkha-alayam – A Place of Misery

When the world is seen in relationship to the Divine everything is glorious; otherwise, the material world is described as a place of misery and distress (duhkha). The living entities work under the influence of the three modes (gunas) of material nature and struggle with the three types of misery.

The three gunas – goodness, passion and ignorance - are likened to the three primary colors, which, when mixed together, form many other colors. In the same way, our mentality and motivations are tinged by these modes of material nature in various combinations.

The three types of miseries:
Adhiatmik - miseries that arise from the body and mind
Adhidaivik – miseries from natural occurrences (heat, cold, hurricanes, floods, drought, etc)
Adhibhautik - miseries caused by other living beings

8) Moksha – Liberation

Traditionally, there are two types of liberation: the personal and impersonal. Those on the impersonal path want to shed their identities and merge into Brahman (the divine light). Those on the personal path acknowledge God as the Supreme Person and seek to renew their eternal relationship with Him. Both groups are referred to as transcendentalists. The impersonalists, however, view that liberation is attained through one's own merits and achievements. The personalists view that liberation is attained through the mercy of God.

Mahabharata: The Eternal Quest

Glossary of Principal Personalities, Places, & Terms

*Ab/hi/man/yu   Arjuna's son, husband of Uttara
*Adityas   twelve predominate Celestials who wield extraordinary power
*Agni   the fire-god
*Agni-hotra   a ceremony involving building a fire in a pit performed to please Agni
*Akshauhini   a division of warriors consisted of 21,870 chariots, 21,870 elephants,
                65,610 horse soldiers, & 109,350 foot soldiers
*Alamvashu   a Rakshasa
*Alayudha   a Rakshasa chieftain
*Amba   eldest daughter of the King of Kashi
*Ambalika   third daughter of King of Kashi, mother of Pandu
*Ambika   second daughter of King of Kashi, mother of Dhritarastra
*Andhakas   a subgroup of the Yadu dynasty
*Anjalika   a powerful weapon
*Apsaras   exotic female dancers of the Celestials
*Arghya   an ceremony to honor someone – an offering of gifts & refreshments
*Arjuna   third eldest of the Pandavas, famous for his skill in archery (aka
                Gudekesh- one who conquered sleep)
*Artha   means economic development
*Ashram   means a place for spiritual activities; a hermitage or a place to perform
                austerities
*Ash/wat/ta/ma   the son of Drona, Kaurava ally
*Asuras   demoniac races
*Badarik   (aka Badrinath) a place in the Himalayas where many sages (including
                Vyasa) lived in seclusion and contemplation
*Baka   a Rakshasa
*Balaram   Krishna's elder brother
*Bhagavad Gita   literally the song of God, Krishna's teachings to Arjuna
*Bharata-varsa   See #3 Vedic worldview
*Bhima   second of the Pandavas, famous for his strength and use of the club
*Bhismadev   the eldest member and guide of the Kuru dynasty (aka the Grandsire)
*Bhumi   the Earth-goddess, Mother Earth
*Bhuminjaya   son of Virata, brother of Uttara
*Brahma   the top-most Celestial, who has four heads and is charged with creating
                this material world. He is aka Dhata – one who bears everything.
*Brahmaloka   the top-most Celestial planet (see Heavens) in the universe, the planet
                of Lord Brahma
*Brahma-muhurta   auspicious pre-dawn hours conducive for meditation
*Brahman   the divine light, an aspect of the Supreme Lord. Yogis often seek to
                merge, or become One, with the Brahman
*Brahmin   (also brahmana) the order of priests & scholars who have accepted vows
                to uphold Dharma (there are also brahmin Rakshasas who have departed
                from saintly activities and use their learning and powers for evil intentions)
*Brahmastra   a devastating, celestial weapon belonging to Brahma
*Charanas   a race of Celestials
*Celestials   residents of the heavens (aka devas), they have very long durations of
                life, in pervious ages (yugas) they were more inclined to visit the Earth

Mahabharata: The Eternal Quest

*Chakra	Krishna's razor-sharp disc weapon named Sudarshan
*Chakra Vyuha	a circular and deadly military formation
*Chitra	a son of Dhritarastra
*Danavas	a race of cultured demons
*Darshan	means to have direct audience with
*Devaki	Krishna's mother & wife of Vasudev
*Dharma	see #4, Dharma, in Vedic worldview
*Dharmaraj	the god of justice (aka the lord of death)
*Dhri/ta/ras/tra	the blind King of Hastinapura, brother of Pandu, father of Duryodhan & his 99 brothers, proxy (or regent) of Kuru dynasty after Pandu's death
*Draupadi	daughter of Drupada (aka Panchali being from Panchala), wife of the Pandavas
*Dris/ta/dyum/na	son of Drupada, brother of Draupadi and Sikhandi
*Drona	military leader and teacher (example of one who is both a brahmin & kshatriya)
*Drupada	King of Panchala, Pandava ally
*Durvasa	a sage with great mystic powers but quick to anger
*Dur/yo/dhan	eldest son of Dhritarastra
*Dus/ha/sa/na	a son of Dhritarastra
*Dyu	leader of the Vasus
*Gandhar	a northwestern kingdom (in region of present day Kandahar)
*Gandamadana	a mountain range in the Himalayas
*Gandhari	princess from Gandhar, wife of King Dhritarastra
*Gandharvas	a race of Celestials who are expert in singing, dancing and fighting, (aka sky warriors)
*Gandiva	invincible bow of the gods given to Arjuna
*Ganesh	Shiva's son who has the head of an elephant, scribe to the Celestials
*Ganga	goddess of the Ganges River
*Ghatotkaca	Rakshasa son of Bhima and Hidimbi
*Ghee	clarified butter used in rituals & for cooking
*Gods	gods, demigods, the Celestials who are the controllers of universal affairs (i.e. wind-god, fire-god, sun-god)
*God	the one Supreme Lord, God of gods, the Lord in the Heart, the source of all beings and all the worlds (aka Krishna, Narayana, Vishnu)
*Has/tin/a/pu/ra	capital city of the Kuru dynasty, (literally- city of elephants)
*Heavens	the higher regions, the abode of the Celestial races, (not to be mistaken with Vaikuntha, the eternal kingdom of God), also referred to as the shinning world of the heroes where celestial maidens would eagerly greet & serve the heroes who died in battle; one of three regions in the universe; the other two being the middle (or earthly) regions and the lower (or hellish) regions
*Hidimba	a forest Rakshasa
*Hidimbi	Hidimba's sister, Ghatotkaca's mother
*Indra	the king of the heavens, the leader of the Celestials, famous as wielder of the thunder-bolt weapon (aka thousand eyed god, rain-god)
*Indraprasta	the capital of the Pandavas' new kingdom, named after Indra
*Jayadratha	king of the Sindhus, husband of Dhritarastra's sole daughter, Kaurava ally
*Kali-yuga	see #2, The Four Ages, in Vedic worldview
*Kalinga	kingdom on the eastern coast & Kaurava ally
*Kama	means desire

Mahabharata: The Eternal Quest

*Kamadhenu a cow of plenty which can fulfill all desires (kama)
*Kamboja   a northwestern kingdom & Kaurava ally
*Kamsa   King of Mathura
*Karma   means work or the reactions (good or bad) of one's work
*Karna   a personality of unknown origins, Kaurava ally (aka King of Anga)
*Kauravas   refers to Duryodhan & his 99 brothers & their allies
*Keechaka   the commander of Virata's army
*Khandava   a forest near Indraprasta
*Kripa   a general & military teacher of the Kurus, Kaurava ally
*Kri/ta/var/nam a general of the Yadus who fought for the Kauravas
*Krishna   Krishna manifests in the material world through Vishnu, but yet is higher than Vishnu, residing in Vaikuntha (Krishna is aka: Acyuta – the infallible one; Adhoksaja - the beginning and the end of all things; Hrsikesa – master of the senses; Bhagavan - complete in all six opulences - knowledge, wealth, strength, fame, beauty and renunciation); Krishna appears as a cousin & friend of the Pandavas
*Ksha/tri/ya the class of warriors/administrators in society
*Kunti   wife of Pandu, mother of Yudhisthira, Bhima and Arjuna, Krishna's aunt
*Kuru   an ancient king & founder of the Kuru dynasty; also a member of the Kuru dynasty (both the Pandavas and the Kauravas were Kurus)
*Kurukshetra a valley in northern India and a place of pilgrimage for thousands of years since the time of King Kuru
*Kuvera   the god of wealth & lord of the Yaksas
*Lomasa   a sage and storyteller who can travel throughout the universe
*Madri   second wife of Pandu, mother of the twins Nakula & Sahadev
*Mahabharata the ancient history of Bharata-varsa, greater (maha) India
*Maharatha means a chariot warrior who can fight alone against thousands
*Mantra   means to free the mind, an invocation, prayer consisting of God's names
*Mathura   City where Krishna was born, ruled by Kamsa
*Matsya   kingdom ruled by Virata, Pandava ally
*Maya   means that which is not or that which has no real existence
*Maya Danava an extraordinary architect of the demon races
*Muni   means one who has erudite knowledge & great mystical abilities
*Nagas   a race of serpents & followers of Varuna
*Naimisa   forest and pilgrimage place in northern India
*Nakula   one of the younger Pandava twins, expert swordsman & horseman
*Nanda   chief of the cowherds in Vrindavan, Krishna's foster father
*Narada   a sage with the ability to travel effortlessly throughout the universe
*Narayana   a name for Vishnu meaning the shelter of all beings
*Nara-Narayana an ancient incarnation of Krishna (Narayana) & Arjuna (Nara – means human) who were renowned rishis & warriors
*OM   a vibration evoking the Divine; those who perform austerities and chant the Om vibration can enter into Brahman
*Panchala   kingdom ruled by Drupada, its capital is Kampilya; Pandava ally
*Pandu   a son of Vyasa, a king of the Kuru dynasty
*Pandavas   refers to the fives sons of Pandu and their allies
*Parasara   a sage, father of Vyasa
*Parasurama a powerful warrior/sage
*Pariksit   son of Abhimanyu & Uttara, grandson of Arjuna & Subhadra
*Pasupata   the powerful & deadly weapon of Shiva
*Prabhas   a pilgrimage site on the western coast near Dwaraka

Mahabharata: The Eternal Quest

*Pranams	a show of respect by placing palms flatly together, fingertips up
*Prayaga	a city & pilgrimage site on the Ganges River (aka Varanasi)
*Pu/ro/cha/na	an advisor of Duryodhan who also executed his schemes
*Rajasuya	a rare imperial ceremony, the coronation of an emperor
*Rak/sha/sas	a race of crude demons & man-eaters
*Rama	an incarnation of Visnu whose story is found in *The Ramayana*
*Rasakund	a celestial beverage
*Rishi	means a sage – usually one who dwells in the mountains or forests
*Rudras	eleven manifestations of Shiva
*Sabha	means an assembly building or meeting hall from where the affairs of a state are conducted; also a gathering of people to make legislative decisions
*Sadhu	means a saintly person
*Sahadev	one of the younger Pandava twins, expert in logic
*Sakuni	Prince of Kandhar, Gandhari's brother, uncle & confidant of Duryodhan, Kaurava ally
*Samadhi	means a state of deep meditation, absorption in the divine
*Samsaptakas	a legion of fierce warriors
*Samsara	means the repeated cycle of birth and death
*Sanjaya	personal aid and confidant to Dhritarastra
*Santanu	a king of the Kuru dynasty, father of Bhismadev
*Sari	one long, colorful cloth used for a woman's dress
*Sati	the act of a loving wife voluntarily entering the funeral pyre of her husband to follow him into the after life. In India, by the middle ages, sati became a murderous act when wives were often forced into the fire of their dead husbands by envious relatives wanting her assets. The British finally banned this practice altogether.
*Satyaki	a Yadu warrior and commander, kinsman of Krishna, ally of the Pandavas
*Satyavati	mother of Vyasa, wife of Santanu
*Shanti	means peace
*Shiva	the lord of destruction
*Shri	an address of honor and veneration
*Siddhas	a race of Celestials, literally means one who is perfected in yogic or mystic powers
*Sikhandi	born as a daughter of Drupada & later became a man
*Sindhu	the river valley in northern India, now known as the Indus River Valley (a name given to it by Alexander the Great, who also gave the region the name "India"). The people on the eastern side of the Sindhu Valley were known as Sindhus which eventually turned into "Hindu"
*Sisupala	king of Chedi who was belligerent towards Krishna
*Sthuna	a Yaksa wizard
*Subhadra	Krishna's sister, Arjuna's wife, mother of Abhimanyu
*Sudarshan	the name of Krishna's razor-sharp discus (or chakra)
*Sudesna	wife of Virata, sister of Keechaka
*Surya	the sun-god (aka Vivasvan)
*Svayamvara	contest wherein a maiden selects an eligible husband from among her suitors
*Svetadvipa	the island on the Pole star where a manifestation of Vishnu resides in the top-most regions of the material universe
*Tirtha	means a place of pilgrimage
*Urvasi	a leading Apsara, a heavenly dancer and celebrity
*Uttara	daughter of Virata, wife of Abhimanyu, mother of Pariksit

Mahabharata: The Eternal Quest

*Vaikuntha   God's abode (see Vedic Pantheon above)
*Varanavat   resort town in northern India
*Varuna   the god of the ocean
*Vasavi   an invincible weapon of Indra
*Vasistha   a sage with extraordinary mystical powers
*Vasudev   Krishna's father & brother of Kunti
*Vasuki   king of the Nagas
*Vasus   eight Celestial brothers who are guardians of King Indra's court
*Vayu   the wind-god
*Vedas   see #5 in Vedic worldview
*Vedic   pertaining to the Vedas,
*Vidura   step-brother, adviser & confidant to Dhritarastra
*Virata   the king of Matsya, Pandava ally
*Vishnu   God, the Lord of lords (means He who pervades the universe - the Maintainer)
*Vrindavan   a village, not far from Mathura, where Krishna grew up
*Vrishnis   a subgroup of the Yadu dynasty
*Vyasa   author of the Mahabharata & complier of the Vedic wisdom (aka Dvaipayana meaning born on a island in the middle of a river), son of Satyavati & the father of Dhritarastra, Pandu & Vidura from separate women
*Yadus   Krishna's dynasty (aka Yadavas)
*Yaksha   an inhospitable race, not quite Celestials, who are followers of Kuvera
*Yamaraj   the lord of death (also see Dharmaraj)
*Yasoda   Krishna's foster mother in Vrindavan Village, wife of Nanda
*Yavanas   a barbaric race, literally means meat-eaters
*Yudhisthira eldest of the Pandavas, fathered by Kunti & Dharmaraj (aka Ajatasatru, one who is without an enemy)

About the Author

Andy Fraenkel was born in Germany in 1947 and came to America with his parents at the age of five. He is a multicultural storyteller, author, and workshop leader. He is also a recipient of a *West Virginia Artist Fellowship Award* and an *Ohio River Border Initiative Grant*. He has performed and offered workshops in a wide variety of venues: schools, colleges, churches, libraries, and museums.

He has performed and given presentations at numerous conferences and special events, including Parliament of the World's Religions Centennial Event (1993), Religious Communications Congress (2000), Dharma Conference (2003), and the National Storytelling Conference (2006).

He is also a presenter of the Vaisnava/Krishna tradition, He offers Katha - a traditional Vedic/Hindu format of dramatic storytelling which includes a sprinkling of spiritual teaching and the chanting of Sanskrit mantras, meant to be both entertaining and enlightening.

Andy also coaches those who want to hone their theater, storytelling and writing skills.

For more information visit
www.sacredvoices.com
www.Mahabharata-Project.com

"The roots of religion are found not in philosophy nor ritual, but in story. The need to understand one another's cultures and traditions is greater than ever. Storytelling is an age-old tool to help us understand our life's purpose, to build community, and to appreciate the world around us. We humans are storytellers by nature, and the stories we accept shape our character and actions."   Andy Fraenkel

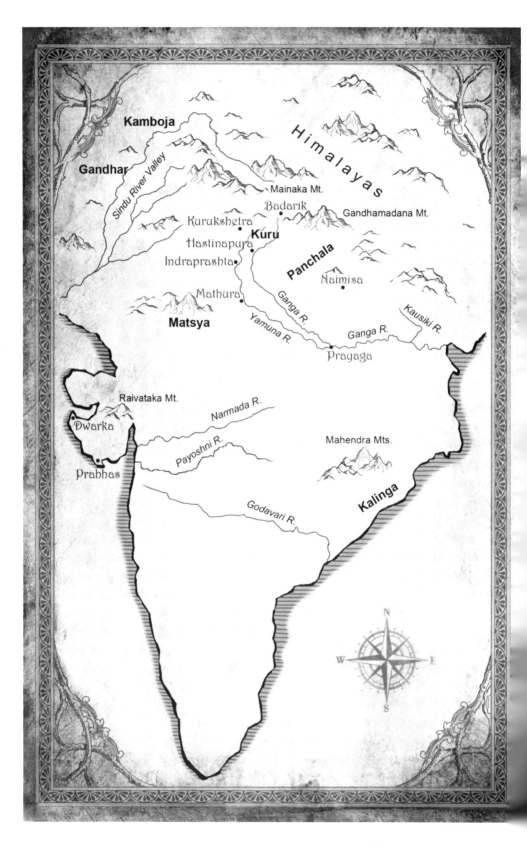